The Hippie Narrative

The Hippie Narrative

A Literary Perspective on the Counterculture

SCOTT MACFARLANE

McFarland & Company, Inc., Publishers
Jefferson, North Carolina, and London

Many thanks to the following professors
for their superb suggestions as this book evolved:
Kay Sands, Frank X. Gaspar, Steve Heller, and Amy Sage Webb.
Thanks also to my friend Robert Touchstone
for his close read of the final draft.

LIBRARY OF CONGRESS CATALOGUING-IN-PUBLICATION DATA

MacFarlane, Scott, 1955–
  The hippie narrative : a literary perspective on the
counterculture / Scott MacFarlane.
      p.   cm.
  Includes bibliographical references and index.

  ISBN-13: 978-0-7864-2915-8
  (softcover : 50# alkaline paper) ∞

  1. American fiction—20th century—History and
criticism.   2. Counterculture in literature.
3. Bohemianism in literature.   4. Hippies in literature.
5. Postmodernism (Literature)—United States.
6. Nineteen sixties.   7. Nineteen seventies.   I. Title.
PS374.C68M33   2007
813'.5409355—dc22   2006036391

British Library cataloguing data are available

On the cover: Concertgoers at the Woodstock Music and Arts
Fair at Bethel, New York, 1969 (Associated Press photograph)

Manufactured in the United States of America

McFarland & Company, Inc., Publishers
  Box 611, Jefferson, North Carolina 28640
  www.mcfarlandpub.com

For Mom,
who took my sister and me
to see Jimi

and

for Brenda,
born in the summer of 1967

Can they—the scholarly historians—reveal what truly happened?
No, the writer is now convinced that he alone
can snatch that essence from its wild background
and isolate it from commotion and myth.
And the writer is willing to spill everything. If you care to listen.
—Tom Robbins, *Another Roadside Attraction*

Table of Contents

DENOUEMENT

Introduction

The Summer of Love was three years away when Ken Kesey, the author of *One Flew Over the Cuckoo's Nest* and *Sometimes a Great Notion*, drove up to the Texas home of Larry McMurtry in an old, wildly-painted school bus dubbed *Furthur.* McMurtry, the aspiring author who would write *The Last Picture Show, Lonesome Dove, Terms of Endearment, Texasville,* and several other novels, couldn't shield from his suburban neighbors the hippieish antics of Kesey and fellow travelers, the Merry Pranksters. Kesey, not quite thirty-years-old, was riding the success of *Cuckoo's Nest* and on his way to New York for the 1964 World's Fair and a publication party for his second novel, *Sometimes a Great Notion.* Unlike McMurtry, who had yet to come into his own as an author, Kesey was already burned out on the novel as a form. Kesey felt "as though if I looked back on this period in 500 years I wouldn't look at the literature to see what was going on. I'd listen to the rock and roll music, I'd go to the movies, I'd read the comic books" (Perry, Babbs, 59).

In 1959 Kesey had moved from Oregon to study creative writing at Stanford University with Wallace Stegner and fellow students McMurtry, Robert Stone, Wendell Berry, Gurney Norman and others. He lived somewhat communally with many of the Pranksters in a row of rundown cottages near the Bay Area campus and discovered the mind-altering power of LSD while part of a CIA sponsored lab experiment at a nearby Veterans Administration hospital where he would also work and glean writing material for *Cuckoo's Nest.* In 1965 and '66, after their bus journey, Kesey and the Pranksters helped sponsor several public "acid tests" throughout California where the crowds tripped on the psychedelic drug. LSD and therefore the "tests," were legal in California until October 6, 1966, though busts for marijuana, which was not, were prevalent. When Tom Wolfe decided to write *The Electric Kool-Aid Acid Test,* published in 1968, he said that the project was prompted in part by his idea that the protagonists, Ken Kesey and the Merry Pranksters, had all the psychological traits of a new religious group in the making.

In 1981, unwittingly, my wife and I traversed much of the same cross-country route taken by Kesey and the Pranksters. We lived in an old Volkswagen bus for a year traveling from the West Coast to New York City with our three-year-old son in tow. Kesey had been proselytizing a new order of consciousness-raising during those years that preceded the flourishing of the counterculture. In 1981 we were selling artist wares from town to town and on the lookout for that special alternative community where we might settle. In retrospect, we were exploring the waning vestiges of the hippie epoch.

While on the road, we visited the annual Rainbow Gathering in Usk, Washington, the Alpha Farm in Oregon, an ashram in California, Arcosanti in Arizona, and the plantation of a Mississippi hippie. That winter we painted faces at Mardi Gras in New Orleans. We stayed a couple days at The Farm commune in Tennessee, attended a harvest festival in the Smoky Mountains, and I worked as a laborer to help build a Geodesic dome for the 1982 World's Fair—*You've Got to Be There*—in Knoxville. When our straitlaced relatives in Phoenix, Dallas or Richmond saw us arriving curbside in that well-dented, orange microbus, they were likely just as chagrined as McMurtry's neighbors were when the Merry Pranksters showed up on his doorstep. In New York City, I took a "real" job, shaved my beard, and cut my hair.

The Electric Kool-Aid Acid Test, though written by outsider Wolfe about Kesey and the Pranksters, is regarded as a consummate narrative regarding the counterculture. At the time, Wolfe, like Kesey, was heralding the death of the novel. Unlike Kesey, who didn't publish another novel for 28 years after *Sometimes a Great Notion,* Wolfe wrote prolifically, championing a melding of journalism and literature. This style blended journalistic "objectivity" with the intersubjective techniques of literary realism, and came to be called the "New Journalism."

Wolfe was partly right that Kesey and the Merry Pranksters had all the makings of a new religious group, but only if Dionysus was the god being worshipped. In Kesey's Bacchanalia, the ecstatic awakening came from this new kind of "wine." Kesey, chief among the Pranksters (with piloting help from Neil Cassady, the real life model for Jack Kerouac's protagonist in *On the Road*), possessed the charisma, but lacked the projection of all-knowingness that accompanies most religious cult-leaders. Essentially, he was a young writer with a mischievous bent and fresh, celebrity-sized ego who was experimenting with lifestyle possibilities and sharing his latest mind-bending discoveries. Ken Kesey has been aptly called "America's First Hippie." What resulted from his controversial consciousness-raising turned out to be more pervasive than had he started a cult. As a literary celebrity and provocateur, he helped catalyze the counterculture. In 1964, no one, including Kesey, could have predicted the religious, political, economic and spiritual upsurge that would confront the American mainstream during the several years that followed.

In 1976, my student union at the University of Washington invited Kesey to speak. He told some outrageous anecdotes and, at the end of his presentation, asked everyone in the audience to squeeze his or her own jugular vein and breathe in-and-out in rapid succession. Still the Prankster, his outlawed Kool-Aid vats of acid were replaced by a mass hyperventilation test.

Even though the legacy of the hippie is routinely lampooned because of the flamboyant dress, theatrical war protests, promiscuous sex, psychotropic drug use, trippy lingo, and communal lifestyles, the dissident subculture promoted by Kesey and the Merry Pranksters helped change social attitudes toward healthier eating, recycling, spiritual expressiveness, cultural and ethnic diversity, environmental accountability, unjustified war, and contributed toward an outburst of artistic expression and innovations for the personal computer. The counterculture is often misunderstood in its entirety, discarded as a cultural aberration and ridiculed as a "utopian" sociological phenomenon, but in many positive and negative ways, American society was inalterably changed.

The counterculture is a broad-reaching phenomenon and difficult to discuss in its many permutations, but contrary to what Kesey stated at the peak of his literary success when he turned his back on his own artistic gift for words, the era's literature affords us the vantage point for best surveying the era. The key works discussed here offer a fascinating look at the cultural nuances and interiority of this time. Taken mostly chronologically, one work at a time, these literary perspectives reveal the actual story of the hippies as the phenomenon played out through American society in the 1960s and '70s. In this way *The Hippie Narrative* is both a literary and cultural study.

A literary critique produces a different perspective on the era than conceptualizing it through the period's rock music, rebellious politics, defiant sociology, or drug use, although these many narratives approach those subjects in differing ways. This is not to suggest that the written narrative form was the most popular communication medium of the time; the din of electrified rock music exemplified the era. However, literature, through cultural nuance and interiority of character and situation, allows a more rounded sense of the hippie Zeitgeist that shaped and inspired the period.

The literature of the hippie phenomenon also provides a fascinating look at the rise of what came to be called "postmodernism," a phrase that gained wide use in the 1980s to describe the contemporary state of literature, architecture, film, and visual arts, as well as the culture of "advanced" modern society. There are several postmodernists who contend that postmodernism first surfaced during the counterculture of the '60s:

> In the West it was a period of questioning and challenging rules and norms, and of embracing spiritual and artistic modes from other cultures that had previously been ignored. Certainly, if we look for a movement that seems to encapsulate post-modernism, the hippie movement fits the bill. The hippie movement was about creating a new culture, which rejected absolutes and rationalism. Hippies took on board various forms of spirituality, rejected materialism and capitalism, and departed from cultural norms for relationships and living arrangements. In hippiedom there was an "anything goes" type of mentality. It was a tribal movement without the restraints of the previous generation [Catez Stevens, "Post-Modernism..."].

Within this context, the rise of postmodernism is viewed as both a period concept emanating from the changes of the '60s and, in literature, as a term linked to poststructuralism. A few disaffected students in France first promulgated this literary deconstructivist theoretical approach after violent protests failed to overthrow the French government in 1968. Instead, Michel Foucault, Jacques Derrida and others refocused their failed efforts to exact socialist change in the government into intellectual endeavors that sought to upend most of the prevailing notions of literary theory and critique.

The Hippie Narrative takes a constructivist rather than deconstructivist look at the era's key works of prose. More nuts and bolts than discursive, this approach offers an intriguing way to appreciate the evolution of postmodernism and highlights certain fundamental limitations found in contemporary postmodern literary critique.

Any book about the counterculture must engage the subject of psychedelic drugs. For example, the surreal passages in Cuckoo's Nest were influenced by Kesey's use of hallucinogens. The Electric Kool-Aid Acid Test featured LSD, and Fear and Loathing in Las Vegas was an autobiographical story being filtered through an overindulgence of all manner of illegal substances. Drugs pervaded much of the literature of the era. Even though there were drug-free hippies—especially the most spiritually focused—the hippie phenomenon was wed to the realm of psychedelia.

The counterculture was also the product of a pervasive disaffection that often had little or nothing to do with drugs. Drug use, in many cases, has served as a simplistic rationale for discarding the whole of the countercultural phenomenon. I'm not a proponent of illegal drugs, but this book attempts to take a dispassionate look at the impact and influence of these illicit substances as pertains to the dynamic of the era when seen through its most significant literature.

Not only do we distort our understanding of this era through, for example, a simplistic dismissal of drug use, but there seems to be an aversion to looking at the heart of the cauldron that precipitated the changes in our society as a whole. *New York Times* movie critic Karen Durbin stated in a 2001 movie review that "the cultural and political upheavals of the 1960's and '70s were as traumatic and transforming in their own way as the Civil War had been a century before. But it's as if we don't want to think about that time, much less risk revisiting its great and terrible vitality" (Durbin, *New York Times*, August 19, 2001).

I propose that the literary narratives of the era offer an insightful way to appreciate its "great and terrible vitality." What follows is a look at narratives that afford a lasting and bon a fide reflection of the era. As literature, these works also provide a fresh look at the emergence of postmodernism. *The Hippie Narrative* highlights those narratives that should be viewed as the literary canon of the counterculture. These works of literature are genuinely representative of the era and render a keener understanding of a difficult time that was grounded in defiant hope and utopian dreams. My own worldview was changed by the counterculture and the era profoundly changed the social and literary landscape of America. *The Hippie Narrative: A Literary Perspective on the Counterculture* highlights the nuance of this vitality, and the story of the hippie phenomenon as it unfolded.—Scott MacFarlane, October 2006.

Act I

Narrative Foreplay

1

Ginsberg, Kerouac and Burroughs

"The Vectoring Legacy of the Beats"

The torch has been passed.
> —*Allen Ginsberg, circa 1963, being interviewed*
> *after first hearing Bob Dylan perform "Hard Rain."*
> *The 2006 PBS documentary,* No Direction Home.

Much has been written about the Beat literary movement. The Beats of the 1950's espoused a Bohemian lifestyle centered on poetry, literature and jazz music. Beat philosophies expressed distaste for the hypocrisy and unfettered materialism in America and its movement evolved outside the mass media spotlight of the 1950's. Even though the anti-establishment Beats greatly influenced the counterculture that followed, the Beat movement haunted the fringe of American life while the counterculture came to be at the epicenter of American social debate. Also, participants in the counterculture of the late 1960's and '70s vastly outnumbered those who considered themselves Beats in the 1950's.

In *The Beat Generation and the Popular Novel in the United States, 1945–1970*, Thomas Newhouse describes "underground narrative" as "the literary response in fiction to the spiritual malaise that grew from dark cold war realities affecting artists and intellectuals immediately after the Second World War, a response that reached its fullest expression in the counterculture of the 1960's" (4). *The Hippie Narrative* limits its use of the term "counterculture" to its most common connotation linked to the youthful outburst of social disaffection of the late '60s and '70s, especially in the United States. Newhouse aptly identifies the "underground narrative." However, as a minor point of clarification, the Beat movement had waned by the early 1960's and was not contemporaneous with the counterculture. The Beat literary movement reached its apex in the late 1950s with the publication of *On the Road* by Jack Kerouac and *Naked Lunch* by William S. Burroughs. Though Beat philosophy vectored through American society and highly influenced the counterculture, the counterculture supplanted the Beat movement. Consequently, the "literary response" of "underground narrative" may have been in its "fullest expression" during the counterculture of the '60s, but not as direct expressions of the Beat literary movement. With the stylistic exception of Richard Fariña's 1966 novel, *Been Down So Long It Looks Like Up to Me,* the works studied here differ in several ways from the works of the Beats. Specifically, the more broadly derived works examined as hippie narratives share the characteristics of being less frenetic, not as concerned with creating an appearance of spontaneous delivery, and more prone to whimsy than the darker tone seen in the Beat era.

There is no evidence to support a unified literary movement in the countercultural era similar to that of the Beats. However, there are a set of narratives presented here that, over the period from 1962 to 1976, are genuine reflections of the era, and consistent with this "underground" expression of "spiritual malaise." In this notion of "underground," the Beat movement and the hippie phenomenon shared the same archetype. Namely, both the Beats and hippies can be seen as reacting to mainstream culture with a Dionysian, or Bacchanalian mode of response. This ecstatic disaffection is at the core of what made both the Beat movement and the counterculture part of an "underground" phenomenon. For example, Rowland Sherrill says in *Road-Book America: Contemporary Culture and the New Picaresque,* "the generations coming of age in the decades after mid-century were not simply different but visibly and vociferously in possession of a different set of ideas about American life than those of their elders and those of more "traditional" young people" (301). These were an "underground" set of ideas.

Again, the core rebelliousness and anti-authoritarian stance of the Beat and hippie underground is best understood through the archetype of Dionysus or Bacchus, god of the vine. The Ancient Greek playwright Euripides wrote the archetypal tragedy *The Bacchae* in 410 B.C. *The Bacchae,* as allegory, is apropos for tracing and comprehending the rise and decline of the counterculture. Dionysus offered his followers an ecstatic release from societal constrictions under the rule of King Pentheus. The Bacchae or Maenads, the followers of Dionysus, were lured away from the stifling confines of the city to the mountains where the followers could dance freely and drink from streams flowing with honey and wine. Of course, as Euripides's play goes on to narrate, the danger of excess existed for the Bacchae (just as it did for the Beats and hippies). The utopianism of the counterculture movement, like the dancing and reveling Bacchae, resulted in many hippies discovering how unattainable it was to easily change the world or to retreat to a mountainside where the honey and wine would always flow sublimely. (For example, the family homestead that is to be reclaimed by the young hippies at the end of Gurney Norman's 1971 novel, *Divine Right's Trip,* is on a mountainside that has been ravaged by strip-mining.)

King Pentheus, mistaken for a beast, pays for his intrusion on the mountain Bacchanalia. Pulled down from the thick tree limb where he is spying, the king is killed, unwittingly, by his own mother, a Maenad. And, though the bloody carnage is considerable, in the end, the fate of the Maenads is a tragic procession where they return to the City/State whence they had come.

This Bacchanalian response to the prevailing authorities is articulated in an essay, "Dionysus and the Beat Generation" by William Everson (also known as Brother Antoninus, a respected Beat poet):

> [...] The insistence of the Beat Generation to combine jazz and poetry is quite symptomatic of the Dionysian tendency. Even the Beat novel is an open effort to sustain lyric intensity over the whole course of the work [181].

Opposing Dionysus in this metaphor for the Beat/Hippie experience is the god Apollo:

> Dionysus in his own realm of field and forest is nothing dangerous; he represents simply the flow of unconscious life in the whole psyche. But over against him stands Apollo, god of light and consciousness, the guardian of civilization and culture, education, commerce and civic virtue. To the civilizing Apollonian attitude, with its premium on rational consciousness and ego-integrity, nothing is more abhorrent, and hence more dangerously seductive, than the dark irrational urge. Ego fears to lose everything before the ecstatic force, and it organizes all its powers of persuasion and coercion to check the spontaneous effect...
>
> [...] Dionysus is unkillable. Unless his voice be heard [...] sooner or later the god will break out. And the humiliated outrage [...] bodes ill for consciousness and Apollo [...] [181–2].

The Bacchae ends with the death of King Pentheus. Had the Greek play continued, it is unlikely that the City/State to which the Maenads returned would have remained the same. Metaphorically, the Bacchanalia in this play ended in a similar way that the idealism and hopes of the counterculture ended. American society was not the same afterwards, but changed by this powerful Apollonian/Dionysian dialectic.

The Apollonian/Dionysian dialectic differs from a Marxist dialectic. Literary theorist Frederick Jameson, for example, proposes that the postmodern state reflects the stage of Late Capitalism that modernized man currently inhabits:

> In his contribution to *The Sixties without Apology,* Jameson suggests that the upheavals of that period parallel the culminating moments of the transition

> from monopoly to multinational capitalism, a shift that was largely complete by
> the early seventies. The postmodern, or so Jameson argues, is the culture appro-
> priate to this last phase of capitalism, just as realism and modernism, respec-
> tively, had been appropriate to its earlier forms [Chabot, 32].

Only the future will reveal, of course, whether Late Capitalism of the
multinational variety self-negates and synthesizes into the Socialism of
the Hegelian model. Soviet and Chinese economies have moved the
opposite direction in the last decades. Perhaps contemporary postmodern economies will evolve into a socialist/capitalist hybrid resulting from
a consciousness revolution yet to be fulfilled, one emanating from the
egalitarian idealism begun by the hippies, an idealism built upon alternative models of co-existence attempted during the counterculture. On
the other hand, current multinational, military-industrial, market capitalism might persist for millennia.

As concerns an Apollonian/Dionysian dialectic, however, it is historical observation, rather than speculation, to depict what happened
to the hippie epoch. The hippies discovered the hard way that a Bacchanalian utopia couldn't be sustained. The idealism to change the world
in the full-scale manner envisioned through the alternative lifestyle was
more easily imagined than accomplished. In this regard, it also should
be pointed out that such idealism was thwarted or co-opted by a
consumer-driven system of state capitalism not predisposed to tolerate,
for any extended period of time, the more anarchic aspects of the counterculture.

When Jameson asserts that realism and modernism were cultural
reflections of earlier stages of Capitalism, his linkage of literary style to
a depiction of culture is overly convenient. Literary styles of realism,
modernism, or postmodernism conform to period concepts only as
rough generalizations. The New Journalism of the '60s, for example, is
often excerpted for anthologies of postmodern literature, but its innovations were rooted in the literary techniques of *realism*. This is discussed
in greater depth in the chapter on *The Electric Kool-Aid Acid Test*.

Postmodernism, a catch-all term used widely since the 1980's, has
been defined as "a cultural condition prevailing in the advanced capitalist societies since the 1960s, characterized by a superabundance of disconnected images and styles—most notably in television, advertising,
commercial design, and pop video ... postmodernity is said to be a culture of fragmentary sensations, eclectic nostalgia, disposable simulacra,
and promiscuous superficiality[...]. [T]he postmodernist greets the
absurd or meaningless confusion of contemporary existence with a certain numbed or flippant indifference, favoring self-consciously 'depthless'
works of fabulation, pastiche, bricolage, or aleatory disconnection"
[Baldick, 174–5]. Several of the Beat and countercultural literary works

examined here display these postmodern attributes of style. Also, post-modernist literature draws heavily from underground narrative, but by no means is most current postmodernist writing rendered in an underground "Dionysian" vein.

For clarification, the term underground narrative, whether applied to the Beats or hippies, does not presuppose a lack of success in the marketplace and it is not about the literature having been clandestine or hidden. Rather, a work of underground narrative connotes a message and story that is positioned to challenge the mainstream culture and its values. It is a view from the margins of society. "Underground" also implies disaffection with the establishment. For example, *On the Road,* the Beat classic by Jack Kerouac, is a picaresque, underground novel about a protagonist living and traveling on the fringes of society, questioning mainstream values, yet the book, nearly a half-century later, is still a bestseller in the literary mainstream marketplace. Likewise, most of the works put forth in this book as hippie narratives were quite successful commercially as well as critically.

The "underground" of the late '60s and '70s ranged from covert to overt. Participants at the most violent end of the countercultural spectrum, including radical student leader Bernadine Dohrn who was wanted in connection with several Weatherman instigated bombings, were often able to disappear for several years in the 1970s within a network of underground connections. More overtly, FM radio, on the new bandwidth made available in the late '60s, provided a less restrictive medium for featuring defiant rock albums and alternative ideas.

A case can be made that the catchphrases of the counterculture offered the defining "underground" narrative of its era. This concept of narrative allows for a fragmented sense of story—in postmodernist fashion—and included lyrical rallying cries, mantras, ironic pronouncements and chants of social protest. Literature, as Kesey noted, was not the dominant mode of expression. Rock and folk music offered what, today, would be called soundbites: *"give peace a chance," "what are we fighting for...?" "let's get together, right now," "let's go get stoned," "the times they are a changin'," "goin' up the country," "fish filled with mercury," "they paved paradise and put up a parking lot," "hare, hare, my sweet lord," "four dead in Ohio,"* or *"we can change the world."* Such phrases were part of a constant flow of messages over the airwaves. These fragments of narrative helped frame the ethos of the counterculture, the "story" by which many young people lived. Of all these messages, the hippie belief that "we can change the world" most distinguished the counterculture from the Beat sentiment that preceded it. In this regard, the hippie outlook was more utopian and collectivist than the Beat movement.

This outlook was also reinforced through underground media. In the late '60s alternative newspapers appeared in cities around the U.S. Weeklies such as New York City's *Village Voice,* the San Francisco *Oracle,* or the Seattle *Helix* became known, collectively, as the "Underground Press." Alternative "comix," such as R. Crumb's "Mr. Natural," lampooned the excess of its own lifestyle. Publications such as *The Last Whole Earth Catalog* or *Mother Earth News* opened up the viability of alternative styles of living distinct from the mainstream's rampant consumerism. *High Times* promoted marijuana cultivation and appreciation. *Rolling Stone Magazine* focused on the era's music.

The counterculture was far more pervasive, politicized, and diffuse than the Beat movement, though the two were linked as part of the same Dionysian upsurge. No one literary author or group of authors ever claimed to represent the counterculture. No group of writers claimed ownership of a countercultural literature. Moreover, "counterculture" was not an easily defined term.

Postmodernism, as a concept, is even more evasive. The first credited use of the term can also be linked to the Beat literary movement. Irving Howe wrote an essay in 1959 called "Mass Society and the Postmodern" where he describes a new kind of fiction in America that was a symptom of post–World War II cultural transformations. His use of the term demonstrated itself through Beat literature as a sequel to modernism. The works studied here as "hippie narratives" were also products of these same cultural transformations and greatly informed by the literature and attitudes of the Beats. Howe's concept of the "postmodern" in 1959 was nearly synonymous with Newhouse's description of "underground narrative," yet, the term "postmodern" evolved after the desiccation of the counterculture in the late '70s, when the "underground," with all of its collectivist good intentions, had atrophied as well. Cultural shifts in values, attitudes, and behaviors—derived in many ways from a fading counterculture—contributed to the contemporary postmodernism that came to be widely recognized by this period concept in the 1980s. In literature, "underground narrative" in works such as *Trout Fishing in America* helped inform the stylistic sensibility of contemporary "postmodern" prose.

Unlike the Beat movement, the counterculture was not a singular movement consisting of authors, poets and musicians with activities centered on writing and jazz. The Beats espoused mind expansion through drugs, including psychedelics, but the powerful hallucinogen LSD was not a part of the bohemian underground until the mid-'60s. For the Beats, the music of choice was jazz and, to a lesser extent, folk. Hard-driving, amplified rock music, rooted in the backbeat of the blues, took center stage about 1966. Hard rock epitomized the spirit of the emerging counterculture. The counterculture was also much broader in its scope of participation and focus of activity. The spiritual, political and lifestyle ramifications were more sweeping. The Beats were at the cutting edge of fighting government attempts at censorship, but the hippies were much more a direct focus of mainstream derision and significant public opposition and persecution. For example, Kesey and Timothy Leary were incarcerated on marijuana charges as a way for the authorities to muffle their advocacy of psychedelics, especially LSD. As Kesey pointed out in a 1992 interview with writer Todd Fahey:

> People don't want other people to get high, because if you get high, you might see the falsity of the fabric of the society we live in. [pause] We thought that by this time that there would be LSD given in classes in college. And you would study for it and prepare for it, you would have somebody there who would help you through it; you would know what to sing, where to be, how to stand out among the trees. We were *naive*. We thought that we had come to a new place, a new, exciting, free place; and that it was going to be available to all America. And they *shut it down*. [...]
>
> People ask, "what happen to you guys?" And I always tell them, "we got *arrested*." Just everybody I know got arrested and had to serve time [www.fargone-books.com/kesey.html].

Such treatment by the authorities likely dissuaded many authors from grandstanding for the counterculture. In fact, while the term "Beat" was embraced by Kerouac, Ginsberg and Burroughs, the term "hippie" was a pejorative to those in the counterculture as well as to members of the mainstream. "Hippie author," unlike "Beat writer," was not an enviable label. Nonetheless, several exemplary works were published from 1962 to 1976 exhibiting a countercultural sensibility and certain stylistic commonalities. These narratives—especially works written by Richard Brautigan, Hunter S. Thompson, Gurney Norman, William Kotzwinkle, and Tom Robbins—articulated an "underground" posturing, yet differed from the Beat style of writing. The most notable difference was one of playfulness, or whimsy, a quality commonly lacking in the more self-serious Beat writing.

Starting with the surreal passages and innovative treatment of time in Ken Kesey's first two novels, all of the works viewed in *The Hippie Narrative* were moving away from depictions of conventional realism. Along with a discernible hippie underground tone of narrative, certain works, such as Brautigan's *Trout Fishing in America,* reflected a significant departure from conventional linear form.

Strictly speaking, the Beats shared a discrete sociological movement of identifiable participants who promoted one another as members of this same movement. Allen Ginsberg, Jack Kerouac and William S. Burroughs were constantly touting one another as fellow Beats. By comparison, many diverse movements contributed to the counterculture, such as the anti-war movement, the psychedelic movement, the natural foods movement, the back-to-the-land movement, various alternative spirituality movements, or the environmental movement. The enormity of change combined to offer an alternative culture and lifestyle, perhaps too new, complex and vast for most authors of the time to immediately distill.

Also, between the mainstream American culture and this alternative counterculture, the separation was highly permeable. No one individual belonged to all these alternative movements and, to varying degrees, people moved back and forth between the mainstream and the counterculture as though the boundary was a membrane. A junior accountant, for example, might work behind a corporate desk all week, but trip out at a rock festival or protest the Vietnam War on the weekend. Many young people, of course, were a hardcore part of the counterculture and rejected most trappings of mainstream society.

Ironically, the Beats, though a singular movement, were often referred to as the Beat Culture, while the counterculture (and its many movements) was referred to in its day by the singular term, "The Movement." This imprecision of labels is part of what makes it difficult to discuss this era. This difficulty is no more pronounced than in the use of the pejorative term "hippie." "Hippie," as best can be determined in *The Hippie Dictionary*, derives from the Beats calling the youthful newcomers to their scene in San Francisco in the mid–'60s, "hippies," as in little hipsters. "Hippie" is used here to describe the adherents of the counterculture who subscribed to pacifist tenets, and who, in various capacities, participated in the alternative lifestyle of the era. The pejorative venom associated with the term has dissipated in the decades following the burgeoning of the counterculture, even though the simplistic lampooning continues. "Hippie" does describe, better than any other term, those who immersed themselves in the idealism and disaffection of the counterculture. Actually, the authors of the narratives studied here who were directly involved in the counterculture—Kesey, Brautigan, Thompson, Norman, and Robbins—were born from 1935 to '37, and a bit too old to be classified with the teens and young adults in late 1966 who fit the description of little hipsters. The bulk of the hippies were "baby boomers" and born from 1945 to 1957, and, starting in late 1966, the seldom used term "hippie" was broadcast nationally and internationally by a mass media that was looking for an easy label to describe the hordes of young people taking part in the eruption of psychedelia in San Francisco especially. Hippie Dippy, indeed; the term spread quickly and stuck. Yet, it is the works of these authors born at the oldest end of "The Movement" that best exhibited in literature, a countercultural grounding of style and content.

Being a hippie and participating in the counterculture—unlike ethnicity or gender—was a purely voluntary pursuit. The hippie, in voluntarily challenging the establishment, differed from other groups of the time. The Black Panthers, for example, were fighting for enfranchisement, fighting for the rights and opportunities being denied them because of race. By 1970, women began demanding rights and opportunities denied them because of gender. The hippies, by comparison, were comprised mostly of enfranchised youth who challenged the shortcomings of the establishment from the inside. Had such large numbers of enfranchised, but disaffected, youth not rallied for social change through this Dionysian upsurge, then it is doubtful so much change would have occurred in such a short period of time.

The walls of "The Establishment" were being assaulted from inside and out, a fact not missed by Emmett Grogan, one of the chief orchestrators of the Diggers, a San Francisco group that used mime, guerilla theater, and free meals to further a covert socialist agenda masquerading as trippy anarchy. Grogan's autobiography, *Ringolevio: A Life Played for Keeps,* is one of the most elucidating memoirs of the Haight Ashbury scene. In one passage, he has returned to his hometown New York and is speaking to a gathering of radical hippies on Manhattan's Lower East Side, addressing how the dreams of the socially disenfranchised differed from those of the disaffected hippies, a contradiction encompassed within the same spirit of period unrest:

> [W]hen hippies come along riffin' about how unhip it is to make it into middle-class society 'n how easy it would have been for them to make it, but they didn't because it was insignificant, these low-money people get confused and upset because here are these creepy longhaired punks who grew up with meat at every meal and backyards to play in and the kind of education which is prayed to God for, and they threw it all away for what?
>
> [...] So you better face the straight goods, brothers an' sisters. You ain't the new niggers or spics, 'n you're never gonna be. You have too much to fall back on [...], you're still the children of the ruling classes, whether you like it or not. As far as they're concerned, you're just having an adventure—an adventure in poverty which, if you aren't careful, may prove to be more real than you're ready to deal with [324–325].

Grogan's book also demonstrates the lack of cohesive leadership in the counterculture when, as a street radical, he vehemently attacks the intellectual Leftists, the many opportunistic merchants of hippie wares, dreamy idealists, certain black radicals, and those who wanted to be media icons of this alternative movement. This Digger is blunt about who he believes is sincere or hypocritical and self-serving. For example, he talks about political radical Jerry Rubin as, "the baby fat runt himself, Jerome Rubin" (274), or other period politicos led by Abbie Hoffman as, "Abbot Hoffman and his East Village cronies in their quest for personal recognition as national figures in a mock-revolutionary movement of masquerade, just 'for the hell of it'" (344). Timothy Leary and Richard Alpert are called "LSD shamans," "a pair of charlatan fools, [...] every time you turned around—on the covers of magazines, on the radio and TV, all over the fucking place—representing them, the young people, the alternative culture. Two creepy, whiskey-drinking schoolteachers!" (268–269). All was not love, peace and harmony in the deepest reaches of the underground.

Grogan and the Diggers were fueling the caldron of change in a way that tried to avoid too much media focus on themselves as individuals, knowing that such attention would bring too much harassment from the authorities and weaken or derail their ulterior mission. Their antics, anarchistic on the surface, epitomized the more activist ilk of hippie. Or as Grogan admits:

> The elements of guerilla theater and street events were merely accessories contingent upon the fundamental reality of Free Food, the free stores, the free goods, and the free services made available to the people. The San Francisco Diggers attempted to organize a solid, collective, comparative apparatus to provide resources sufficient for the people to set up an alternative power base, that wouldn't have to depend on either the state or the system for its sustenance [303].

The Diggers' efforts were more grassroots and tangible than other radical campaigns of unrest, yet Grogan's memoir demonstrates how in the midst of the anarchy, the egos of the more prominent participants, including his own, played a significant role in the chaotic disunity of the politicized factions of "The Movement." Interestingly, one of the people who Grogan says he liked was Beat poet Allen Ginsberg. Chameleon-like, Ginsberg found himself in the spotlight of the counterculture, just as he had been a leading figure of the Beat movement the decade before. He was politicized, but not highly doctrinaire, an activist and spiritualist, yet fundamentally an artist.

As an artist, Ginsberg's Beat poem "Howl" established the DNA of the underground narrative. "Howl," published in 1955 (and later nearly banned for its profanity), served as the Dionysian clarion cry of the Beat Generation. The cadence and pace used to describe the types of drugs identified in "Howl," mimics, respectively, either a hallucinatory or amphetamine induced pace:

> Peyote solidities of halls, backyard green tree cemetery
> dawns, wine drunkenness over the rooftops,
> storefront boroughs of teahead joyride neon
> blinking traffic light, sun and moon and tree

Or,

> [...] from Battery to holy Bronx on benzedrine
> until the noise of wheels and children brought
> them down shuddering mouth-wracked and
> battered bleak of brain all drained of brilliance
> in the drear light of Zoo [...] [9].

Ginsberg employs the dithyrambic verse favored by the Beat poets "(a wild poetry of spontaneous enthusiasm)," as described by Everson.

The poet, with this seminal work, establishes a disaffected voice of outrage by employing vernacular from the underbelly of American society. The jaded imagery, alienation, and various altered states presented here were emblematic of the "underground" sensibility, and an early articulation of postmodern fragmentation. In this regard, the piece is seminal to the sense of "spiritual malaise" afflicting America after mid-century. This poet's emulation of pace to state-of-consciousness is also seen in later examples of countercultural prose, notably Hunter S. Thompson's *Fear and Loathing in Las Vegas*.

By comparison to "Howl," the novel most commonly presented as epitomizing the Beat literary movement is Jack Kerouac's *On the Road*. Structurally, the story follows a traditional narrative arc, and, though the lingo and lifestyle are Bohemian, the world is rendered through a depiction of conventional realism. In fact, this novel also epitomizes the modern American picaresque novel. The prose style that makes *On the Road* quintessentially Beat, is Kerouac's use of the sustained lyrical intensity which Everson noted. *On the Road* is dithyrambic from start to finish. First published in 1957, the novel laid the groundwork for the countercultural Dionysian sensibility that followed:

> It was remarkable how Dean could go mad and then suddenly continue with his soul—which I think is wrapped up in a fast car, a coast to reach, and a woman at the end of the road—calmly and sanely as though nothing had happened. "I get like that every time in Denver now—I can't make that town any more. Gookly, gooky, Dean's a spooky. Zoom!" I told him, I had been over this Nebraska road before in '47. He had too. "Sal, when I was working for the New Era Laundry in Los Angeles, nineteen forty-four, falsifying my age, I made a trip to Indianapolis Speedway for the express purpose of seeing the Memorial Day classic hitch, hiking by day and stealing cars by night to make time [...]" [219].

This manic, pedal-to-the-metal pace continues throughout the book. Kerouac uses a run-on sentence structure (and two different people quoted in the same paragraph) to help create this effect. Note the Beat bebop-like lingo, life outside the law, and the oblique and irreverent reference to Dean's spirituality. In its picaresque rendering, *On the Road* featured roguish characters on the fringe of society to pose imploring questions about the meaning of life in industrial America.

The picaresque novel goes back at least to Cervantes' *Don Quixote* and his tilting at windmills. The form was employed by Mark Twain in

The Adventures of Huckleberry Finn to show a roguish posture toward the Antebellum establishment of the mid–19th century South with its institutionalized slavery. *On the Road* is the quintessential example of the modern picaresque form, episodic in how it explores themes of alienation, homoeroticism, and the expression of personal freedom that defied the role of being a cog in a highly industrialized society. Although the novel challenged the conventions of mainstream American life through the protagonist as anti-hero, stylistically, this was a conventionally rendered work that subscribed to a continuous narrative dream (Gardner, 31). *On the Road* serves as an example of Late Modernist writing; its random, episodic quest also shows the beginning of the "numbed or flippant indifference" notable in Postmodernism.

    On the Road became a philosophical bible for the counterculture. In the Beat world of the outcast, Newhouse further states that: "many of the underground narratives [...] are the work of writers who chronicled the lives of social types and who sought to establish an alternative mode of community that many felt had been destroyed by the Second World War" (4). For many hardcore hippies, this countercultural drive to establish alternative modes of community took root in experiments to create communes. As has been suggested, this stronger communal urge—a more widespread sense of collectivism—also differentiated the hippie phenomenon from the Beat experience.

    Both *On the Road* and William S. Burroughs' urban and drug-wracked *Naked Lunch* are autobiographical fiction. *Naked Lunch* paints, brazenly, the life of a heroin junkie. This book is often designated as a seminal postmodern work because of its use of cut-ups resembling the postmodernist pastiche and ironic parallel assemblages. Burroughs would cut passages at random from different sources and piece them together to find new meanings through the juxtaposition.

    The following passage, for the time it was written in 1959, is notably iconoclastic in its metaphorical likening of Presidential power to homosexual lust and the need for a fix:

> The President is a junky but can't take it direct because of his position. So he gets fixed through me.... From time to time we make contact, and I recharge him. These contacts look, to the casual observer, like homosexual practices, but the actual excitement is not primarily sexual, and the climax is the separation when the recharge is completed. The erect penises are brought into contact—at least we used that method in the beginning, but contact points wear out like veins. Now I sometimes have to slip my penis under his left eyelid [62].

Such writing was boldly irreverent in the late '50s and opened the door to a wide array of writing during the counterculture that also tore at the mainstream sense of propriety. The use of juxtapositioning—President/junky/homosexual—was absurdly ironic, a cornerstone of later postmodernist writing.

These excerpts from the three most prominent works of the Beat era show how a roguish tone of irreverence was well established. In literary canons, Ginsberg, Burroughs and Kerouac enjoy the benefit of being notably linked to their movement. The writers from the counterculture do not enjoy such recognition, and have never benefited from even an informal literary clustering.

Yet, as early as 1962, and heavily influenced by the Beat movement that preceded it, several literary gems began to appear with enough similarity in voice, tone, roguishness, iconoclastic whimsy and anti-establishment sentiment to consider grouping them as a distinct body of literature. While rock music was the dominant form of artistic expression for the generation that followed the Beats, there is a nuance and interiority portrayed by these literary works that render a visceral and more thorough sense of the era. This depth and subtlety cannot be garnered by any other medium. Likewise, the poetry and literature of the Beats offer a similar visceral sense of that era.

Starting with the first two novels by Ken Kesey, the interim period between the Beats and the hippies is examined. Kesey and the Merry Pranksters were the consummate proto-hippies, living a communal lifestyle starting in the early '60s. Much of the core dynamic of the countercultural upheaval that would follow is found in *One Flew Over the Cuckoo's Nest* and *Sometimes a Great Notion.*

2

One Flew Over the Cuckoo's Nest (1962)

Shock Therapy, Surreally

Published in 1962 to popular and critical acclaim, *One Flew Over the Cuckoo's Nest* depicts a rebellious conman, Randle P. McMurphy, newly committed to the Oregon State Mental Hospital as he methodically challenges the control of Nurse Ratched. Known as Big Nurse, she polices her ward in a rigidly uptight and authoritarian manner. The straightforward plot is told from the point of view of Chief Broom (Bromden) who has been institutionalized in the Big Nurse's ward for many years. He leads everyone in the hospital to believe he is deaf and dumb.

At every turn, McMurphy tries to undermine the Nurse's strict routine of control and to usurp her influence over the men on the ward. McMurphy's moxie inspires the Chief to gradually rediscover his own self-empowerment and inner humanity. This accretion of change in the Chief runs parallel to the growing conflict between the head nurse and her disruptive new patient and serves as the primary undercurrent of the narrative. When the conflict between Ratched and McMurphy comes to a head at the end of the novel, the Chief is fully actualized as an integral participant in the drama. In other words, the outer dramatic tension of the novel builds with the pacing of the Chief's inner psychological change. From the outset of the novel, the Chief, like an eye-in-the-sky, is a first-person cipher relaying the outer drama. By the end of *Cuckoo's Nest*, the Chief is the central protagonist of the story.

In this, Kesey's first published novel, he juxtaposes external plot with internal awakening by interspersing surrealistic, first person passages. Against the backdrop of the Big Nurse's authoritarian control and McMurphy's rebelliousness, the Chief's struggle against psychic dissonance unfolds. The surrealism is carefully placed in reasoned intervals,

oscillating with lucid passages, to show the reader what the Chief is struggling with internally.

Kesey began writing this novel in 1960 when at Stanford University
in Palo Alto, California. He participated in a graduate creative writing
program with numerous other talented authors, including eventual
Pulitzer Prize winner Larry McMurtry (*The Last Picture Show, Lonesome
Dove*), Robert Stone (*Dog Soldiers, Children of Light*) and Gurney Norman
(*Divine Right's Trip*). *One Flew Over the Cuckoo's Nest* is sometimes grouped
with the Beat writing of the era, but the narrative doesn't exhibit either
the frenetic pacing or picaresque structure of most Beat narrative.
Cuckoo's Nest is more deliberately and traditionally crafted, although it
does share the soul-wrenching alienation and anti-authoritarian tone of
disaffection seen in the key Beat narratives of this era. Also, Kesey claims
to have evoked the character of Chief Broom after ingesting peyote. The
first three pages of the novel, which opens as follows, were written after
such a hallucination, and the surrealistic passage survived the many drafts
of the manuscript:

> They're out there.
>   Black boys in white suits up against me to commit sex acts in the hall and get
> it mopped up before I can catch them.
>   They're mopping when I come out of the dorm, all three of them sulky and
> hating everything, the time of day, the place they're at here, the people they got
> to work around. When they hate like this, better if they don't see me. I creep
> along the wall quiet as dust in my canvas shoes, but they got special sensitive
> equipment detects my fear [...] [9].

Kesey establishes his Native American protagonist as unsettled and paranoid and always observing.

When Kesey entered Stanford, he was a non-drinking athlete from
rural Oregon. He quickly adopted a more bohemian lifestyle. He moved
to Palo Alto in late 1958 with his wife and they took up residence on Perry
Lane, considered the Left Bank of the Stanford area. The neighborhood
of rundown World War I housing was hip and intellectual as well as a
gathering point for an underground expressiveness not seen at this time
in Kesey's Oregon. During that first year Kesey worked on a novel called
Zoo, which he stopped writing when he began *Cuckoo's Nest*. *Zoo* featured
a football star that encounters the communal Beat life in San Francisco's
North Beach neighborhood. Considering that Kesey was an excellent
wrestler at the University of Oregon, autobiographical implications were
strong.

In other words, Kesey, in his mid-twenties, was exposed to the anti-
authoritarian prose of the Beats—the most vibrant new literature of this
era—as well as to the rigors of Wallace Stegner's outstanding creative writing program at Stanford, where he honed the many elements of traditional

literary crafting. In *Cuckoo's Nest*, it's clear that Kesey's immersion in this demanding writing program had the greater impact on his authorial techniques than did the Beat literary influences. At Stanford, pre–Xerox machine, before copies of work were easily distributed, each writer would read sections of his or her prose to the others in the workshop and then listen to feedback. Typed portions of the manuscript were then submitted for comment to the professor leading the workshop. Kesey had the benefit of seasoned feedback for his novel-in-progress. In the workshop environment at Stanford, peer writers and literary professors helped Kesey craft his manuscript in a way that optimized the dramatic impact of the work. As Stephen L. Tanner notes in his book *Ken Kesey*: "By skillfully drawing upon proven conventions within the literary tradition—a timeworn yet timeless pattern of myth, a conscious and elaborate manipulation of images, a standard conflict-and-resolution plot with hero and villain—Kesey has created a novel that in terms of social and cultural tradition is highly unconventional. His degree of formal skill is noteworthy among recent novelists [...]" (44).

While Kesey gives credit to one of his writing professors at the University of Oregon and to this time at Stanford for his formal skill as an author, the Beat scene, combined with his Oregon upbringing, provided the thematic and tonal underpinnings of the novel. The disaffected and surrealistic content of his work, in its unconventionality, borrowed heavily from his increasingly bohemian extracurricular activities. Also, growing up in Oregon, mid-century, informed the author's sense of a pioneer ethic that was being eroded by increased modernization. The plight of the rugged individualist and the yearning for self-reliance are at the thematic core of both *Cuckoo's Nest* and Kesey's second novel, *Sometimes A Great Notion*.

Another strong influence on Kesey's writing and personality was his penchant for drama and the illusion of magic that he developed as a school kid. Tanner contends that this interest in magic explains why Kesey was so receptive to try drugs after he moved to California. Whether the reason is this simple or not, both of his novels feature physically strong male characters with clearly defined dramatic motives who must come in from the metaphorical wilderness and confront the social pressures of a radically changing world. Kesey's main characters are forced to either adapt to the change with a new kind of self-reliance or suffer great personal loss.

In 1960, Kesey signed up to participate at the Menlo Park Veterans Hospital as a paid guinea pig of sorts in a drug research program called MK-ULTRA, first funded by the CIA in 1953. Here the researchers studied him after he ingested their psychoactive drugs. He was tested on LSD, Ditran, mescaline, and IT-290, an amphetamine. Kesey soon worked at the hospital part-time, an experience that greatly influenced the characters and workings of his novel.

Malcolm Crowley, former editor for Faulkner, Hemingway and others, and a workshop leader in the Stanford program, said of Kesey's manuscript:

> From the beginning he had his narrator in the person of Chief Broom, a schizophrenic Indian who pretends to be deaf and dumb. He (Kesey) had his own crazy visions—induced by eating peyote, as he later explained—and these could be attributed to Chief Broom. Thus when the Indian looks at Big Nurse, "She's swelling up, swells till her back's splitting out the white uniform and she's let her arms section out long enough to wrap around the three of them five, six times ... she blows up bigger and bigger, big as a tractor, so big I can smell the machinery inside the way you smell a motor pulling too big a load." That hallucinated but everyday style, smelling of motor oil, was something new in fiction. Kesey's narrative problem, the central one, was how to use Chief Broom-or-Bromden's visions as the medium for telling an essentially simple, dramatic, soundly constructed story [Northwest Review Books, 2–3].

Even taking in account the story's ultimately successful reliance on surrealism to propel the interior narrative of the story, this novel, as Crowley and Tanner allude, is traditionally rendered.

Traditional narrative entails an application of what Aristotle calls energeia, "the actualization of the potential that exists in character and situation" (Gardner, 185). The dramatic impact of *Cuckoo's Nest* results from a series of causes and effects building toward a resounding climax in the "showdown" between the Big Nurse and her unwieldy patient. Kesey creates a continuous fictional dream, another indication of traditional narrative, from which the story never departs. Kesey's use of surrealism to tell the Chief's story renders an intermittent dreamlike quality to his continuous fictional dream. The surrealism is deployed in a way that serves the growth of the narrator and, thereby, the underlying plot of the novel.

Kesey's work is fundamentally tragic in how it laments the loss of individualism. Some analyses of *Cuckoo's Nest* assert that it is comic and others that it is a romance. Others portray McMurphy and the Big Nurse as surrogate mother and father figures for Chief Broom, while another line of metaphorical treatment views the Chief and McMurphy as part–Indian and part-cowboy who join forces against a new common enemy, modern totalitarianism as personified in Nurse Ratched. Some point to the Christ imagery with McMurphy as a Jesus figure, his fellow patients on the ward as the disciples, and Chief "Broom as the one who is ultimately "saved." Though not mutually exclusive, the variety and depth of these symbolic analyses can be debated, but the richness of the interpretations reflects mostly on the resonance of Kesey's work. Kesey, in the mid–'70s called *Cuckoo's Nest* "a simple Christ allegory that takes place in a nut house" (*Spit in the Ocean* 7, 140). The novel was also, very much, a product of its time. The interpretations used here focus on those elements of the work that best portray the changing world being depicted, and which portend the tumultuous years that will follow the book's publication.

From a literary perspective there is evidence in *Cuckoo's Nest* of the irony exhibited in later postmodern works, but the novel is never metafictional, a common later trait. In the continuous and vivid fictional dream, the author never, in other words, draws attention to his presence or the narrative structure he is creating; Kesey doesn't attempt to deconstruct the novel for the reader. Even its surrealism is well integrated into the dramatic buildup of tension. The novel is dystopic, and in the end, Kesey constructs a fully actualized dramatic arc that culminates with a semblance of hope found through self-reliance. This sense of hope is offered metaphorically when the Chief makes his grand escape. In the escape is the message of a grand narrative, a literary approach that fell out of favor in the postmodern era for its perceived Eurocentric and masculine bias (Simpson, 29).

The theme of choosing between security and freedom plays out in the story through both McMurphy and the Chief. This choice is evident with the other patients as well. In the latter part of the novel, the reader learns that virtually all of the acute (but not chronic) patients are in the hospital's mental ward voluntarily. McMurphy, as a transferred prisoner, is involuntarily committed, and this is the trump card that Nurse Ratched holds over him. The Chief and several of the other patients on the ward garner inner strength and self-confidence through McMurphy's show of will against this formidable institution as embodied in the person of Nurse Ratched.

In literary terms, the structured order of Kesey's narrative is an attempt to show, rationally, how self-reliance can be made to prevail over totalitarianism in its many facets. Kesey—reactionary *and* traditionalist— articulated the price paid for many of the modern impositions on individuality and the human spirit. So, even though the surface structure of the dramatic work exemplified the traditional narrative form, the content and sentiment of the novel, especially its interiority as developed through the Chief's bouts of surrealistic delusion, show an underground sensibility of disaffection and defiance.

Cuckoo's Nest exhibits strong impressionism and subjectivity, including its many stream-of-conscious passages, and bridges the gap between *high* and *low* culture. The novel features the Chief's gradual psychological self-empowerment as a way to convey, surrealistically, the more overt drama. This exceptional use of point of view is the foremost reason why *Cuckoo's Nest* is widely regarded as outstanding literature. The literary richness in Kesey's rendering of a straightforward narrative dynamic derives from the voice he creates for the Chief, one vacillating between lucid narrative observation and subjective inner turmoil. As such, the Chief is an unreliable narrator. This unreliability allows both the Big Nurse and McMurphy, through the Chief's point of view, to become believably caricaturized: a larger-than-life amplification of a fascist, authoritarian ruler of the ward who must struggle, systematically, to control the larger-than-life, anti-establishment conman. The reader is led to believe that McMurphy may only have allowed himself to be committed because he wanted to avoid a prison work camp elsewhere. *Cuckoo's Nest* is a dramatic, comi-tragic romp played out against the backdrop of the more serious social questions that Kesey poses relative to mental health care, free will, modernization, self-reliance, and individuality.

It has been well noted how Kesey wrote *Cuckoo's Nest* from the experiences he had while working part time at the Menlo Park Veterans Hospital. Often missing in discussion about *Cuckoo's Nest* is how profoundly his work reflected the societal pressures of modernization in the Pacific Northwest, specifically the curtailing of a spirit of rugged individualism. The pioneering spirit to fulfill America's manifest destiny and civilize the entire continent from the Atlantic to the Pacific, suffered cultural reverberations of containment following World War II. It's no accident that Kesey, in *Cuckoo's Nest*, located his Mental hospital not in the urban Bay Area, but in his more rural home state of Oregon.

In a 2001 obituary for Kesey, Bob Welch, columnist for The Register-Guard in Eugene, wrote:

> What I liked best about Ken Kesey has nothing to do with psychedelic buses or LSD or Merry Pranksters.
> What I liked best about Kesey was his words. Specifically, the way those words brought to life Oregon,
> [...], like someone who understood this place—at least the old, rural, pre-factory outlet version—better than most.
> [...] It was as if Kesey and Oregon were one, like saltwater and freshwater at a river's mouth, nothing to define where one started and the other ended but clearly part of one another [Eugene *Register-Guard*].

This attachment to Oregon and the modernization affecting the state is presented through the proverbial Indian and cowboy joining forces to fight the loss of the Wild West. McMurphy possesses a seemingly indefatigable will to design his own roguish life as though life is forever a hustle at the edge of the frontier. He is ever the battler of those looking to contain him. The Chief, victim of a tamed frontier, the embodiment of a lost voice being called back from the void between worlds, draws power from McMurphy's spirit. There are many surreal passages throughout the novel where the Chief, as narrator, struggles with the memories of his past, of fighting through a metaphorical fog that he believes is real. The fog has been induced by years of being institutionalized in the mental ward and suffering treatment with electroshock therapy.

Less recognized in the construction of the novel is the factual basis on which Kesey developed the Chief Broom character. Kesey portrays "Broom" as a half-white, half–Indian, whose father was a Chief of the now-vanished Columbia Indians of the Columbia Gorge between Washington and Oregon. Tanner points out that the hallucinated origin of the Chief Broom character was overstated by the author: "Kesey did know a good deal about Indians and had thought and written about them. For an assignment in his radio and television class at [the University of] Oregon he had written "Sunset at Celilo," a script about an Indian who returns from the Korean Conflict at the time when the dam was being built at The Dalles and his tribe was being forced to leave their village" (22).

Kesey uses the building of The Dalles Dam as a core source of the Chief's severe alienation from the world. At the beginning of the novel, the Chief acts deaf and dumb, yet serves as the eyes of the story. Even though the conflict between Randle McMurphy and Nurse Ratched is centerstage in the Chief's first person observations, the Chief is ultimately the story's protagonist, and the one who changes most by the end of the novel.

The Dalles is situated on the arid, eastern edge of the Cascade Mountain Range on the south shore of the Columbia River, second largest river system in North America. The Dam and fog serve as the key motifs employed by Kesey to express the Chief's profound disengagement from society. The plight of the Chief's people is poignant. This helps Kesey establish the Chief's severe schizophrenic withdrawal in a manner that, plausibly, can be overcome within the energeics of the novel.

To put this in perspective, early in the book the Chief says that "the mill put me in kind of a dream [...] reminded me somehow of the men in the tribe who'd left the village in the last days to do work on the gravel crusher for the dam (38–9)." In 1957, while Kesey was still living in Oregon, Vice President Richard Nixon came to The Dalles to dedicate the opening of The Dalles Dam, a public works project that was part of the massive Columbia River hydro-electrification effort, and the second dam upstream from the Pacific Ocean behind the Bonneville Dam, which was built in the 1930's. What made The Dalles Dam so significant was the inundation it caused.

Before the arrival of the white man—starting with the Lewis and Clark Corps of Discovery expedition in 1803–1805—Celilo Falls served as the single most significant trade center in the greater Pacific Northwest for both plateau and coastal Native Americans. Celilo Falls was eight miles upriver from where The Dalles Dam would be built. Archaeological findings document 11,000 years of continuous occupation at Celilo Village beside the Falls. The massive falls, with a flow four times greater than Niagra, slowed the migration of huge schools of salmon returning to the river to spawn. In the eddies and foaming water, local Indians erected scaffolds to tend hoops, dipnet and spear the large fish ascending the waterfalls. Even though modernization had caused significant changes in the lives of the "fish" Indians there—known as the River People—the building of the dam and the reservoir it created, all but eliminated a way of life that had been in place for millennia before the arrival of the white man. There are factual inaccuracies in how Kesey depicted his Columbia Gorge Indians, such as his claim that the Columbia Indians became extinct with the Dam—the River People and a relocated Celilo Village still exist. However, in writing this clearly fictional work, the author tapped into the profound angst caused by this dam. When the novel speaks of Indians working those last days on the gravel crusher for the dam, there is a powerful subtext. This line rings with connotations of a condemned man working to build the scaffolding from which he knows he will be hanged, or a Jew forced to build a concentration camp where he suspects he will be gassed.

Several of the stalwart leaders of the River People openly wept on the day Celilo Falls vanished under the backed up Columbia. Chief Tommy Thompson, who was the real life Salmon Chief of Celilo Village at the time the Dam was finished, heard the news in a nursing home downriver. "There goes my life," he said. "My people will never be the same." The Chief died two years later.

The loss that Kesey tapped into with the Chief Broom character was rooted in tragedy wrought by this dubious act of modernization. With a ship canal already bypassing the Falls, the merits of building this dam were too conveniently rationalized, even in the context of the unfettered progress of this time. Celilo Falls was touted as one of the eight wonders of the Western Hemisphere, a magnificent geologic, natural and cultural resource. The destruction of this geologic formation shows the type of mindset that was so vehemently opposed in later years by those in the counterculture. It explains how the environmental movement, as a reaction, gained its legitimacy in the late 1960s and '70s. In *Cuckoo's Nest*, this tragic background of the Chief was largely subtextual; the overt storyline questioned the mental health practices of the time, especially electroshock therapy. Yet, on more than one front, a careful reading of *Cuckoo's Nest* reveals the systemic factors that helped give birth to a reactionary counterculture, one responding to the institutional, industrial and military self-indulgence being exhibited by the leaders in America.

The flooding of Celilo Falls is symbolic of an "establishment" deemed so in control it was out of control. Nowhere was this prospect more frightening than with the threat of a "trigger-happy" nuclear annihilation. The response from the youthful shadows would come to include protest, exuberant fun, and wild mind-altering excess in the face of this structured threat.

Cuckoo's Nest, like the counterculture, represented an archetypal enactment of a Dionysian sentiment. The coming Bacchanalia of the counterculture would challenge the "enlightened" modern order of the day. In *Cuckoo's Nest*, the spirit of protest is best exemplified through Kesey's portrayal of McMurphy's laughter, a robust laugh of humanity in the face of authority and in a ward where nobody laughed; this is an infectious laugh that helps transform Chief Broom. This symbolic laughter became manifest in the theatrics of his Merry Pranksters, and in the "play as power" protests of the hippies. Within the "soul" of this counterculture, a spectrum of alternative notions related to a socio-spiritual quest for enlightenment, was about to turn the "enlightened" ideas of modernization on its head. This is at the core of the consciousness revolution, the utopian belief that "we can change the world" by starting with ourselves through a more enlightened approach to living on the planet.

In the bowels of a hydroelectric dam, through the person of Chief Bromden, Kesey creates surrealistic images of a turbine producing electricity. The author then blends a vision of such imagery into the many electroshock therapy treatments the Chief had endured before McMurphy arrived at the hospital. To produce his surrealistic effect, Kesey employs the metaphor of fog repeatedly. In these passages, Chief Broom struggles to fight for lucid thought and memories from within his paranoia of fog. Chief Broom of these Columbia Indians worked as a trained electrician before he was committed to the state mental hospital. The inclusion of this perverse irony by Kesey was not an accident.

On the last page of the novel, the Chief has escaped the mental ward and talks about returning to the Columbia Gorge where he imagines the scaffolding that he's heard are now on the cement sides of the Dam: "I'd give something to see that. Mostly, I'd just like to look over the country around the gorge again, just to bring some of it clear in my mind again.

"I been away a long time" (272).

The Dam and the fog are key motifs that Kesey uses to portray the Chief's complete withdrawal from the world. In light of how he chose to end the novel with the Chief gamely returning home, and as dramatically as Bromden's home had changed, Kesey underscores how he felt about this character as central to the construction of his novel. The movie version, which Kesey chose never to see, relegates the character of the Chief to secondary status as part of the ensemble of men in the ward. Highly successful as a movie, it is well acted, but without the interior point-of-view of the Chief, the movie version of *Cuckoo's Nest* is a two-dimensional rendition of the novel. As two well-received products, a comparison of this book and movie offers a superb argument for the inherent limitations when adapting literary works into film. For Kesey, the evolution and self-actualization of Chief Bromden was more integral to *One Flew Over the Cuckoo's Nest* than were the roles of McMurphy and Nurse Ratched. This triangle of characters is like a firm tripod in the construction of the narrative, but, unlike the movie version, ultimately, the story belongs to the Chief.

Any analysis of *Cuckoo's Nest* should factor in the societal-historical context of the time period when Kesey wrote the novel. Cold War tension was at its height. The book was published during a year of political brinkmanship when President John F. Kennedy forced Soviet Premier Nikita Khrushchev to back away from installing nuclear missiles in Cuba. Martin Luther King's "I have a Dream" speech had yet to be given, though the Civil Rights movement was beginning to gain momentum in the Deep South. Betty Friedan's *The Feminine Mystique,* would not be published until the following year. In the book, Friedan called women's growing unhappiness with narrow roles "the problem that has no name."

Kesey does not deal with either black characters struggling for enfranchisement, or women reacting to being confined within idealized images of femininity (as Friedan put it). In *Cuckoo's Nest* the black and women characters are the ones in charge of the confinement. This novel has been harshly criticized for its depiction of women as seen through the Nurse Ratched character. Nurse Ratched *is* castrating and she *is* a fascist control freak. This is obvious. However, the core story could just as easily be about the Big Nurse presiding over a women's mental ward and facing a similar revolt by these women against the containment of their human spirit. She would be no less a villain in this regard, or if she was a man.

At the end of the novel, when the Chief has regained his will and resolve, Kesey introduces another nurse character. She is very minor to the story, a Japanese-American who appears just as McMurphy and the Chief are to be given the electroshock treatment ordered by Nurse Ratched after they have been in an all out fight with the two black orderlies on her ward. Showing empathy for the two men, this newly introduced nurse gives McMurphy a cigarette and the Chief a stick of gum, remembering that he liked gum:

> The nurse—about as big as the small end of nothing whittled to a fine point, as
> McMurphy put it later—undid our cuffs [...]
>   "It's not all like her [Ratched's] ward," she said. "A lot of it is, but not all.
> Army nurses trying to run an Army hospital. They are a little sick themselves. I
> sometimes think that all single nurses should be fired after they reach thirty-
> five."
>   "At least all the single *Army* nurses," McMurphy added. [...]
>   "Yes, I'd like to keep men here sometimes instead of sending them back, but
> she has seniority [233–234].

Through the voice of this sympathetic nurse, the author certainly imposes a very sexist view that women who are not married by age thirty-five are destined to a dangerous sort of hardness. This is not an enlightened feminist view in a pre-feminist era, but there to help Kesey reinforce the authoritarian theme he has established. The comment is intended to render Ratched as a victim and product herself of a cold, unrelenting regimen; her career as an Army nurse has dehumanized her.

In Kesey's portrayal, Ratched's nurturing role as a Nurse is constantly dwarfed by a more insidious and militaristic need to be in control. Her faint touches of humanity seep onto the page only in glimpses as seen in the way she keeps a personal interest in Billy Bibbit, her dear friend's son, who is a virgin at age thirty. After the Big Nurse discovers Billy sleeping with one of McMurphy's hooker friends, she first chastises and then consoles him against her large bosom, of which we are reminded often. McMurphy's intent with the hooker was to help his fellow ward mate get laid. Ratched consoles Billy, but at the same time lets him know that she is obligated to tell his mother. When Billy slits his own throat shortly after this encounter, the Big Nurse, predictably, blames McMurphy.

The sexist implications are strong in this scene, but so is the plausibility of the drama unfolding in this way. Through detailed character development, Kesey has set up the individual personalities at play in this dramatic encounter. Ratched, Bibbit, and McMurphy, by this late point in the novel, are all pathetic characters, yet three-dimensional and each yielding to a respective energeic fate. There is a difference between noting sexist depictions and condemning a work based on a retroactive political correctness. Or, as Tanner states:

> Miss Ratched is a villain not because she is a woman, but because she is not
> human. McMurphy's ripping open of her shell-like uniform is not a revengeful
> attack on a castrating bitch: it is a symbolic gesture indicating that the human
> must be liberated from the machine if the oppression of the Combine is to be
> eliminated. [...] Big Nurse may reflect to some extent a "pre–Liberation" female
> personality of the late 1950s—the woman feeling much alone in asserting herself
> in a male world and therefore finding it necessary to be overly aggressive and
> domineering in order to prove her worth [47].

The brief, surreal depictions of the Chief's white mother are enigmatic. There is a temptation, though inconclusive, to draw a parallel between his mother and Nurse Ratched. The Chief's detachment from the Big Nurse is consistent throughout the novel—she largely ignores his deaf and dumb presence, relegating his care to the black orderlies. The reader simply isn't given many clues about the Chief's relationship with his mother. The most telling exposition about Mrs. Bromden is when the Chief recalls how three federal negotiators came to the village to buy off the tribe for the land to be flooded by the Dam. One of them, notably a woman, suggests that they mail the offer to the wife (Broom's mother), instead of the father (then, the Chief). The implication in this surreal passage is that the Chief's mother, the white woman, sells out the tribe. This aspect of the story is literally and figuratively foggy, but sexist and racist undertones are certainly present.

Along with the Dam and the fog, "The Combine" is the other primary motif used by Kesey to create the surrealistic basis of the Chief's world. Kristen Rooks, in an online study guide, suggests that readers of *Cuckoo's Nest*:

> compare Ken Kesey's concept of the Combine—as demonstrated by President Eisenhower's policies, and corporate America's views on an efficient, well-organized, and compliant society—with Chief Bromden's concept of the Combine—an all-powerful, all-seeing secret group in the mental hospital, which watches and controls everything [http://school.discovery.com/lessonplans/programs/cuckoo/].

This suggestion offers valuable insight into Kesey's distrust of a perceived institutional cabal controlling American society at the time he wrote this novel. Rooks goes on to to define "The Combine" as:

> A combination especially of business or political interests. Also, a harvesting machine that heads, threshes, and cleans grain while moving over a field [*http://school.discovery.com/lessonplans/*programs/cuckoo/].

The state of Oregon is split roughly down the middle by the Cascade Range. The lush green maritime climate of western Oregon, where the mental hospital is, differs significantly from the arid side, east of the mountains, where Chief Broom grew up. Much of the rolling hills above The Dalles are covered with wheat. For this reason "The Combine," a large and complex machine seen rolling through the wheat fields at harvest time, was an appropriate metaphor for the Chief to employ in his surrealistic associations. The Chief, whose world was limited to the hospital environment for so many years, associates the Combine with Nurse Ratched's ward and her manner of controlling the patients. In other words, the Big Nurse systematically heads, threshes and cleans them as part of her ostensible "cure."

None of the characters in the novel, overwhelmingly male, were given a candy-coated portrayal. Three of the men on the ward die, a few, most notably the Chief, gain the strength to leave, and a few remain at the hospital as acute or chronic patients. Kesey's caricatures flow from the Chief's surreal perception of the ward. The manner in which the author portrays and develops the diverse psychological characteristics of the other men on the ward, hints at his personal fascination with group dynamic, later seen in the communal synergy he embraced. Following the success of *Cuckoo's Nest,* Kesey exhibited charismatic qualities helping to corral a small tribe of people into joining him in 1964 on a cross-country trip across the United States in a wildly painted school bus. Upon their return, the Merry Pranksters instigated through their acid test parties a popular disbursement of LSD. This will be discussed later in the chapter on Tom Wolfe's *The Electric Acid Kool-Aid Test,* but the evolution of Kesey's personal life is consistent with the type of story and type of primary male characters he constructed for *Cuckoo's Nest.* Kesey was an alpha male of sorts, gregarious, a natural leader, and not unlike McMurphy.

There was certainly a fair amount of pranksterism instigated by McMurphy in *Cuckoo's Nest* as he asserts more freedom under the authoritarian regime of the Big Nurse. Toward the end of the novel, McMurphy is blamed by Nurse Ratched for the deaths of two of the patients in the ward, but by this point the Nurse has been fully implicated every bit as much as McMurphy. This is not to say that McMurphy's brand of leadership and hustle would be acceptable anywhere. Beneath his bravado, ironically, McMurphy needs a foil such as Nurse Ratched from whom to draw psychological power. He oversleeps and refuses to escape at the end because, seemingly, he needs the power he has found as the leader of the pack. He also knows from repeated past failures that he cannot make it on the outside. A metaphorical treatment that views McMurphy as a Christ-figure will attribute more lofty ideals to the decision not to flee. In this view, he dies for the "sins" of his "disciples." Tanner describes McMurphy as "a coarse and vulgar personality, but the victory wrought by him is not merely a triumph of coarseness and vulgarity. His crude strength and cocky self-centeredness are manifestations in caricature of an underlying moral strength and a salutary self-respect" (51).

Pranksterism is an apt label for the style of personal protest that reached its peak of expression at the height of the anti–Vietnam War movement. This eccentric theatricality was distinctive to this period, especially as a method of drawing attention to a cause. For such protesters, "play as power" was, of course, an attempt to be heard and seen against the enormity of American military might. The outlandishness of such behavior as a mode of protest subjects it to easy lampooning. However, such lampooning obfuscates the pragmatism underlying much of this flamboyant and unorthodox behavior. Such theatricality championed fun in face of institutional excess. A great part of the allure of the counterculture was the fun it embraced within this notion of play as power. This behavioral strategy is very much present in Randall P. McMurphy as he operates within the confines of Nurse Ratched's ward in the Oregon State Mental Hospital.

In *Cuckoo's Nest*, Kesey employs pranksterism in several scenes designed to unnerve or subvert the authority of Nurse Ratched and to empower McMurphy as the de facto leader of the ward. This comes to a head in a culminating scene late in the novel when two hooker friends of McMurphy's drive down from Portland. As mentioned, Billy Bibbit loses his virginity in the scene; Mr. Turkle, the night watchman, is lured into the chaos with liquor and the promise of sex.

Here the reader is offered the best hint of Kesey's personal immersion into experimentation with drugs. The cigarette being smoked by the night watchman is "funny"; it's referred to as a joint. McMurphy helps them break into the stores of drugs in the ward. A gallon jug of codeine cough syrup is mixed with the vodka brought to them by one of the women. In the midst of the wildness, Harding, the intellectual wardmate, holds two fistfuls of drugs and, though already high, warns that "Miss Ratched shall line us all against the wall, where we'll face the terrible maw of a muzzle-loading shotgun which she has loaded with Miltowns! Thorazines! Libriums! Stelazines! And with a wave of her sword, *blooie!* Tranquilize all of us completely out of our of existence" (255).

While working at the Veterans Hospital, Kesey "liberated" a vile of pure LSD from a Doctor's desk. With this "elixir" that Kesey said lasted them quite some time, the Pranksters began their psychedelic journey as proto-hippie catalyzers of the counterculture.

Cuckoo's Nest struck a responsive, humanistic chord far beyond a bohemian readership. By questioning the loss of humanity in the face of modern, scientific institutions, Kesey captured—through his metaphorical depiction of an insane asylum—much broader societal forces institutionalizing the human spirit. The defeat of rugged individualism, as seen through McMurphy's valiant conman resolve, was amplified through the complete loss of culture embodied in the Chief's deaf and dumb retreat.

Cuckoos Nest demonstrates, through Kesey's use of surrealism, the urge within the literature of the early '60s to break away from traditional form. Yet, as a whole, this novel, along with its concerns, is traditional. In its tone of challenge toward authority and the use of unconventional realism, this book reflects some of the social dynamic that led to the emergence of the counterculture. *Cuckoo's Nest* also helps explain why

Kesey assumed a McMurphyesque role in working to catalyze a style of life that challenged the sterility and conformity of modern America. Or as author Robert Stone said about his fellow Stanford writing program participant:

> When the world leaned on him, he upped the ante and fought back. In a way he became a character in his own book. He became McMurphy. McMurphy sacrifices himself on behalf of his people to take on the world. Ken did that [On The Bus, 156].

Cuckoo's Nest was a manifesto for personal freedom and empowerment through self-reliance; it lamented the loss of the traditional in the face of the modern; the story questioned notions of conformity, especially in terms of who and what should be considered insane. A paranoia about the establishment cabal is notable in the personal and group revolt. Moreover, a mostly pacifistic and, at times, theatrical method of revolt is underscored; revised notions of personal freedom are explored; and, a group psychology of leadership and hierarchy is dramatically highlighted. In these ways, *Cuckoo's Nest* served as a template for Kesey's personal exploits.

As Stone points out, Kesey's methods, via the prank, were not dissimilar to McMurphy's. The Merry Pranksters disseminated psychoactive drugs, questioned authority in a theatrical, non-violent manner, and set the stage for more widespread communal experimentation. Kesey was a natural tribal leader, the egalitarian chief of the commune, the master Prankster, a big kid, ala Randle P. McMurphy. With *One Flew Over the Cuckoo's Nest,* Ken Kesey had a script for his life, except that the narrow confines of a mental hospital were now the constraints of modern America in the 1960s. Kesey, a privileged white male in the most affluent modern society in the world, was at the cutting edge of a social phenomenon that was unthinkable in the years that preceded him. He challenged, for reasons of institutional excess brought forth in *Cuckoo's Nest,* the very establishment that privileged him.

Within the conventional narrative of *Cuckoo's Nest,* the seeds of a broader cultural and literary change are evident. Kesey's second novel, *Sometimes A Great Notion,* to be discussed next, expounds on many of the same themes as *Cuckoo's Nest.* Much more than in his first novel, with *Great Notion* Kesey pushed the boundaries of literary structure.

3

Sometimes a Great Notion (1964)

A Frontier Duality

Sometimes A Great Notion was significantly more difficult for Ken Kesey to construct than the straightforward narrative of *One Flew Over the Cuckoo's Nest*. While *Cuckoo's Nest* is mostly confined to scenes within a hospital setting, *Great Notion* is the portrayal of an entire small Oregon Coast logging community in the early 1960's. It features the dynamic of one extended family. The novel pivots on one element. Kesey scribbled a note to himself in 1962 while beginning to draft the novel. It said: "Try to make Hank give up" (Northwest Review, 24). This provides the through-line of *Great Notion*, the focal point upon which several narrative points of view, timelines, and dramatic plotlines converge.

Hank Stamper is the heir apparent, the "crown prince," of the family logging operation. His father, Old Henry Stamper, is the family patriarch, the man Hank must try to live up to. The Stamper's family business operation has a logging contract to fulfill. Several booms of logs must be floated down the Waukonda Auga River to the major mill in town no later than Thanksgiving Day. The rub in the story is that this delivery will keep the corporate owners of the mill from having to negotiate with the other unionized loggers from the town who are on strike. By keeping the mill supplied with logs, Hank Stamper becomes the focal point of the striking loggers' animosity.

Hank and his cousin Joe Ben Stamper try to round up workers by contacting every shirttail relative they can think of to help them meet the quota for the log contract. This includes a postcard sent to Hank's half-brother, Leland Stanford Stamper, who is a dozen years younger. Twelve years before the current story with its logging conflict, Lee and his mother had moved to Greenwich Village in New York City. Lee's mother, Myra, left the Stamper home because of the affair she had been

having with her stepson, Hank, which started when the boy was in high
school. Lee, through a peephole, had known of the affair as a child, and,
now as a 24-year-old, decides to respond to the request for labor so that
he can exact revenge on his big brother. When Lee arrives in the coastal
town, he is still grieving his mother's death by suicide a year earlier.

Great Notion employs numerous points of view by telling the story at
various times through Hank, Old Henry, Lee, Joe Ben, Viv, Indian Jenny
or the union men—Jonathan Draeger and Floyd Evenwrite. Some of the
novel is first person, some third person limited; some is in past tense,
some in present tense; the author's own P.O.V. occasionally appears with
metaphorical asides and what seem like second person declarations. The
creative impact—once the reader grasps the authorial design—is a complex mosaic, a refractory structure that converges from several simultaneous directions on Hank Stamper. The effect is one of a fragmented
narrative omniscience coming together to create a singular portrait. As
Paul Perry points out in *On The Bus: The Complete Guide to the Legendary
Trip of Ken Kesey and the Merry Pranksters and the Birth of the Counterculture:*

> the techniques Kesey used [in *Great Notion*] are experimental, in the masterful
> tradition of the works of a James Joyce or William Faulkner. Tenses change in
> mid-paragraph, as do points of view; yet these shifting perspectives (acid
> inspired?) make for a more complete picture of the blustery world of the Stam-
> per family [44].

The impression during the early pages is one of disjointedness, but the
focal point never wavers from Hank, to breaking his will. The tension
and conflict in *Great Notion* come at Hank like different sized sticking
pins, different points of pain, being pushed into a voodoo doll. This is
not an easy read; the Newsweek review when the book came out called
it "lumbering. [...] Kesey's book, for all his intensity of purpose, attempts
to be all inclusive and ends up elephantine" (Perry, 55).

The portrait is indeed elephantine and its method challenging, but
Great Notion ties together brilliantly as a fascinating portrait of the changing American West Coast culture in the early 1960s. Kesey's many narrative threads approach the climax from these different directions, but
there is strong profluence, or forward fluid movement in the story and,
ultimately, the dramatic arc yields a poignant climax with a denouement
that is satisfyingly tragic.

Published in 1964, the novel identifies significant stress fractures in
American society that, over the course of the next decade, will become
major chasms.

The manner in which the *Great Notion* both highlights and challenges masculinization and Eurocentrism creates an ironic push-and-
pull that is part of the novel's lasting strength. The story is all but
drenched in male testosterone and steeped in the Eurocentric expan-

sionist spirit of America taming its Wild West through the exertion of rugged individualism. The story is of man conquering nature, of man extracting the resources of the land, of "never giving an inch" to the river or the rough wooded terrain or to any person or thing getting in the way. The motto was Old Henry's reaction to his own father who had left Henry and Oregon when Henry was a boy to return to the predictable sameness of Kansas. Old Henry has passed this "notion" of "never give and inch" down to his son, Hank. Throughout the novel, Hank struggles to live up to Old Henry's resolve.

The essence of the novel hinges on the relationship of the two brothers. Old Henry is crippled from a logging injury and has left Hank in charge of the family business and affairs. Hank is up to the task; he was the stud athlete at the local high school years ago, a fact not lost on Floyd Evenwrite, the local union leader who was not named an All-State Team selection because of Hank's superior ability as fullback on the football field. Consequently, Floyd has a grudge to bear beyond the current strike.

Many people in the town knew of the teenager's affair with his stepmother, but if Old Henry knew, the father never let on. Young Leland knew though, and Hank, we find, knew about the peephole. The monolithic Stamper home perches on the eroding bank of the River and is accessible from the main highway only by boat. Twelve years earlier, when Myra and Lee move out, Hank helps to ferry them from the Stamper house across the river. The young Leland tells his older half-brother:

> "You ... just ... wait," he says, squeezing out the threat. "Mmm. Mm boy, Hank, someday you'll get it for what you..."
>
> "Me? *Me?*" Hank erupts, twisting in his seat. "You're lucky I don't bust your scrawny little *neck!* Because let me tell you, bub..."
>
> "You just wait till..."
>
> "–if you wasn't a kid and I found out what you'd been..."
>
> "–till I'm a big guy!"
>
> [...]
>
> "*What!*" Old Henry silences the outburst. "In God's *creation!* Are you two talking about!" [40].

Likewise, when Lee returns to the Stamper home as a man, the relationship between the brothers, especially Lee's covert intent for revenge, takes up where it left off. This conflict is at the core of the novel. Over the course of *Great Notion*, Lee, at first callously, wants to take out his deep-seated loathing for Hank by seducing Vivian, Lee's independent-minded, though traditionally supportive sister-in-law. Later, however, a growing fondness for Viv impels him to sincerely want to win her heart and steal her away from Hank.

Kesey talked about how he went about writing *Great Notion* in a 1963 interview with Gordon Lish in *Genesis West* magazine:

> For one thing, I want to find out which side of me really is: the woodsy, logger
> side—complete with homespun homilies and crackerbarrel corniness, a valid
> side of me that I like—or its opposition. The two Stamper brothers in the novel
> are each one of the ways I think I am ... In college, for example, the guys on the
> wrestling team used to say, "You write? You act? What in the hell you doing over
> with those people?" Over in the drama or writing department they were always
> bugging me about associating with a gang of thumpheads. Look, I don't intend
> to let anybody make me live in less world than I'm capable of living in. [Ken]
> Babbs once said it perfectly: *A man should have the right to be as big as he feels it's in
> him to be* [Perry & Babbs, 39].

Psychologically then, *Great Notion* is rooted in an autobiographical exploration of Kesey's own internal duality of character. He is the assertive,
athletic, masculine Oregon boy who goes to the urban Bay area and finds
himself expressing more of his sensitive, disaffected and experimental
side.

Lee represents a classic passive-aggressive personality pitted against
Hank's persona of the classic unyielding alpha male. Insidiously, Lee
ushers the outside forces of change into the midst of the extractive, conquering, patriarchal Stamper family enterprise. When he wrote the novel,
Kesey was conflicted by similar contradictory pressures, living this changing dynamic within himself. Unlike McMurphy and Big Nurse, neither
Lee nor Hank are broad-stroked caricatures—Lee is an effective, though
inexperienced, worker in the woods conflicted by growing familial attachment and revenge; Hank shows great restraint, a complex resolve, and
even a hip interest in jazz music, for example. Likewise, Hank loves his
little brother and saves Lee's life both when Lee was a young kid and
when he returns as an adult. At times Lee finds it hard to despise his
brother and suffers from never believing he can live up to the strength
and resoluteness of the older sibling. Hank, as the novel develops, is
increasingly aware that his younger brother has designs on his wife.

Stephen Tanner in *Ken Kesey* notes that "Kesey's real interest is in
strength and weakness and the relationships between them" (80). To
give dramatic definition to the relationship between Hank and Lee,
Kesey draws parallels for this dynamic in the extended family and community. As animosity heats up in the community over the log contract,
the members of the community increasingly despise Hank Stamper. Thematically, this parallels Lee's despite for Hank. When Hank gives up on
trying to deliver the logs near the end of the novel, the same community members find themselves not celebrating Hank's defeat, but
depressed. Hank, even when despised, is a pillar of strength that the
community hates to see weakened, because it makes each of them feel
weaker. The author delves deeply into the idea that in strength there is
weakness and in weakness strength. This culminates overtly when both
Hank and Lee come to terms with the paradox within themselves.

In the early 1960's, Kesey was living on the cusp of dramatic cultural upheaval and change. By exploring, so intensely, these two parts of his own inner dynamic, it's no wonder the author felt emotionally exhausted by the time he finished *Great Notion*. He had given this novel everything he felt he had inside. Naturally, he was disappointed that *Great Notion* was not as well received as *Cuckoo's Nest*. This undoubtedly factored into why he chose to veer away from novel writing for nearly three decades. The difficulty factor for writing *Great Notion*, like an Olympic dive, was significantly greater than with *Cuckoo's Nest*. The second novel, with its complexity, also gave greater insight into the nuance of social change brewing in the first half of the 1960s.

In *Great Notion*, Hank is closest to his cousin, Joe Ben Stamper. For part of the novel, Joe Ben, his wife and five children live in the big Stamper home until Joe Ben's own home can be finished. Joe Ben is Hank's best and most faithful worker. More significantly for the construction of the novel, Joe Ben is a devout evangelical Christian with an uncanny ability to see the positive in every life occurrence that besets the Stamper clan throughout the novel.

Kesey's wife Faye, who he married in 1956 before they left Oregon for Stanford, was a devout Christian throughout their 45-year marriage. Kesey's exploration of faith in *Great Notion* is viewed through Joe Ben— not only the impact of the cousin's faith on Hank, but on Lee as well. The surface sexism, racism, masculinization, Eurocentrism, and Christianity help Kesey explore many cultural phenomena predominant in America at the time. For example, Joe Ben is a simple man, but the author subtly elevates the theme of faith through the impact Joe Ben has on Hank. After Joe Ben drowns near the end of the novel, Hank finally loses his will and optimism to continue the battle to meet the logging contract. The implication is that Hank has been garnering strength vicariously through Joe Ben's faith-driven optimism.

Midway through the novel, Lee agrees to go to church with Joe Ben, with the ulterior motive of meeting up with Vivian afterwards. At the tent service, Lee experiences an epiphany of sorts. He is talking to himself:

> Nitwit, you have a pot hangover is all. The "aftergrass"[...] because when the high first started to come on—to the tune of "Onward Christian Soldiers" played dance-time on a steel guitar as Brother Walker screamed for converts to stand and seek their salvation—I didn't relate it to being high the night before and, for a few maddening moments, teetered on the verge of trooping forth up that sawdust path to metaphysical glory [287].

Lee, the East Coast intellectual in the midst of this West Coast individualism, serves as Kesey's modern skeptic. In contrast—through Hank's reaction to Joe Ben's death—the author acknowledges the power of faith. During Joe Ben's memorial service late in the novel, Hank notes how community members at the service focus more on him than on the newly departed. Hank, in this scene, is fully aware of his position at the eye of the community storm. He is also appreciative of the value Joe Ben had on his own bearing in life. At the end of the service, Hank observes the local real estate agent who is standing next to Joe Ben's preacher:

> a dealer in dirt and a peddler of sky, chance comrades for a while because of their shared destination and their corresponding views of destiny, both beaming their brightest and dreaming of great transactions of earth and air—tingling and cheerful, real pinnacles of optimism, masters of the bright outlook ... but still only amateurs compared to the dead man they were on their way to bury [508].

With Kesey's layering of attitudes toward faith and spirituality through Lee, Hank, and Joe Ben, the author reveals the changing state of religion in the Western world in the early 1960's. Living a bohemian life near San Francisco at the end of the Beat era, Kesey was familiar with the Beat philosophies that welcomed eastern spiritual perspectives.

Kesey renders a world through dramatic actualization by creating realistic characters with realistic traits and manners of speech and individual belief systems. His portrayals in *Great Notion* are not judgmental "truths," but fascinating characterizations that develop via the plot dynamic. This is manifest in how Kesey handled spiritual skepticism within *Great Notion*. The author articulated this cultural/spiritual shift—the spiritual outlook on the artistic fringes in America—in a 2000 interview, the year before he died:

> Here's another [phenomenon] that happened in the 60's, Buddhism. The whole eastern thinking came in. [...] [T]he whole Zen attitude of going with it, flowing with the energy. Christianity needs Buddhism to do its work, otherwise it becomes clogged up in it's thinking. Buddhism needs Christianity, otherwise it becomes too insulated, too turning into itself. All of these philosophies and religions that are operating need each other but they don't know it, so they're fighting amongst each other. But you hang around with good acidhead Christian Buddhists and you know all that stuff you learn is really valuable and the part of the revolution. We are part of the revolution. You can look back in history and see revolutionists. People who did things were selfless and increased human knowledge. The revolution, when you boil it down to a kernel, its ever lasting kernel is love [www.sputnik.ac/interview%20page/trip.html].

The Beat sensibility in *Great Notion* belongs to Lee Stamper. Expositional references are made about Lee's mother Myra, an East Coast Stanford grad and early beatnik who, for some inexplicable reason is wooed back to the West Coast by the assertive courting of a man three decades older than she. Henry Stamper, after Henry's first wife and Hank's mother died, had gone back East to find a new wife.

In Oregon, Myra's and Henry's young boy Leland is bookish, reclusive and clings to his mother. He all but lives in his bedroom where he spies on the affair between his mother and halfbrother.

At the beginning of the novel, Lee is coping quite poorly with his mother's suicide the year before when she jumped from the 40th floor of a building in New York City. At the time that Leland receives the postcard from Oregon, he is a failing grad student in English Literature at Yale and an emotional wreck looking to kill himself. After he sets off a natural gas explosion in his apartment that fails to end his life, he remembers the postcard, sells his Volkswagen bug and buys a ticket for a crosscountry bus trip. In a fog of Dexedrines and phenobarbs, Lee makes his way to Oregon.

When Lee and Hank first reunite after twelve years, Hank is swimming across the river while Lee is trying to steer the motorboat that had nearly gotten loose on the highway side. Hank, swimming to rescue the boat, doesn't know who's steering the skiff, who is trying to stop for him. When he figures out that whoever is driving doesn't know how to slow the boat, Hank grabs hold and pulls himself onboard. When he catches his breath and sees that it's his brother Lee, his first words are: "You had three tries, bub [...] and missed me every time; now don't that frost you?" (92).

Lee's design for comeuppance unfolds and changes over the course of the novel. He fits in surprisingly well with the hard working family, and his sense of accomplishment in the woods confounds his obsession for primal revenge. Once reacquainted with these Stampers, Lee finds he likes the work and his family more than he's comfortable admitting. He always keeps a bit of distance, however, and sequesters himself in his room, smoking the pot he has hidden in a cold cream jar in his shaving kit. This is the early '60s before marijuana use became commonplace with American youth. In one of Kesey's surrealistic passages, Lee can't find rolling papers until he remembers they are wrapped within a short story he had penned about Fuckleberry Hen.

Like Kesey, Lee enjoyed his altered states. Also like Kesey, Hank was the alpha male. Again, marijuana prior to 1964 was not widely prevalent, although hip in certain circles and definitely illegal. Kesey interjects into *Great Notion* the world outside this rather insular and isolated logging community. Lee and his hipster attitudes, the pot he smokes, and the encounter he makes with the greaser high school boys are examples of how Kesey infuses the small town novel with the changing world beyond.

The local greasers give Lee a ride to the beach after he leaves the church tent service. The boys are looking for trouble, and a hip repartee between Lee and the teens ensues. The conversation is rife with pointed hipster subtext—they know that Lee is a Stamper, and he, in as cool a manner as he can muster, lets them know that he has their number, too, so to speak. The boys drop Lee off near the beach without incident. Kesey, in traditional dramatic fashion, lets the reader think Lee is off the hook. The author then brings back the same trouble with even greater force. A short time later, when Lee is trying to find Viv at the beach, the boys and the hot car appear in the novel again.

On the beach Lee sees that the boys have gotten their car hopelessly stuck in the sand. When Lee walks past, the toughest kid bullies him. He forces Lee to walk into the rising tide. He insists that Lee push the car free before it's submerged: "An' if Hank could do it I bet you could do it too, hey? So let's see you put a shoulder an' try. Come on, hey?" (297). The boys are taking out on the younger brother, the animosity that has been building in the community toward Hank Stamper:

> "You better not ... my brother will..."
> "Your brother will what, Mr. Stamper? Your brother isn't here. All alone, you said." ... [...]
> "Look."
> "Who's that?"
> "Christ-o-Friday, it's him..."
> "Split everybody! Split!" [298].

Hank, not Vivian who Lee is expecting, shows up walking across the dunes. Lee, soaking wet and cold, is saved. This section of current story is juxtaposed with the backstory of when Lee was a young boy and Hank rescued him from being buried in a cave-in on the sand dunes.

With the backstory of this childhood rescue, Kesey shows the contemporary pacifism of Lee, and amplifies Lee's unwillingness to fight overtly, despite his covert obsession for revenge. Hank has foiled, for the time, Lee's growing intent to seduce Vivian, whom Lee sincerely desires now. Through Lee's dependency on the older brother's protection, these scenes highlight Hank's role as the alpha male, both in the community and in the Stamper family. The foreshadowing of a showdown between Hank and Lee is palpable at this halfway point of the lengthy novel. Both men are struggling; the overt pressures on Hank from all these directions are taking a toll, while with Lee, the internal desire for revenge has shifted toward an obsession to steal Vivian away from Hank, even though he knows he should love a brother who cares for him and protects him. However, Lee allows his fraternal resentment to prevail.

Hank is aware of Lee's interest in Viv, but unresolved in Hank's mind is the affair he once had with Lee's mother, Myra. This is seen in how Hank insists that Viv wear her hair long, and how he wonders what it might look like black, the length and color of Myra's. Hank and Vivian are also plagued by the inability to get over the miscarriage that Viv had before Lee returned. The miscarriage will likely mean that they will have no children. And there are still too many logs left to cut, too much pressure from the locals who want the Stampers to back off the contract with the mill; then, there is the father who, though crippled, would never tolerate such backing down. Hank and Lee, for countervailing reasons of strength and weakness, are both at the edge.

More overtly than he did in *Cuckoo's Nest*, Kesey develops in *Great Notion* the motif of wilderness in cold war America. The cultural reverberations of containment and modernization are curtailing a pioneering spirit. Kesey presents this in *Cuckoo's Nest* via exposition. The effect is seen in the mental states of the Chief and McMurphy. The wilderness motif is shown mostly through Chief Broom's surreal reflections on the world he has lost. In *Great Notion* wilderness is not expositional; it's an immediate and visceral part of the current story. Wilderness is central to this novel. The extractive, resource dependent community is feeling the pressure of capitalist maneuvering. The union activists are at odds with the exigencies of the corporate mill owners. There are diminishing natural resources in this wilderness. The cauldron of this novel relates to such containment. There is battle at the frontier edge of the continent for how the rewards of the wilds will be reaped. However, Kesey demonstrates that man must never discount the inherent power of this wilderness. One enormous fir kills both Old Henry and Joe Ben. The untamed exacts a price on the tamer. This parallels the author's treatment of strength and weakness.

Kesey described the importance of this theme in a 1994 interview with Robert Faggen in the *Paris Review:*

> What I explore in all my work [is] wilderness. Settlers on this continent from the beginning have been seeking wilderness and its wildness. The explorers and pioneers sought that wildness because they could sense that in Europe everything had become locked tight ... When we got here there was a sense of possibility and new direction, and it had to do with wildness. Throughout the work of James Fennimore Cooper there is what I call the American terror. It's very important to our literature, and it's important to who we are: the terror of the Hurons out there, the terror of the bear, the avalanche, the tornado—whatever may be over the next horizon [Faggen interview].

For Kesey, the last frontier to conquer was in the mind. Hank personified the conquering of a more literal frontier, Lee this more figurative one.

Kesey was well into his LSD experimentations when he wrote *Great Notion*. In the same 1994 interview Kesey acknowledged:

> So you want to take some more LSD and see what else is there. And soon I had the experience that everyone who's ever dabbled in psychedelics has. A big hand grabs you by the back of the neck, and you hear a voice saying, "You want to see the books? Okay, here are the books." And it pushes your face right down into all of your cruelties and all of your meanness, all the times that you have been insensitive, intolerant, racist, sexist. [...] You start trying to be a little better person. Then you get the surprise. [...] There's only a big hollow, the great American wild hollow, which is scarier than hell, scarier than purgatory or Satan. It's the fact that there isn't any hell and there isn't any purgatory, there isn't any Satan. [...] That's the new wilderness. It's the same old wilderness, just no longer

up on that hill or around that bend, or in that gully. It's because there are no more hills and gullies that the hollow is there, and you've got to explore the hollow with faith [Faggen interview].

In *Great Notion,* Kesey's depiction of racial attitudes, women, and masculinity is presented through the frame of the retreating frontier of the Northwest. This sense of change is both figurative and literal in a wilderness that is as much internal as external.

Ironically, Lee and Hank exhibit different strands of insensitivity—Lee is tragically hip, Hank is tragically masculine. Yet nowhere is Kesey's exploration of the *wilderness* plight of the human soul more evident than through the author's depiction of Vivian. In comparison to the totalitarian simplicity of Nurse Ratched in *Cuckoo's Nest,* Vivian is more complex, sympathetic and sophisticated. As depicted in *Great Notion,* Viv reveals Kesey's prescience for the feminist movement to come.

Viv assumes her role of wife and household cook without complaint. The stress in her marriage—her growing discontent with Hank's masculine hardness and his inability to communicate their suffering over her miscarriage—weigh on Viv, though she deeply loves her husband. And, over time, she grows to love Lee for his sensitivity, intellectual curiosity, and warmth that her husband cannot give. Viv's love of both brothers can be viewed as one more metaphor for the haunted yin and yang of Kesey's own inner masculine personality. This duality converges at the conclusion of the novel.

When Lee and Hank come to blows over Viv, Lee joins the masculine fight, the sustained will to conquer. At this point, Lee doesn't care whether he is conquered, just that he must fight the fight and stand his ground if he is to find his own humanity. The fight helps Hank, too, who is deflated by Joe Ben's death and the mounting pressure from all these different directions. At the time Hank chooses to finally attack Lee for his indiscretions with Viv, Hank has literally given up on the log contract. During the fight, Hank doesn't want to bludgeon his brother, whom he could undoubtedly kill. After the blows, Hank chooses to resume his mission to deliver the logs. Ultimately, both are Stampers and neither of them, at the end of the novel, with Old Henry dead, will give an inch. Both want Viv, but underlying this, both want Myra back, too. Lee's sin with Viv is Hank's sin with Myra.

When Viv first met Hank, it was in the Midwest when she tended to him in jail. This was after Hank, the returning Korean War vet, was arrested for brawling. So it wasn't the masculinity, newfound in Lee and resurgent in Hank, that ran Viv off at the end of the novel. Vivian's reason for leaving them both is due to the haunting presence of Myra. Vivian asserts her individuality as her own woman. This is not to suggest that Kesey was profoundly sensitive to the female plight of his time, for he certainly wasn't, but the character of Viv resounds with a verisimilitude. Viv is not abandoning the masculine world; she is abandoning two men haunted by perverse masculine obsessions. Kesey noted as much in a 1971 interview with Paul Krassner:

> Women's Lib was the real issue in *Notion*. I didn't know this when I wrote it, but think about it: It's about men matching egos and wills on the battlefront of Vivian's unconsulted hide. When she leaves at the end of the book, she chooses to leave the only people she loves for a bleak and uncertain but at least *equal* future [*Kesey's Garage Sale*, 218].

Conversely, at the end of the novel, when, instead of leaving, Lee decides to help Hank move the log booms down the river, it is clear to the reader that Hank and Lee have become, metaphorically, one and the same. They are battling the same wilderness, joined as brothers. Viv, in this assertion of independence, chooses to confront her own wilderness rather than be haunted by the oedipal specter of this other woman. Myra, the mother and stepmother/lover, is "a dark fire, a cold fire, that melted them all almost beyond recognition. Burned them until they barely knew themselves or each other" (597). The specter of Myra serves as a metaphor for all that haunts us as humans. More than the woods and the frontier, she was the insurmountable wilderness of this novel, the wilderness that had shifted from the literal edge of West Coast America to the figurative frontier hollow of the human psyche.

Kesey recognized this. In a 1992 interview with Todd Fahey, he said:

> That stuff that happened in the Sixties, all of us who were part of it ... you can tell when you break new ground. If you're a farmer, you can tell that this sod has never been broken before, the plow is laying open great, purple earth and something comes out of it and you can *smell* it. When you're a writer, when I was working on *Sometimes a Great Notion*, I could tell I was breaking new ground; there's an energy that comes out, that's probably not unlike the energy that comes out of nuclear fission—It wasn't just me. It was not *anybody*. It wasn't rock and roll; it wasn't art; it wasn't cinema or dance. *Something was happening* at that time, and it was a wave that some of us were able to surf on. And none of us started the wave; I don't think there's any way you could start the wave. The wave is still going [Fahey interview].

A difficult question surrounds how extensively Kesey's copious use of psychedelic drugs impacted the writing in *Cuckoo's Nest* and *Great Notion*. As recently as 2005, Cintra Wilson in her on-line column for *Salon* included Kesey as one of her favorite novelists, with "*Sometimes A Great Notion* being a foremost example of the great contributions LSD made to serious literature."

Kesey, however, never suggested that LSD or the other hallucinogens were a substitute for his individual efforts and abilities. In his 1963 Gordon Lish interview, Kesey was asked how drugs aided creativity: "The kaleidoscopic pictures, the geometrics of humanity, that one experiences under, say, mescaline, aren't concealed in the white crystals inside the gelatin capsule. They are always in the mind. In the world. Already. The chemical *allows* the pictures to be seen. To know the world you need to see as many sides of it as possible. And this sometimes means using microscopes, telescopes, spectroscopes, even kaleidoscopes" (Perry & Babbs, 39). Elsewhere he said that drugs did not create the lyrical and fantastic descriptions in *Cuckoo's Nest* "anymore than Joyce's *eyeglasses* created *Ulysses*" (Tanner, 98).

The difficult brilliance of *Great Notion* is apparent. Tanner notes that "*Great Notion* itself is a singular achievement of intellectual power" (86). Tanner, though, is reluctant to attribute more than a modicum of this achievement to Kesey's drug explorations: "There is no evidence that drugs contributed in any substantive way in his literary creation aside from intensifying his conviction that reality is complex and has larger boundaries than is often recognized" (102). Yet, in Tanner's astute literary analysis of *Great Notion*, he addresses in specific detail Kesey's experimental techniques as an author: "*Great Notion* aims at conveying the total reality of a primary event. This involves multiple perceptions, both objective and subjective, and involves merging and telescoping time. The usual linear order of language is inadequate for Kesey's objective, so he tries a variety of unconventional methods" (58–9). Tanner adds that "[h]e is trying to capture the significant elements in events that are not revealed by the unusual objective and sequential manner of narration. Any event or feeling is related to others, and the reality of that event or feeling can be fully known only when the relationships are perceived or experienced as a simultaneous whole"(61).

Considering the level of psychedelic drug use admitted by Kesey during the writing of *Cuckoo's Nest* and *Great Notion,* a more compelling argument than Tanner's infers that there is no evidence to show that these drugs *did not* have a profound influence on this talented author's artistic creation. The "kaleidoscopic" structure of the overall narrative is consistent with the effects of induced hallucinations where fragmented visual imagery coalesces into a refractory whole. For Kesey, it is likely that such visions through the "eyeglasses" of psychotropic drugs, translated verbally into what Tanner calls "so many diverse elements working harmoniously to convey a definite theme." His psychedelic experiences probably explain why the author labored so diligently to portray a simultaneous whole by merging and telescoping time. Tanner goes on to note that this singular accomplishment "require[d] an effort and concentration that Kesey has shown no inclination to undertake again" (84).

On this latter point Tanner is most critical of Kesey's indulgences in drugs for the fact that his personal excesses resulted in the loss of a great literary talent after just two novels. *Great Notion* was published before Kesey turned thirty. Many authors, including Beat author William S. Burroughs with his heroin addiction or Aldus Huxley on mescaline in *Doors of Perception*, have written while influenced by drugs. Assuming that Kesey had a goal to write an easily read follow-up best seller to *Cuckoo's Nest*, then the author went too far with his experimentation with narrative techniques. However, at the time he wrote *Great Notion*, he was pushing his boundaries as a literary artist. With psychedelics he was also pushing the boundaries of his personal perception. Again, to suggest that the latter did not inform the former is implausible.

Moreover, setting aside Tanner's implication that a talented artist *owes* artistic production to the world at large, Kesey pointedly chose to move away from writing literature and to live his art through his theatrical Prankster adventures. The fact that the filming of these adventures was a fiasco does not discount the validity of the artistic effort. When looking at Kesey the author, it's fair to wonder whether his unwillingness to tackle a new novel was due to burning out on drugs. This is likely too simplistic, however. Psychedelics did not render the author brain-dead or psychotic. Kesey, as witnessed by the many interview comments used in this and the preceding chapter, remained very articulate and intellectually engaged until his death from liver cancer at age 66.

Writing novels of this complexity requires tremendous focus and introspection. The chaos created by his chosen communal lifestyle, growing family, and his increasing celebrity from *Cuckoo's Nest*, made writing difficult for Kesey in the mid–'60s. *Great Notion* was well underway when *Cuckoo's Nest* was first published. After the intense psychic toll exacted from writing *Great Notion*, Kesey was legitimately exhausted. He was perhaps afraid that he would never be able to improve on what he had accomplished. And, as he said at the time, he had a greater interest in exploring other artistic modes of expression. He began to live his art. He was burned out on novel writing, and in his thirties and forties he chose not to try a writing project as ambitious as his first two. Kesey never claimed that any of his fiction later in his life approached the level of accomplishment of *Cuckoo's Nest* or *Great Notion*, although the fact that he took up the novel again when he wrote *Sailor Song* in 1992 shows that he came to again honor his own artistic strength and gift as a storyteller.

For all his keen insight into Kesey's literary works, Tanner falls prey to his desire to protect Kesey from being too closely associated with the counterculture that the author's activities helped spawn:

[Kesey's] drug-taking, unconventional behavior, bizarre clothing, the famous bus trip, the pranks—these were not motivated by the same attitudes that animated countercultural activists or hippie dropouts. Kesey was radicalized to some extent while at Perry Lane, enough to be acutely aware of the sterility of the suburbanized, homogenized, and depersonalized aspects of American society; but his base of criticism was closer to that of Hank than that of Lee. Consequently, he looked toward an old-fashioned frontier tradition of self-reliant individualism for solutions and not, as many of his young protégés, toward a thin-blooded intellectualism, radical politics, or withdrawal into youthcult. His drug explorations were more a search for new sources and forms of artistic expression than they were a political or cultural rebellion; they were more a quest for heightened consciousness than an escape from an unsatisfactory society [90].

Tanner grossly overstates his case here. Extolling heightened consciousness, as an awakening to a new wilderness, became Kesey's rebellion. Kesey was as animated and expressive about this as any later hippie. The hippie, in order to be hippie, shared this core motive. Kesey was the prototypical hippie, a seminal figurehead, an intrepid catalyst for the countercultural epoch.

There is no substantiated reason to suggest that Kesey's outlook on the world was more like Hank's than Lee's. Rather, the complex balance of *Great Notion* resonates from the internal conflict of these two, rather equally weighted, personas. In this regard, Tanner fails to appreciate Kesey's maxim that "you're either *on* the bus, or *off* the bus." This phrase from his Lee persona, derived from the cross-country adventure depicted in *The Electric Kool-Aid Acid Test*. Being "on the bus" highlighted the notion of *counter* in the *counter*culture. Kesey, in his lifetime, never wavered from the idea that the individual consciousness revolution at the heart of his hippie sensibility was the most substantive cultural contribution of this countercultural epoch.

Tanner also contends that Kesey's search through drugs for new sources of artistic expression contrasts with the purely escapist pursuits of his "youthful protégés." This statement is patently elitist. Judgment placed on Kesey's drug use is one matter, but to suggest a loftier motive for Kesey presupposes that his activities were superior to the individuals who later experimented with these same drugs in the years that followed. *Great Notion* was brilliantly "elephantine," but the issue of drug use today, where public discourse is overwhelmingly anti-drug, has created an elephant in the room that is usually ignored and rarely discussed candidly. The use of hallucinogens in the late '60s and beyond involved the same sort of experimentation as Kesey engaged in, and for a host of personal and cultural reasons—including spiritual, artistic, consciousness-expanding, hedonistic or purely escapist. Considering the frequency of his drug use, Kesey, at different times, probably used psychedelics for all these reasons. To his credit, Tanner did not allow a judgmental attitude toward the counterculture to influence his literary analysis of Kesey's work.

After spending six months in jail for marijuana use and with a young family to raise, Kesey left California for Oregon in 1967, just as the hippie label being promulgated by the mass media stuck. These growing legions of hippies looked like Merry Pranksters, acted like Merry Pranksters and now had a label—hippie—that was a pejorative to both the mainstream and countercultural adherents alike. Kesey, returning to Oregon, was not the pied piper leading legions of "youthful protégés." The "wave" Kesey spoke about was cresting without the gravitational pull of a formal leadership. A scattering of viewpoints were being put forth of which Kesey's voice was not insignificant, but a minor one compared to the rock stars of the time. He threw several large parties where LSD was given out, and he spoke to groups as a successful, albeit eccentric, new author. His first two novels were not overtly "hippie." The term wasn't in use in 1964. Kesey's notoriety as a "leader" of the counterculture did not come until publication of *The Electric Kool-Aid Acid Test* in 1968 when Wolfe's novel, more than any other factor, made Kesey a larger-than-life countercultural persona.

Tanner is correct in stating that Kesey was not highly political. The author was not a leader of the New Left Movement or a major antiwar activist. With his age, growing family, and a draft deferment from the late '50s, Kesey didn't have to worry about being inducted into the Vietnam War. Tanner, however, fails to appreciate the traditionalist roots of Kesey's strain of hippie, the mode of disaffection so well articulated in both of his novels that questioned unfettered modernization and progress just for the sake of progress. Kesey, in his personal life, was irrefutably part of championing a new Dionysian upsurge, a fresh utopianism—arguably escapist and self-indulgent—but also one that evolved with a youthful hope of changing the world through alternative possibilities. This was a movement that was open to transcendence, and that honored self-reliance. Kesey was a young literary celebrity with rural roots who was at the forefront of wanting to explore a new manifestation of the American frontier. At the end of the '60s, many prankster-types, theatrical or earthy, retreated back to the land and, ironically, into rural enclaves such as the coastal community depicted in *Great Notion*.

A receptivity to notions of frontier and new possibilities may explain why the peaceful type of "revolution" embraced by Kesey and many others flourished more in the West Coast states than anywhere else in the world. Kesey's themes of wilderness, individualism and self-reliance in *Great Notion* help indicate why—into the '70s and beyond—the Pacific Northwest better tolerated a countercultural way of life in its midst than, for example, the more gentried and racially-polarized Deep South. Kesey, as a fellow traveler, shared a sincere optimism with those in the West Coast counterculture that a frontier type of personal freedom in a modern world could become manifest in conjunction with an expanded consciousness. It was not one versus the other, but belief that all of this was possible. Kesey rode the cutting edge of this consciousness change and, prodigal or otherwise, his character Lee was an example of the changed persona returning home.

Kesey, by turning away from writing novels and orchestrating his own Bacchanalian lifestyle, was part of "the countercultural activists and hippie dropouts," to use Tanner's phrase; he helped shape and promote the core attitudes of the counterculture. By the mid–'70s, when giving a speech at a local library, Kesey's attitude had shifted, not away from the idea of consciousness expansion, but from the potential dangers of drug excess:

> Here's the way I feel that these drugs affected us. They cut off our periphery time sense, so here we just were, floating. Our minds were scattered. We weren't worried about where we were going or where we had been. After a length of time of this, we wanted to go somewhere. We saw that there is a light ahead; there are things to be done, in each community and in each heart. So we started trying to make it toward this light, but we couldn't steer the boat. We had turned loose the tiller; the boat was awash in the sea. When you're lost in super-stition and dope, you're lost. A lot of people were [*Spit in the Ocean 7*, 143].

This spells out the shift in the counterculture from a reactionary disen-gagement to a more constructivist engagement that can be viewed as a lifestyle activism. This movement toward "the light ahead," and with the things to be done "in each community and in each heart" is at the essence of the Apollonian/Dionysian dialectic.

Seemingly, to elevate Kesey's literary accomplishments, Tanner argues for a softening of Kesey's link to this counterculture. To use a Hank Stamper style of metaphor, the author, in this regard, had broad shoulders throughout his life—Kesey was uncommonly candid about his drug use and the type of "revolution" he espoused. And, as pointed out earlier, no one individual embraced the entirety of this diverse move-ment. In his interview with Todd Fahey, Kesey stated:

> You think of the stuff that came out of the Sixties: the environmental movement, the feminist movement, the power of the civil rights movement; but most of all, it's the psychedelic movement that attempted to actually go in and change the consciousness of the people, either back to something more pure and honest, or forward to something never before realized, knowing that the places we were in, the status quo, was a dead-end—a dead-end spiritually and, as we are finding out, a dead-end economically [Fahey interview].

Charles Reich, in his now dated and overly optimistic assessment of the sweeping cultural changes of the "youth revolution" in *The Greening of America (1971)*, claimed that, "*Sometimes A Great Notion* probably comes the closest to being in the fullest sense a work of the new consciousness" (432).

It will never be possible to prove with *Great Notion* the extent to which psychedelic drugs impacted Kesey's prose. The circumstantial evidence, much of it forthcoming from the Author himself, indicates a profound impact on the innovative narrative structure of the novel. Part of the fascination in delving into *Great Notion* is in figuring out how much the author's own personality draws from both Hank and Lee. And, like *Cuckoo's Nest,* the novel exhibits passages with a surreal tone and fragmentation of rich imagery consistent with what one would expect such drugs might have on a man with Kesey's gift for words:

> The rain had let up and leveled out to its usual winter-long pace ... not so much a rain as a dreamy smear of blue-grey that wipes over the land instead of falling on it, making patient spectral shades of the tree trunks and a pathic, placid, and cordial sighing sound along the river. A friendly sound, even [339].

Great Notion was as innovative and complex as the changing world it worked to depict, a grand novel in the Faulknerian tradition. It doesn't conclude with tidy narrative truths, but is a novel powerful in the way it challenges the ethnocentricity and masculinization that it simultaneously forefronts. By exploring the two predominant veins of his own personality, Kesey opened his narrative to the cultural fracturing of his time. Always lurking in the shadows of its grandness is Vivian (and the feminist problem with no name). Although the town he depicts is vastly white, he alludes to the pressures of racism, and, through Joe Ben and Lee, Kesey intones a new openness to religious possibility, especially in how Joe Ben's faith girded Hank's masculine resolve. Through its grandness, *Great Notion* portrays a community and cast of characters that turn the screws on Hank—the quintessential alpha male—from every conceivable direction. Stylistically, thematically and structurally, the work is masterfully innovative. *Great Notion* is of lasting importance, in part, for its structural innovations and, in part, for the insight it provides into the evolving cultural mindset of the '60s.

4

Been Down So Long It Looks Like Up To Me and *The Crying of Lot 49* (1966)

A Chic Cabal

Richard Fariña's only novel, *Been Down So Long It Looks Like Up to Me* was set on a fictional, upstate New York campus in 1958. The work was written mostly in 1963, and not published until 1966. In the Beat tradition of dithyrambic prose, the story features the frenetic collegiate romp of protagonist, Gnossos Pappadopoulis—a luminous, drug-indulged, charismatic, often unsympathetic hero. The novel tracks the escapades of the Ivy-league hipster through an onslaught of encounters on the shadow side of campus life. The stream of drug use is constant and the book is filled with both pop and high culture allusions ranging from comic book superhero Plastic Man to the deities of Greek mythology. The author imposes the qualities of Odysseus on Gnossos who engages, with manic coolness, the ennui of an estranged existence. The pacing resembles a barrage of speedy jazz riffs more than the folk music that Fariña embraced with critical, though modest, commercial success as a musician after he left Cornell University in 1959. Yet, both jazz and folk music as well as high and low intellectualism were a part of the Beat scene. One edition of Fariña's book proclaims it "The Classic Novel of the 1960s." Set in 1958, this is, strictly speaking, not of the '60s, yet the attitudes of Fariña's students foreshadow the mood of Campus unrest during the period of anti–Vietnam War protests.

Gnossos raps with the cutting edge lingo of those in the Beat movement, and, etymologically, the novel is fascinating in terms of how much of the language associated with hippies was well in vogue before the late '60s. *Joint, hip, groovy,* and *dig it* were all part of Gnossos's *scene.* Most interesting in this regard is Fariña's use of the slang term *chic* to describe the female coeds. Had the spelling of *chic* not been supplanted by *chick* in the late '60s, one wonders whether the term would have fallen on disfavor in the 1970's during the feminist movement. *Chic* has a more flattering connotation than *chick*. Etymologically, Fariña's work shows that the slang used in 1958 at the hip fringes of culture mushroomed into widespread usage in the late '60s. Likewise, many expressions from the hippie epoch are part of mainstream American vernacular today.

Most critical literary reviews of *Been Down So Long* were unfavorable. *Time Magazine* went so far as to call both Fariña's work and *The Crying of Lot 49*, Thomas Pynchon's 1966 novel, "gibberish literature" (www. richardandmimi.com/litcrit.html). Fariña's constant stream of allusions—hip and otherwise—risked disengagement by the reader. The constant sophomoric antics by Gnossos, coupled with a hyperactive pacing, were often wearisome. Moreover, for the first half of the novel there is no solid sense of motive driving the character or the plot, situations through which our main character can resolve conflict, inner or outer.

Gnossos is like a ship fast adrift. The ornate denseness of the third-person limited prose impresses the reader with Fariña's erudite and "with it" vocabulary, but the incessant onslaught results in a purple prose of the hippest variety. His collage is vaguely picaresque with its roguish characters, except that the drama is not episodic; once Gnossos falls in love, the plot, at long last, revolves around this and the building tension on campus, with Gnossos trying to make sense of his role there. School, for Gnossos, is a haven from the dangerous world outside. Here he chooses to withdraw with paregoric Pall Malls (opium-laced cigarettes) and marijuana especially.

Halfway into the novel, as indicated, Gnossos, a campus lady's man, falls in love. An element of human sensitivity then develops in the protagonist. In contrast to constant indulgence in drugs and partying, a thread of Winnie-the-Pooh references proves to be more refreshing than cutesy, especially in this romance. Yet, in keeping with the low and high reflections on culture, Thanatos always lurks for Gnossos. The novel is a disaffected modern man's dance with death against the backdrop of buzzed escape and cultural depthlessness. As hinted with the Pooh allusions, Gnossos is reluctant to assume the responsibilities of adulthood.

He is, however, proud of his Greek heritage, especially its food and the pantheon of heroes, though the reader is never given any point of reference to his family life, except that he is Greek. It is revealed that Gnossos is much traveled, has seen disturbing things, experienced dangers from which withdrawal into the fringes of campus culture is a welcomed respite, but not much in the way of specifics. Had the author incorporated even one key element of Gnossos's dark history outside the insular campus life, something to overtly haunt the protagonist, then one could suggest that this would have better propelled the story. More than oblique hints, a sense of Gnossos's history with contraband, insurrection or similar danger would have created reader empathy for his disaffection and a stronger thread throughout the novel. This would have created greater juxtapositional irony at the end of the book when the outside world, again, imposes itself fully on Gnossos.

As the novel unfolds, the outside world is held at bay. We do know that Gnossos does well in school with no evidence of him ever studying. Study would not be hip, it seems, and his scholarly abilities surprise his many friends. In this, he is the archetype of student protesters in the '60s when campuses were notorious for students who would relegate studies to a secondary status behind political protest. In this campus romp, Gnossos is in the midst of a social tumult of the students own making.

By the second half of the novel, Gnossos is in love with the chic Kristin whose predominant characteristic is that she wears knee-high socks. Campus unrest develops over discontent about dating curfews. Here, with Kristin's involvement, Gnossos is sucked into orchestrated efforts to change the policy. The man masterminding the protest effort is Oeuf, a young dean with lofty career ambitions:

> Nurse Fang entered quietly and filled Gnossos' empty glass, adding an ice cube with a pair of surgical tongs from the bucket. She touched Oeuf on the pulse, "Some of the Junta waiting to see you, sir. And I'm available for the addressograph, effective eleven hundred hours."
> "In a moment."
> She left, ass-bouncing, and Gnossos said, "No."
> "No what?"
> "I still couldn't. It's not my scene. Too political."
> "It's been that way *de novo*, old sport."
> "I don't give a shit."
> "Ms. Cloud [Kristin] is with us."
> "What?"
> "So is Fitzgore. And your ace buddy Heffalump, at least until he leaves for Cuba. We will win, Gnossos, and *vae victus* when we do. You want a Prix de Rome? A Pulitzer Prize?"
> "What about grass? I'm only asking, mind you."
> "We've got a trustee who just won the proxy fight at Sandoz."
> "Sandoz?"
> "The lab of the same name. Largest manufacturer of synthetic mescaline in the world. You want to do research?"
> "Stop!" Gnossos jumped up and paced the carpeted floor from one wall to the other. [...] "You're evil shit, you know that Oeuf?" [209–210].

Here, at the two-thirds mark in the novel, a layered plot finally develops when the relationship with Kristin is linked to the campus insurrection, when Gnossos's network of student ties becomes politically expedient for Oeuf. Yet, at the same time, for reasons that are never completely clear,

Gnossos slits the tip of his condom so he can impregnate Kristin. Later, the ploy seems to work when Gnossos seduces Kristin.

Nurse Fang's "ass-bouncing" in the novel is representative of the period's sexism. More disturbing is an earlier scene in the story that, today, would constitute date rape. Gnossos has had sex with a young woman prior to when he met Kristin. To his dismay, Gnossos learns in this latter part of the novel that the young woman is an heiress worth billions. The innocence here is perverse. Fariña's contrived comeuppance is that this is a *chic* that Gnossos could have married. The author ignores the issue of forced sex. The initial encounter wouldn't escape reproach today.

As it plays out in the novel, the date rape of the heiress is yet one more engagement with a minor character that won't be anchored easily in the story. Those in the cast surrounding the protagonist constantly rush in and out of his life with such madcap deportment that little sense of empathy is established for any of them. This superficiality reflects on Gnossos. Even when Oeuf calls Gnossos "Old Sport," Fariña infuses this Ivy League scene with detachment. "Old Sport," a favorite term of F. Scott Fitzgerald's Gatsby, resonates with its allusion of superficiality and arrogance. Gnossos, however, never stays still long enough for the reader to care or not care about his situations of privilege or sense of pop irony.

Gnossos also gets his comeuppance on spring break after Oeuf successfully recruits him into the cause of the Campus uprising. Before he leaves, Gnossos writes a letter to the school paper calling out the college president to come clean with the real reason for more strict policies in campus housing—to control dating behavior. The ensuing stir and galvanizing unrest happens while Gnossos is gone. En route to Cuba with four fellow students, Gnossos finds out that Kristin, who is not with them and who was ostensibly a virgin when they first had sex, has given him a wicked dose of the clap through the opening he had cut in the prophylactic. This is not Fariña's customary humor of allusion—the insider's irony where the reader finds it funny only if privy to the context outside the novel—but one of the few times where the author sets up the situation within the confines of his book to allow the irony to emerge from context of the story.

Here our hero's drip, drip, drip of affliction is amusing because the clap is unexpected and well earned by the author—low humor that amplifies Gnossos's maneuverings to gain exempt status from key obligations in life. Immediately, Gnossos knows the culprit. Oeuf, the Machiavellian orchestrator of the protest, is the only one in their circle who is similarly afflicted. The payback is pronounced, but in terms of significance, this pales compared to what comes next. In the Cuba scene, Fariña sets up a profound juxtaposition, namely, the revolutionary zeal of privileged students combating dating policy compared to the armed overthrow of Batista's Cuban government by Fidel Castro's forces. In his introduction to the novel, postmodern author Thomas Pynchon, a friend of Fariña's from their student days at Cornell, argues that:

> of the many dark scenes in the novel[,] the darkest of all, and I think the best written, is the sequence that takes place in revolutionary Cuba, in which Gnossos's best friend is accidentally killed. Although a few pages of campus rioting come later, the true climax of the book is in Cuba. Back in his Hemingway phase, Fariña must have seen that line about every true story ending in death. Death, no idle prankster, is always, in this book, just outside the window. The cosmic humor is in Gnossos's blundering attempts to make some kind of early arrangement with Thanatos, to find some kind of hustle that will get him out of the mortal contract we're all stuck with [xiii].

Fariña was immersed in the folk music scene and heavily exposed to a Beat sensibility. This might explain why the voice through most of the novel reads so frenetically, like one is holding onto the coattails of a manic pied piper. This hipster/protagonist, however, happens to be a discontented student. Douglas Cooke, in a 2001 critique posted on his Fariña website, further suggests that:

> There are perhaps too many mini-resolutions in the novel, too many epiphanies, too many karmic adjustments rather than one big, cathartic, aesthetically satisfying climax, and along the way we have to put up with too much of Gnossos' posing and pointless partying. As a result, many critics have overlooked the complexity and significance of the novel altogether, dismissing it as an outdated effort now useful only as a document of its time [Cooke, *www.richardandmimi.com*].

Been Down So Long was indeed too unfocused for the reasons Cooke described. Readers shouldn't have to "put up" with protagonists, but should be swept along by them whether they are heroes or antiheroes. The posing or partying was not an inherent problem for Gnossos as a character. Rather, Fariña did not create a palpable sense of the motive or dysfunction driving Gnossos's circumstance. The reader was left trying to keep up with a character who is animated, but for whom we are not given a tangible sense of ordeal or mission. Indeed, the novel is very useful as a document of its time, but the problem wasn't with too many epiphanies or a lack of satisfying climax—the juxtapositional conclusion of the novel was its redeeming literary feature.

Thomas Pynchon's second novel, *The Crying of Lot 49* was published the same year and shares with Fariña's book a strong sense of protagonist paranoia. Pynchon's story is rooted, even more deeply, in a cabalistic mystery that drives the plot. Oedipa Maas, a hip, self-described young Republican, has been designated as an executor of a former lover's labyrinthine estate. She goes to great length to unravel the dead man's connections with a secretive private postal service that held a monopoly in Europe for centuries and may have infiltrated the US at the time of the Pony Express. Ultimately Pynchon, leaves the nature of the clandestine group unresolved—it simply may be a figment of chance coincidences, which Oedipa discovers, or, perhaps, the tip of a highly secretive cabalistic organization. Pynchon is considered by many to be the foremost postmodern novelist—especially in light of *Gravity's Rainbow* in 1973. *The Crying of Lot 49* is characteristically dense, but this narrative structure is among his most conventionally rendered. Both *Lot 49* and *Been Down So Long* give a palpable sense of the national mood in America on the cusp of a burgeoning counterculture. *The Crying of Lot 49,* however, features a straightlaced protagonist caught up in a swirl of seemingly internecine intrigue that introduces her to a bizarre network of defense contractors, academics, musicians, and hipsters.

Oedipa, in this new age of The Pill, may be politically conservative, but she takes lovers outside her marriage, cavorts with The Paranoids— a young, pot-smoking, Beatles wannabe garage band of the ilk popping up throughout America in 1965–66; she drinks and flirts, but refuses to be part of her Freudian psychologist's experimentations with LSD. The protagonist visits North Beach and Berkeley in her search of clues, but, despite the chaos she finds, Oedipa is the composite of a young, 27-year-old Californian of the early '60s, of this state that was, and still is, simultaneously among the most conservative and liberal in the country. At one point in the novel when she is tracking down leads, Oedipa wanders through the University of California campus at Berkeley:

> It was summer, a weekday, and midafternoon; no time for any campus Oedipa knew of to be jumping, yet this one was. She came [...] into a plaza teeming with corduroy, denim, bare legs, blonde hair, hornrims, bicycle spokes in the sun, bookbags, swaying card tables, long paper petitions dangling to earth, posters for undecipherable FSM's, YAF's, VDC's, suds in the fountain, Students in nose-to-nose dialogue. She moved through it carrying her fat book, attracted, unsure, a stranger, wanting to feel relevant but knowing how much of a search among alternative universes it would take. For she had undergone her own educating at a time of nerves, blandness and retreat among not only her fellow students, but also most of the visible structure around and ahead of them, this having been a national reflex to certain pathologies in high places only death had the power to cure, and this Berkeley was like no somnolent Siwash out of her own past at all [...] [*Lot 49,* 75–76].

While Oedipa's conservative background did not predispose her to campus sit-ins and marches, both this protagonist and Gnossos find themselves swimming in suspicious, saturnalian worlds. Both of these books capture the nuance at the cutting edge of a changing culture, though Gnossos is part of the underground while Oedipa is besieged by this changing society that comes to surround her. Ultimately, a cabalistic paranoia—also indicative of this period—grips both Oedipa and Gnossos.

For most of *Been Down So Long*, Gnossos comes across as exactly an idle prankster. In his sheltered, Ivy League existence, Gnossos shows no higher motive than to withdraw into self-anesthetizing; he mocks most campus conventions, engages in witty one-upmanship with all he encounters, and, until Kristin, womanizes freely. The deal he negotiates with Oeuf holds implications of Gnossos securing "exemption" on campus, privilege and protection from any negative "real world" consequences. The big irony of the novel is formulated around Gnossos's loss of exemption. The depth of this metaphor is realized at several levels. He loses Kristin to her betrayal. It's a payback in the karmic sense that Gnossos, as a true hipster, recognizes. At the very end of the book, perhaps set up by Oeuf, Gnossos is given his draft notice—his military induction into the bigger world of geopolitics.

As literature, the frenetic prose is thick with heady vernacular and pop twistedness, but the novel most comes alive when the pace slows into a deeper sense of the protagonist's struggle. In Cuba, Batista's soldiers, on patrol, spray the square in Havana with machine gun fire. A stray bullet kills Gnossos's close friend Heffalump. Two other students traveling with Gnossos have left to join Castro's forces in the Cuban hills. Still in Havana, Gnossos buries his friend and encounters connections that were mentioned briefly much earlier in the novel. For cash, he makes an arrangement with them to smuggle heroin back home:

> That night Louie Motherball wove his magic circle, spun his rhythmic words, hypnotized his psychedelic legion, spoke to opiated faces. Gnossos sat with taxi drivers, prostitutes, refugee Taos Indians, and the recently paid off gnomes. Each of them sucked at a private surgical tube connected to a regulator which pulsated in the contents of a cyclopean bowl [312].

As the novel closes, Fariña connects the pieces of his story with lyrical potency. Back on campus, the life and death stakes of the Cuban world he has just left resonates with ironic insignificance. Gnossos is pulled on stage at the massive campus protest over dating privileges:

> Seven thousand Ivy League smiles flickered and gleamed. Two hundred and twenty-four thousand calcium-white incisors, canines, bicuspids, premolars, eye-teeth, and molars, anxious to bite, ready for the bacchanal, hungry and drooling. A tremble of despotic power shuddered in his loins. A flood of adrenalin buoyed up his blood. [Gnossos] could do no worse than give them provender for a night of romping abandon.
>
> With exquisite deliberation he made two loose fists, held them up, and gave everyone the finger.
>
> And they loved it [322].

Again, this comes at the close of Gnossos's own romping abandon, one that sprinted with the reader for three hundred pages, but took too long to unfold, too long to develop the underlying tensions. As mentioned, some of this might have been alleviated had the reader been given more exposition related to the surreptitious life Gnossos led before the story of his time at college. Louie Motherball, for example, could have been drawn out in backstory so that when he showed up again in Cuba, the reader wouldn't be forced to pull this character from out of Fariña's earlier, unanchored, renderings. The frantic pacing reduces the dramatic tension of the novel. At the end, when tension develops, the pacing slows to accommodate the level of sensitivity. At its deepest, the metaphor of exemption works best when Gnossos is confronted with his best friend's death in Cuba, though, even here, Fariña's writing maintains a hip obliqueness.

Looking back, the prescient quality of *Been Down So Long* helps us understand the attitudes and increasingly disaffected mindset of a rebellious bohemian fringe in America in the period where the Beat movement segued into the Hippie phenomenon and widespread campus revolt. As an author, Kesey explored the theme of wilderness in conflict with modernization; his personal life fused a rugged individualism with a Beat-like primitivism. Fariña, similarly intellectual and hip, delved more directly into the realm of high culture colliding with pop culture through bohemian expressivism and alienation. One wonders if Fariña modeled his tertiary character, Nurse Fang, off of Kesey's Nurse Ratched. Also, both Kesey and Fariña showed a fascination with the icons of comic book America and the fantastical heroism expressed therein. Kesey chose to quit as a novelist before he was thirty years old. Fariña died tragically in a motorcycle accident two days following the publication of this first novel. He was 29.

Like Kesey, Fariña was at the leading edge of what would explode into the counterculture of the late '60s. Both were among the forefront of those who carried forth the bohemian sensibility from the Beat generation. Both authors found themselves in the celebrity realm of this social change. Pynchon, in *The Crying of Lot 49,* captures the cultural fissuring within American society, and, notably, the cabalistic paranoia that was a fixture of the American counterculture. Gnossos and Oedipa, in this respect, share a deep-seated suspiciousness, though in *Lot 49* this unfolds through the web of "coincidences" and connection that Oedipa discovers. Oedipa's growing discoveries (or imagined ones) drive the narrative. By comparison, when the reader meets Gnossos, he is already jaded to the larger world, fully convinced of the surreptitious nature of those in ivory towers, or governments. Chief Broom's "Combine" in *Cuckoo's Nest* is Kesey's way of expressing this same cabalistic concern. All three novels underscore the distrust of authority that came to be so pronounced in the late '60s.

Fariña was a critically accomplished folk musician who demonstrated innovative techniques with the Dulcimer. In 1962 Fariña was divorced from fellow folkie Carolyn Hester after he fell in love with Mimi Baez, Joan's 16-year-old, younger sister. Fariña was eight years older than his new wife, and they, too, formed a musical alliance. Douglas Cooke, on this same website for Richard Fariña and Mimi Baez, puts Fariña's musical and literary pursuits in a larger perspective:

> Gnossos' quest is to find the meaning behind the easy allusions. In the late fifties there arose among youth a yearning for meaning, substance, roots, authenticity. Authenticity above all was idealized by young discontents. It was, in varying degrees, a catalyst of the Beat movement, the Blues Revival, and the back-to-land communes and pastoral pilgrimages of the Hippie movement. But it was a particular fetish of the urban folk revival [Cooke, *www.richardandmimi.com*].

Fariña was exposed to the hippest forms of lifestyle expression through his constant touring at the beginning of the '60s.

As a young novelist, Kesey was far more successful than Fariña at creating and executing metaphorical depth from the beginning of his novels to the end. Pynchon, likewise, stays focused on his cabalistic theme far more skillfully than Fariña. Gnossos, as protagonist, is too unanchored within the narrative. Kesey's central characters had clear motivation; each of his first two novels was built on an unwavering through-line, an element that *Been Down So Long* lacked. It could be argued that Fariña's work was built on juxtaposition like many later postmodern works, but the elements juxtaposed in the novel that hold any appreciable dramatic impact come too near the end, in traditional resolution, but without skillful buildup. In *Lot 49,* Pynchon creates a reverse detective story, where the mysteries accrete, but are never resolved. *Been Down So Long,* provides a resolution, but not a compelling build-up of tension. *Lot 49* yields a postmodern ennui and paranoia and leaves the reader with a cabalistic mystery. The connections that Oedipa discovers are either figmentary or real, no one is certain. Only her suspicions are a given. Pynchon is quite deliberate in how he toys with the detective novel as genre. Instead of a compelling resolution, he leaves the reader with more questions than answers, because mystery is the point of his cabalistic exercise.

Cooke points out that Fariña possessed a "keen eye for the absurd and the pathetic in modern American life, and the use of these absurdities—rather than conventional literary devices—to tell his story" (Cooke, *www.richardandmimi.com*). Yet again, it is only near the end that Fariña shows a strong sensibility for storytelling, and one wonders if his avoidance of conventional literary devices was by intent, or from underdeveloped craftsmanship. Kesey and Pynchon, as young authors, do not beg this same question.

Despite its flaws, *Been Down So Long* was a promising, highly ambitious first novel, with sections of superb prose. The work offers an excellent nuanced sense of the growing cultural alienation shared by so many American college students during this period of time.

One wonders if Fariña felt compelled to set this novel in 1958 because of the significance of the revolutionary scenes in Cuba. The campus tone and wild intensity of the book does feel like a novel of the 1960s. It was published on the cusp of social unrest in 1966, the year that Fariña died. Yet, there actually was a campus uprising at Cornell in 1958 for the reasons depicted in this novel, and Cuba fell to Castro in 1959. Clearly, student attitudes and a propensity to react en masse did not change much from the Cornell campus protests of 1958 to 1967 when the Vietnam War gave American students external cause to galvanize in discontent. This novel successfully captures this propensity. Witnessed through Gnossos's rebellious lifestyle, the novel is a portrait of American culture in transition.

Lot 49, in a different way, captures the broader mood and fissures of California culture in the mid–'60s. In terms of drugs, Pynchon is aware of the same clinical availability of LSD that initially turned Kesey onto psychedelics. Pynchon's novel, actually written in 1964 and '65, mentions Dr. Hilarious's experiments with "LSD-25, mescaline, psilocybin, and related drugs on a large sample of suburban housewives. The Bridge inward" (7). Near the end of the novel, the protagonist Oedipa, who has been losing all the men in her life during her investigation as an executor of a past lover's estate, returns home to her disc jockey husband, Mucho Maas:

> She stared at the pills in it, and then understood. "That's LSD?" she said. Mucho smiled back. "Where'd you get it?" Knowing.
> "Hilarius[...]."
> "But there's a chance you're not addicted yet?"
> "Oed," Looking at her puzzled. "You don't get addicted. It's not like you're some kind of hophead. You take it because it's good. Because you hear things, even smell them, taste like you never could. [...] You're an antenna, sending your pattern out to a million lives a night, and they're your lives too."
> [...] She could not quite get it in her head that the day she had left him for San Narciso, was the day she'd seen Mucho for the last time. So much of him already had dissipated [107–108].

Not only was Pynchon aware of the allure of the heightening effects of LSD, but also of the psychic risk—albeit non-addictive—to those who overindulged in the drug. This contributing element of Oedipa's growing paranoia was not speculative. Though there is ample evidence in *Lot 49* that Oedipa had long since left him, it's clear from this passage that she believed she'd lost her husband for good when he'd crossed that "bridge inward." By the mid–'60s, Thomas Pynchon and Richard Fariña had seen many new worlds beyond their college days at

Cornell in the late '50s—an unfolding cultural shift that was growing more pronounced.

The manner in which *Been Down So Long* and *Lot 49* depict the nuances of culture, specifically the changing attitudes of American society in the late '50s and early '60s, gives these novels a noteworthy place in literary history. Both foreshadow the counterculture. *Lot 49*, moreover, offers a fascinating authorial study as a predecessor work of Pynchon's postmodern masterpiece, *Gravity's Rainbow*, published in 1973.

5

Trout Fishing in America (1967)

It's All in the Presentation

Richard Brautigan left the Pacific Northwest in 1956 at the age of twenty-one to become a writer. He moved to San Francisco. Sometimes referred to as "The Last Beat," the story of how his success unfolded is more linked to the story of the "hippie." But there is more to the substance of Brautigan's most popular works than his association with the hippie phenomenon.

When the attention of the mass media fell on hippies, flower power, and Haight Ashbury during the "Summer of Love," Richard Brautigan's stories and poems were being mimeographed and stacked on the street corners of this neighborhood only to quickly disappear. Emmett Grogan of the Diggers describes in his memoir *Ringolevio* how one day Brautigan showed up with a connection to help the group acquire a donated vehicle:

> a crew of Diggers were discussing the need for another vehicle, when in the front door walked Richard Brautigan, a tall, carrot-haired, thirty-five-year old poet wearing grandpa glasses, a peacoat and a floppy, wide-brimmed, felt hat. He also sported a golden bristled moustache, which drooped over his mouth like a nodding eyelash. Richard called his poems "Tidbits" and he wrote quite a few for the free handbills which were mimeographed and distributed by the Communication Company [...], single sheet newspapers which were handed out along Haight Street several times a day.

This exposure helped generate grass roots popularity for the author in a quieter, but similar, manner to how the free rock concerts of the Grateful Dead or Jefferson Airplane in neighboring Golden Gate Park gave these bands an initial boost of popular exposure. The Diggers were a key orchestrating force behind those free concerts as well.

With all the "flowerchild" media hype, literary agents and publishers were on the lookout for the hot new novel of the hippie scene. However, the "hippies" were such a freshly labeled, youth phenomenon, that there were no teenage, homeless, literary geniuses in the Haight primed to submit a major literary tome crafted in a matter of months. Brautigan filled the void. *Trout Fishing in America* had been written a half-decade earlier. This work wasn't about hippies or the hippie scene, so the mainstream public would have to wait until shortly after the "Summer of Love" for outsiders such as Joan Didion, Tom Wolfe, and Norman Mailer to explain what was "really" going on with all these youth. Compared to these writers, Richard Brautigan wrote with an authentic bohemian sensibility. For many reasons to be discussed, his breakout work—like the music of The Dead and Airplane—appealed to those in a burgeoning counterculture that stretched far beyond its nexus in San Francisco. *Trout Fishing in America* helped fill a vacuum as the great hippie novel, although at 112 pages it was more of a novella.

Brautigan lived in San Francisco as a young, eccentric, struggling writer at the fringe of the Beat scene for a decade before the hippies were widely labeled as such by the mass media. Yet, Brautigan's success was tied to this moniker. Fame struck as the counterculture exploded. The author was in the right place at the right time with the right look and the right expressive sensibility. *Trout Fishing in America* was quickly and widely adored. Fame came with Brautigan becoming an icon of the hippies and, whether he thought of himself as one or not, the author was clearly a part of this scene. In his short story, "A Long Time Ago People Decided to Live in America," written in the late '60s, Brautigan's narrator wants to get laid by someone new:

> A tall, God-I-love-the-tall-ones girl comes walking up the street, casual as a young animal with Levi's on. She must be 5–9, wearing a blue sweater. Her breasts are loose beneath it and move in firm youthful tide.
> She has no shoes on.
> She's a hippie girl.
> Her hair is long.
> She doesn't know how pretty she is. I like that. It always turns me on, which isn't very hard to do right now because I'm already thinking about girls. [...]
> "What's your name?" I ask, maybe I'm going to make a pass at her. That's what I should be doing right now. Actually, I'm about thirty seconds late in doing it.
> "Willow Woman," she says. "I'm trying to get out to the Haight-Ashbury. I just got into town from Spokane."
> "I wouldn't," I say. "It's very bad out there."
> "I have friends in the Haight-Ashbury," she says.
> "It's a bad place," I say.
> She shrugs her shoulders and looks helplessly down at her feet [109].

Brautigan ends the story by having the narrator give the girl a dollar. She reacts as though it's a miracle, gives him a "warm, friendly, and giving" hug, and kisses him on the cheek, but as far as making a pass at her, he's lost his thread of thought and she's gone. Brautigan completes the little twist in his story by telling the reader how "she departs beautifully toward all the people that she will ever meet [...]" (110).

As will be seen when Joan Didion's essay "Slouching Toward Bethlehem" is discussed, Brautigan was not being facetious when the narrator of this story warns of Haight-Ashbury as a bad place. In 1967, as a result of too much media attention and a convergence of nomadic teens, the neighborhood became an out-of-control zoo.

In 1966, Brautigan's writer friend Keith Abbott lived in the Haight, in part, because of the cheap rent. After Brautigan's suicide in 1984, he wrote about his memories of the author's rise to fame. "[Brautigan's] work was dumped on the street corners in San Francisco and was out of print one day after it appeared. This reinforces my sense of the speed of the events that were happening then, and the ephemeral nature of its products" ("Garfish...," Abbott). When psychedelia erupted in late '66, the Haight was the epicenter of media attention.

Although Brautigan rode the coattails, according to Abbott, Brautigan never took psychedelic drugs. After a decade in San Francisco, he found his opportunity to shine as a writer:

> The prevailing literature in San Francisco was leftover beats. The writing was outdated and negative and largely self-destructive. Popular writers, such as Ginsberg and Ferlinghetti, were regarded as forefathers and teachers by my generation. But they were old hat, too. Someone new was needed to write about what was going on ["Garfish...," Abbott].

Locally, Brautigan wasn't new, but his lack of success in the Beat literary movement may have been a blessing for the author. His tone differed from the more staccato, nihilistic writing of the Beat period. To all the outside eyes suddenly fascinated by the upsurge of wild activity in San Francisco, Brautigan's writing was fresh. Then there was Brautigan's own complicity in promoting himself:

> *Trout Fishing* sold out in its first edition. The second edition hit a snag with the printer. I remember Richard very upset with this—the printer wouldn't reprint it as it had dirty words in it—because the time, he knew, was ripe for him. Then a third edition of it came out along with his collection of poetry, *The Pill Versus the Springhill Mine Disaster.* These sold out instantly ["Garfish...,"Abbott].

Even though his success came in conjunction with the enormous attention being given the psychedelic phenomenon, more than one critical analysis of Richard Brautigan's work has lamented how, following his death, the author has been relegated to relative obscurity by literary critics due to this association with the era and its countercultural baggage. Janusz K. Buda in "Richard Brautigan 1935–1984" blames this on Brautigan's "facile and wholly spurious sobriquet of hippie." The critic, who otherwise appreciated the substance of Brautigan's writing, states:

"the hippie phenomenon of the mid-sixties lasted only a matter of months and metamorphosed, depending on one's point of view, into either the political excesses of the Yippies and Black Panthers or the materialistic sterility of consumer culture" (20).

This statement is laughable. For one, it's difficult to feel sorry for a determined and exceedingly poor author who suddenly finds a niche and gains success as a dedicated writer. Secondly, if the counterculture is ever fully appreciated for its transformative impact on society, then it won't be surprising to see Brautigan's works again garnering deserved accolades. As Buda notes, the innovative structure and ironic humor of his books warrant lasting attention, irrespective of any association with the hippies. Thirdly, the success of the novel, which quickly sold in the millions of copies, would not have been so popular had its appeal not extended beyond a phenomenon lasting only months or without book sales that extended well beyond this one city. Buda recognized the catalyst, but failed to understand the phenomenon that gelled into the much larger counterculture, a countercultural market that served Brautigan very well.

The hippie phenomenon was not metamorphosing into the New Left or radical black politics. The counterculture had many overlapping movements. Leftist politicos—such as Abbie Hoffman and Jerry Rubin—tried with limited success to appropriate the energy of the hippie phenomenon into overtly political causes and, while many highly political activists came to consider themselves hippies, many hippies were apolitical or not leftist. After the U.S. government stopped drafting young men for the Vietnam War in 1972, the yippies, the New Left, and Students for a Democratic Society (SDS) could not sustain political momentum. Much of the counterculture, even though it had lost its galvanizing focal point in Vietnam, continued for several years longer. This is evidenced by the evolution of the counterculture in many alternative directions, such as the environmental movement, the New Age movement, natural foods movement, high tech innovation, etc. Hordes of Deadheads continued to follow The Grateful Dead from concert to concert into the mid–'90s, and certain hippie communes, such as The Farm in Tennessee, persisted. There was also continued popularity of the Oregon Country Fair, annual Rainbow Gatherings, and the Burning Man gathering in Nevada. The Bacchanalian spirit of 1967 still flares again at such events, but the phenomenon has gradually dissipated, with only remnant traces of hard-core hippies still to be found.

Buda's notion that the hippies of the late '60s—mostly enfranchised white kids rejecting the establishment—metamorphosed into the Black Panther movement, a group founded in Oakland and consisting of African-American activists who were insisting on opportunities for enfranchisement within a racist, white-dominated establishment, is ridiculous. Even rock star Jimi Hendrix, the most notable black member of psychedelia, resisted attempts by black American activists who pressured him on his American tours to become politically radical. His funeral in October 1970 was not held in New York City because the family feared that it would become a politicized event and a media circus. His body was flown to the U.S. from London, and quietly buried in his hometown of Seattle.

The establishment in America was being challenged on many fronts by a largely leaderless opposition. The counterculture was never monolithic, and the many movements of disaffection did overlap. One of the best examples of this was seen when Sly Stone, a very hip, black San Francisco DJ, formed an integrated, psychedelic band called *Sly and the Family Stone*. For three years in the late '60s, the group's highly popular sound fused soul, funk and rock. Sly's hopeful sounding, danceable energy was a far cry from the hostile activism of Eldridge Cleaver or Bobby Stokes of the Black Panthers. However, with the satirical hit "Hot Fun in the Summertime," Sly and the Family Stone were not apolitical either. This funky, upbeat song highlighted the several summers of rioting that plagued big city ghettos throughout the United States in the mid-and-late '60s.

Nor did the hippies, as Buda suggests, so quickly acquiesce to a consumerist sterility. Buda's reductivism completely misses the cultural subtleties of this sweeping Dionysian upsurge and its ubiquitous sociological ramifications that changed mainstream American culture. For many, the reactionary impulse to reject materialism evolved into efforts to radically change consumer habits. This alternative sensibility gravitated toward finding earth-friendly, ecologically conscientious modes of inhabiting the planet and opposing an unfettered industrialism.

The paradox that hippies do consume and cannot live outside the forces of commercialism is the point articulated by Manfred Pütz in his 1974 article "Transcendentalism Revived: The Fiction of Richard Brautigan":

> The fate of Brautigan himself illustrates the failure to escape the mechanisms of contemporary life. He started as a convinced enemy of commercialism; he did not write primarily to sell; he did not want to become a figure in the professional literary world. Many of his works (mainly the poems) were privately printed and distributed gratis. They contained attacks on an insanely commercialized world. But the system with its immense absorbing faculties is able to commercialize anything—even attempts to annihilate it. In poking fun at the ideology of success Brautigan, too, has become a success. Today the name Brautigan is a trademark of the fashionable, his books are objects of indiscriminate consumption; the man himself is an item of commerce [Pütz].

Pütz makes an excellent point about the "absorbing faculties" of the system; this explains how a Dionysian reactivism is not sustainable.

However, he seems to be on a mission to make Brautigan the whipping boy for the bohemian disposition. Brautigan moved to San Francisco to make his living as a writer. He didn't go to college; the '50s were a time when financial aid was not readily an option. He lived poor and stubbornly persisted in his dream to support himself solely as a writer. He wasn't the "convinced enemy of commercialism." Just because he didn't enter academia does not mean he wasn't a professional in the literary world. Though dirt-poor, writing was his vocation. As will be discussed shortly, his writing was experimental, but certainly highly literary, if literary entails a layering of inventive irony that incorporates subtly embedded allusions to other literature.

Moreover, Brautigan wasn't poking fun at the "ideology of success" as much as at the ideology of progress. The disaffection he felt toward the patterns of modernization that have invaded human consciousness at the expense of the pastoral could not, in Brautigan's mind, be resolved by removing himself from the modern or by trying to "annihilate" it. At best, in his non-didactic manner, Brautigan was working to re-imagine the world. The absurd and quirky connections he made between the modern artifacts of man and the pastoral trout streams, indicate that he saw, in a fresh way, how Americans, collectively, have become. The author wanted to jolt his reader into seeing the world with fresh eyes. Brautigan did not divorce himself from the implications that he, too, was a member of the absurd, modern world with the imperfections and weird hubris he saw. So for him to survive as a writer, to be one of the fortunate few who could garner success by pointing out the consequences of man's modernized existence, was not inconsistent with his writings or his personal goals.

Pütz's attempt to highlight the contradictions of Brautigan's philosophy and success, also fails to recognize that West Coast America in the 1960's still possessed many pockets of true wilderness and remnants of frontier. The counterculture has been called naïve, romantic and utopian as a way to dismiss the era, but the hippie sense that "we can change the world" came as much from an urge toward self-reliance and a belief in possibility, as it did from sheer youthful optimism and hope. The sense of rugged individualism, so evident in Ken Kesey's first two novels, was not dead, though the hippies' largest internal obstacle when experimenting with communal living, was to find individuals who could learn to be collectivist in everyday life. Brautigan had turned to the imagination to shake up the ideology of progress. The author's vision reinforced a certain reactionary sentiment in the mosaic of countercultural perspectives. Out of the upsurge around 1967 came many alternative movements that explored different possibilities for the way man should live, consume and produce goods, extract resources and engage the landscape.

So, yes, the author, with his imagination that articulated the state of man's modern progress, had phenomenal success among those in the hippie generation. He had a unique style, but *Trout Fishing in America* didn't propose any specific solutions or even point any accusatory fingers. In Brautigan's portrait, modern man's mess belongs to all modern men and women.

Bruce Cook of *The National Observer* is quoted on the back of *The Hawkline Monster: A Gothic Western*, a 1974 novel by the author: "Brautigan is good for you. No writer you can think of is quite like him today, nor has any writer anytime—unless you can imagine the kind of things Mark Twain might have written had he wandered into a field of ripe cannabis with a pack of Zig Zag papers in his pocket. That's as close as I can come to Brautigan, a kind of crackerbarrel surrealist whose humor is essentially Nineteenth-Century Western American." Cook's take on Brautigan's hippie sensibility is "right on," except that, ironically, Brautigan didn't smoke pot, either.

Brautigan, in a distinctly American vernacular, employed a colloquial style and the wit of surprise based on the yarn. Here the comparison of this author with Twain is warranted. In other ways, Brautigan's style differs greatly from Twain's. As for the similarity, near the opening of *Trout Fishing in America,* we think we're entering a Huck-Finn-goes-a-fishin' adventure:

> The next morning I got up early and ate my breakfast. I took a slice of white bread to use for bait. I planned on making doughballs from the soft center of the bread and putting them on my vaudevillian hook. I left the place and walked down to the different street corner. How beautiful the field looked and the creek that came pouring down in a waterfall off the hill.
>
> But as I got closer to the creek I could see that something was wrong. The creek did not act right. There was a strangeness to it. There was a thing about its motion that was wrong. Finally I got close enough to see what the trouble was.
>
> The waterfall was just a flight of white wooden stairs leading up to a house in the trees. I stood there for a long time, looking up and looking down, following the stairs with my eyes, having trouble believing. Then I knocked on my creek and heard the sound of wood. I ended up by being my own trout and eating the slice of bread myself [4–5].

Brautigan used Twain's style of dampened colloquial humor to help elevate, in a paradoxical way, his whimsical, dreamy metaphors. To attain this paradox, his sentences were minimalist and declarative in order to suppress the reader's responses until he was ready to invade them with his spectacularly surreal metaphors. While he uses whimsy brilliantly, Abbott states: "what happens in Brautigan's prose is that parasitical imagination invades and occupies the host of precise, orderly prose, subverting, disrupting and eventually usurping the factual prose's function" (*Downstream...*, Abbott, 120).

In other words, Brautigan, in his light style, lulls the reader into complacency—here the illusion of a boy going fishing. This author employs masterful timing with his deftly employed, simple build-up. The surreal phrase "vaudevillian hook," is a surprise nugget dropped in our lap. The understated tone of his lead-in sentences allows us to accept this without protest. Then, when the boy approaches the waterfall, the tension builds through quiet repetition: something is wrong in one sentence, not right in the next, then strange, not moving right, then finally the boy gets close enough. We, the reader, are now close enough, too; we're close enough to be caught by a Vaudevillian hook on that flight of white stairs. This is a whimsical violation of expectation, not dissimilar to the impact of seeing a photo of an anti-war protester who has stuffed the stem of a daisy in the barrel of a soldier's rifle. His hippie style was soft and humorous, but quietly outrageous. Just as the reader is lulled into whatever little scene he is creating, he applies an odd phrase, metaphor, or twist in the action that violates expectation in a way that is often uproariously absurd. Indeed, the reason for this author's success is mostly due to his warped sense of humor. His work is rife with subtle literary allusions and the structure of *Trout Fishing* was highly innovative. Primarily, though, Brautigan is flat out funny.

In his "Review of Trout Fishing in America" in the December 1967 edition of *Ramparts Magazine,* Stephen Schneck lauds Brautigan's style of humor:

> Our comic talents [in America] depend less upon language and technique than upon the untutored rural tradition of the eccentric vision and the absurd juxtaposition of reason and extremism. Authentic American humor (as opposed to the commercial, prefabricated variety) has its roots in the rich American soil. Here we grow things bigger, faster, better than anyone, anywhere else. And our humor is, largely, derived from a major American vice, *exaggeration.* The Fish Story is probably the purest form of American wit: farce is our reality and our métier. [...]
>
> As the inventor of a metaphorical hook constructed with American know-how to catch the slippery American *hubris,* Brautigan fishes in and out of context, casting his unassuming lure in the waters, in the parks, in the mystery of America, at a time when fish and fishermen alike are either crazed or comatose: frozen, frightened nearly out of their American wits.
>
> Anyone who has tried can tell you that this American continent is not an easy place to locate, or state of mind to elucidate. There is no describing us, no explaining us: no one has such scope, no one is so perceptive [...] [Schneck].

Beyond the colloquial humor and vernacular, Brautigan's work did not resemble Twain's. In terms of creating character depth or narrative structure, the 19th century humorist was far more traditional than Brautigan. Moreover, Twain's ear for dialect as a tool in his characterizations was nothing short of brilliant. Unlike the depth of character developed in Huck Finn or Tom Sawyer, in *Trout Fishing* we're never certain who or what Trout Fishing in America is. Brautigan's metaphor as main character is at times the book itself, a person (Trout Fishing in America Shorty), a hotel, the author, even the actual pastime—we're never quite sure. However, there's little doubt that Samuel Clemens, were he alive to read this book, would have been highly amused.

In the placement of odd assemblages of bricolage, or absurd fragments from the flotsam and jetsam of industry, Brautigan's style, especially in *Trout Fishing in America*, compared much more closely to that of Donald Barthelme, an author who also began to publish at the same time as Brautigan. Though the term was little used at the time they were writing, Brautigan and Barthelme were both postmodernist in style and structure. In fact, it can be argued that the experimental narrative structure employed in *Trout Fishing in America* was especially well suited to Brautigan's style of irony. His later attempts to employ this style of humor in parodies of more traditional forms of narrative, never worked as well.

In *Trout Fishing*, Brautigan's narrative structure is not linear; it doesn't lead to conflict resolution, but is circular in the way each chapter coils around one central metaphor. The author uses several incarnations of trout fishing in America to paint a series of absurdist vignettes. At its best, the writing is unexpectedly engaging and, often, mind-bendingly funny. There is actual trout fishing in Brautigan's vision of America, but the pastoral is usurped by the author's overlay of modernized whimsy.

In the short chapter (and all the chapters in this short novel are short) called "The Hunchback Trout," Brautigan goes fishing on a creek that "was like 12,845 telephone booths in a row with high Victorian ceilings and all the doors taken off and all the backs of the booths knocked out" (55). [...] "I waded about seventy-three telephone booths in. I caught two trout in a little hole that was like a wagon wheel. [...] The next good place was forty-five telephone booths in" (56). When the narrator catches a big one, he thinks for a second that it's a frog. "The fish ran deep again and I could feel its life energy screaming back up the line to my hand. The line felt like sound. It was an ambulance siren coming straight at me, red light flashing, and then going away again and then taking to the air again and becoming an air-raid siren" (57).

Brautigan melds the distinction between simile and actuality. He turns "like 12,845 telephone booths" into an actual fishing hole at booth numbers seventy-three or forty-five. Brautigan's line that "felt like sound" becomes an actual ambulance siren, then an air-raid siren. Such is the technique and power of exaggeration at the heart of the yarn. Exaggeration was also a mainstay of Twain's humor as in the story "Roughing It."

Yet, Brautigan lived in a different era than Twain. As his absurdist, whimsical vignettes accrete through the novel, the underlying resonance of his theme—a sense of the wilderness being supplanted by the modernized quirkiness of man—becomes more pronounced. Brautigan is never overtly didactic, yet his surrealism comes with teeth. "The fish was a twelve-inch rainbow trout with a huge hump on its back. A hunchback trout. The first I'd ever seen. The hump was probably due to an injury that occurred when the trout was young" (57). Trout fishing, as presented in Brautigan's America, has lost its pastoral and romantic allure.

While trout fishing was an actual part of Brautigan's life growing up in the Pacific Northwest, his conceit with this novel was to jolt all sense of natural realism in order to invoke, through the absurdity, a broader sense of modern realism as rendered through America's paradise lost:

> There was a fine thing about that trout. I only wish I could have made a death mask of him. Not of his body though, but of his energy. I don't know if anyone would have understood his body. I put it in my creel [57].

Brautigan, at his best, had an uncanny ability to see the extraordinary in the ordinary. In this case he harnesses, through this odd, maimed, survivor of a fish, a sense of energy. Mostly, one comes away from reading Brautigan feeling the vitality of the imagination, the trait he seems to posit as mankind's singular hope for seeing beyond hidebound tendency and modern circumstance.

Snow White, the 1967 novel by Donald Barthelme, uses similar absurdist techniques to recast this fairy tale within a modern context. Like *Trout Fishing in America*, this novel relies heavily on the juxtaposition of ironic imagery to create a non-linear narrative. *Snow White* features seven men who live communally with one woman. Though certain motifs, characters and situations reappear throughout both books, these novels are made up of a series of seemingly unconnected mini-narratives and the respective overall structures have no unified plot. The narrative vignettes coil around one central feature—Brautigan's central metaphor of fishing, or Barthelme's absurdist and loosely traced parody of the fairy tale.

On the back cover of *Snow White*, Webster Schott of *Life Magazine* states: "Probably the most perversely gifted writer in the U.S., Donald Barthelme has created a new form of fiction." Certainly, Barthelme was at the cutting edge with his experimental prose, but he wasn't alone. *Trout Fishing* and *Snow White* were published the same year, but Brautigan actually wrote his novel in 1961 and Barthelme prior to 1965. *Naked Lunch*, published in 1959 by Beat author William S. Burroughs, employed an innovative cut-up style that also broke from the traditional narrative form. *Naked Lunch* depicted non-linear vignettes related to Burroughs's addiction to heroin. Gertrude Stein in the '30s was another author experimenting with form in her prose. Yet, in the wide cultural upheaval of the late '60s, literature was one of many traditions being challenged. A critical mass of individuals had begun to coalesce on numerous fronts to question, attack, and alter the established forms of government, industry, social behavior, and the arts. In this broader ushering in of "post-modernism," Brautigan and Barthelme, as authors, were bending the boundaries of the established literary form.

Specifically, Late Modernism as a literary form, incorporated certain experimentation such as the surrealism in *Cuckoo's Nest* and the compressed use of time and multiple points of view in *Great Notion,* but the Late Modernist form still adhered to the traditional narrative arc with a concomitant dramatic resolution to the story. *Snow White,* in its odd communal depictions, and *Trout Fishing,* with its quirky recasting of a pastoral American metaphor, broke from such literary constraint. Both books reflected the changing sensibility of the times. As a whole, *Snow White* wasn't hippiesque, but Barthelme recognized a changing consciousness, including a fascination with communal living. *Snow White* includes a scene featuring one of the seven men at a party somewhere in urban America in the mid–60s:

> There were a lot of other people talking there, political talk and other kinds of talk. A certain contempt for the institutions of society was exhibited. Clem thrust his arm into the bag of consciousness-expanding drugs. His consciousness expanded. He concentrated his consciousness upon a thumbtip. "Is this the upper extent of knowing, this dermis that I perceive here?" Then he became melancholy as a gib cat, melancholy as a jugged hare. "The content of the giraffe is giraffe meat. Giraffe have high blood pressure because the blood must plod to the brain up ten feet of neck" [*Snow White,* 116–117].

Barthelme and Brautigan exhibit a similar method of delivery through simple declarative sentences to set up the absurdist irony. Both deploy a nontraditional narrative structure.

In a review of Brautigan in the *London Review of Books* in 2000, a comparison of the two authors is made:

> Brautigan shares with Barthelme his extreme minimalism, the deft placement, or misplacement, of emphasis, the shaggy dog endings. But the similarities end there. The colour, texture and tone of their work is completely different, as is the subject matter and its treatment. Brautigan is the looser writer, more radical in form and further out in his imaginative flights, but he is also less capable of achieving a successfully sustained narrative, no matter how brief. Brautigan is continually bailing out in his stories before they arrive anywhere. Or he is trying to charm his way out [London Review of Books, December 14, 2000].

Looking at the whole body of each author's work, this argument is valid, but in comparing *Trout Fishing in America* with *Snow White,* Brautigan's novella is the better sustained and a more fully realized juxtapositional narrative. In part, the thematic stakes in *Trout Fishing* were considerably higher than in *Snow White.* Brautigan's style is more colloquial and Western, and the imaginative flights more outrageously funny. Also, this critique is correct that, over his career, the author never learned to excel beyond his strength at depicting juxtapositional irony. In both *Trout Fishing* and *In Watermelon Sugar*, however, he was exceptionally adept at this cutting-edge narrative form.

John Gardner in *The Art of Fiction*, published in 1982, suggests that "[s]uccessful novel-length fictions can be organized in numerous ways: energeically, that is, by a sequence of causally related events; juxtapositionally, when the novel's parts have symbolic or thematic relationship but no flowing development through cause and effect; or lyrically, that is, by some essentially musical principle—one thinks, for example of the novels of Marcel Proust or Virginia Woolf" (185).

Most fiction is energeic—for example the first two novels of Ken Kesey. Gardner attributes this definition of *energeia* to Aristotle. Most fiction is structured according to "the actualization of the potential that exists in character and situation" (185). The conflict between Nurse Ratched and McMurphy—as to which one of them would control the mental ward—caused a situation that would be actualized through the dramatic narrative of *Cuckoo's Nest*. The energeics of the plot in *Sometimes a Great Notion* hinged on trying to get Hank to give up. The effects played out through Hank during the course of the novel. By comparison, *Trout Fishing in America* and *Snow White* relied on the relationship of the imagistic prose to the theme, not on cause and effect to drive the plot. In this regard, though by no means were they the only experimental novelists of their time, Brautigan and Barthelme were seminally postmodernist.

In his article "Richard Brautigan: A Poetics of Alienation" from *American Literature*, Travis Eachan Triance points out:

> Traditional forms of linear narrative are re-ordered, and cast into a slowly shifting near stasis. It is as if the author decided to utilise as narration, a collage whose forms were imbued with a sort of viscous motion. These images are gradually strung together, through various idiosyncratic allusions, and permutations of language.
>
> Brautigan's prose and poetry are coloured by the whimsical [...] which was characteristic of the hippie generation, these moments are neither indicative of Brautigan's style, nor are they particularly luminous surrounded as they are by the innovative use/misuse of conventional literary forms and devices.
>
> It is this juxtaposition of nostalgic reminiscence, with a parodic, disjunctive rendition of the English language that allows for Brautigan's peculiar "cacophonic simplicity." [...]
>
> Direct and indirect references to earlier American literature [...] make *Trout Fishing in America* a far richer book than reviewers initially supposed. Where in 1971 John Clayton saw only flower-powered utopianism, subsequent readers have found a Spenglerian account of the decline of the West [Triance].

To be appreciated, allusion, of course, depends on the reader being familiar with whatever is being alluded to. While Brautigan's work was replete with literary allusion, it should be pointed out that, as a strength of Brautigan's writing, his humor was not dependent on, but enhanced by its use. The core juxtapositions were set up and well enough contextualized within the narrative to create self-standing comic associations. In other words, his writing was deceptively simple, yet embedded with subtle layering of implication. Or as David Vanderwerken in his article, "*Trout Fishing in America* and the American Tradition," points out:

> *Trout Fishing in America* is loaded with put-ons, parodies, throwaway comments, whimsical irony, pseudo-logic, mock scholarship—for example, the list of fishing books that includes no accounts of "Trout Death by Port Wine" (TFA, pp.44–5), hyperbole, incongruous juxtapositions, and red herrings too numerous to document. For the careful reader, surprises lurk on every page [Vanderwerken].

As an example of underground narrative—the literary response suggested by Thomas Newhouse that reached its fullest expression in the counterculture of the 1960's—Brautigan's novel demonstrates a modest departure from most Beat literature. Like Beat prose, *Trout Fishing* exacts an alienated, disaffected posture. However, the manner of voice and tone he employs is softer, more deliberate, and funnier. As pointed out earlier, most Beat writing is far more self-serious, hyper, and intentionally "hip" than Brautigan's work. Beat literature is less folksy, or, more accurately, it's subsumed in its own hip vernacular. Though each vignette is tightly rendered, the pacing in *Trout Fishing in America* is much more laid back than the frenetic, spontaneous feel of most Beat writing.

Been Down So Long It Looks Like Up to Me, by comparison to *Trout Fishing,* emulated the Beat dithyrambic pacing with a chaotic, ornate, and hip style. However, Fariña's novel suffered from too many oblique allusions, and a manic pace that lacked modulation. By Gardner's terms, the novel exhibited poorly executed *energeics.*

Brautigan's easy pace, coupled with his inventive similes and metaphors, was often uproarious, as well as lighter to read. His whimsy mirrored the Alice-in-Wonderland mood in San Francisco (and beyond) suddenly induced by an influx of potent psychedelic drugs in the mid-part of the decade. By comparison, Gnossos Pappadopoulis was the hippest trickster on campus, but his hyperactive pace of engagement, although replete with great lingo, intelligence and allusion, became more wearisome than amusing to read. Gnossos could be trippy, but was too self-serious to be whimsical. *Trout Fishing in America* captured a fresh, new sentiment, one that viewed its disaffection with detachment and a pained sense of humor. The alienation was quite real, but the manner of adaptation to society was changing. With his colloquial, absurdist whimsy, Richard Brautigan was the first author widely acclaimed for writing with a hippie sensibility.

One might argue that Ken Kesey deserves this distinction, except

that Kesey's novels were set in a time that immediately preceded the hippie scene he helped create. Personal antics that promulgated a turned-
on lifestyle are what have earned Kesey distinction as America's first
hippie. More than Brautigan, Kesey assumed the role of a provocateur.
On a personal and social level, Brautigan was much more withdrawn.

Also, *Trout Fishing* was not anchored in one specific time or place.
As precursors to the hippie phenomenon, *Cuckoo's Nest* and *Great Notion*
showed the societal tensions at play between the "establishment" and
the respective protagonists of these novels who were looking to forge a
sense of identity in a modernizing society. The tensions which were only
brewing in the early '60s, had yet to erupt. With the eruption came the
hippie mode of coping through a distinct countercultural behavior. *Trout
Fishing*, unlike the works of Kesey, was rather dislodged from time, so its
metaphorical parallels were as relevant in 1967 as when the book was written in 1961. This said, Kesey's first two novels and Brautigan's *Trout Fishing in America* shared one great characteristic in common—all three
novels, although every one of these narratives was rendered in a radically different fashion—were thematic expressions of modern man at the
edge of the wilderness in decline.

Both Kesey and Brautigan were born in 1935 and raised in the Pacific
Northwest, although Brautigan's childhood in Tacoma, Washington and
Eugene, Oregon was more impoverished and he didn't benefit, as Kesey
did, from a college education in Eugene and Palo Alto. Like Randle P.
McMurphy in Kesey's *Cuckoo's Nest,* Brautigan received electroshock therapy during the short time he spent at the Oregon State Mental Hospital in Salem as a twenty-year-old. Both authors came to the Bay Area in
the '50s to become writers. Kesey had the privilege of studying with the
formal literary elite of his time, while Brautigan's literary education was
honed on the fringes of the Beat scene. He was never an insider with
the notable Beat writers of the period. He brought to San Francisco his
own distinct sense of humor. He scraped by, determined to be a writer.

Kesey often left his Stanford scene to immerse himself in the same
Beatnik world of North Beach that was inhabited by Brautigan. Prior to
Cuckoo's Nest, Kesey wrote *Zoo,* a fiction manuscript that was never published. It was set in North Beach. Both authors shared the down home
vernacular of the rural Northwest, and absorbed from the Beat scene a
love for surrealistic imagery and the shock of well-phrased words. Kesey's
writing in his first two novels forces the reader to be highly immersive,
whereas Brautigan's style is pared down and sparse. It yields sudden
impact through metaphorical twists that often leave the reader dangling.
With set characters and situations, and adhering to traditional form,
Kesey was nonetheless able to experiment successfully at compressing
linear time in *Great Notion.* The novel, in this respect, was multi-linear,

with numerous characters and situations encroaching during the same timeframe on one central character and situation.

In *Trout Fishing in America* Brautigan anchors himself to one metaphor and allows his imagination to run wild. The wildness establishes an absurdist connection to the central metaphor of the title. Usually his metaphors have less to do with wildness, than with the modern as a perverse new kind of wilderness. In the modernist tradition, Kesey's first two works are grand narratives offering a sense of completion and moral closure, while *Trout Fishing* presents no sense of closure, no denouement, but only a series of little narratives, what the French Postmodernists of more recent times call *petit recit*, which is currently favored among contemporary literary critics over the earlier "grand" form.

Trout Fishing in America doesn't have a traditional climax in terms of energeic resolution. Rather, near the end of the book, the reader finds the novel's most compelling juxtaposition, the one that all the earlier juxtapositioning has been circling toward. This occurs in the chapter called "The Cleveland Wrecking Yard." This is where the novel best depicts the sense of a contemporary America that is, not only losing its sense of the pastoral, but is actually morphing into a wilderness of commoditization. In the novel, parts of an actual trout stream are stacked up within the chain-linked confines of the junkyard:

> "Can I help you?"
> "Yes," I said. "I'm curious about the trout stream you have for sale. Can you tell me something about it? How are you selling it?"
> "We're selling it by the foot length. You can buy as little as you want or you can buy all we've got left. A man came in here this morning and bought 563 feet." [...]
> "How much are you selling the stream for?" I asked.
> "Six dollars and fifty-cents a foot," he said. "That's for the first hundred feet. After that it's five dollars a foot."
> "How much for the birds?" I asked.
> "Thirty-five cents apiece," he said. "But of course they're used. We can't guarantee anything" [104].

This absurdist sense that the wilderness could be turned into a commodity, a junk-yard product to sell, appealed to the hippie philosophy and sense of humor, much of it based on the rejection of materialism and "plastic" society. As such, Brautigan's outrageous sense of humor proved to be highly popular in the late '60s.

John Clayton, the object of Triance's earlier comment on seeing only "flower powered utopianism," commented on this "junk-yard" chapter in a 1971 article "Richard Brautigan: The Politics of Woodstock":

> Another writer might have produced an obvious satire on destruction and commercialization of the pastoral—a trout stream sold by the foot length. Of course the American trout stream has been sawed into pieces, animals extra. But this

> satire Brautigan soft-pedals: if the pastoral stream is no longer available, the pastoral of the imagination *is* available. I am seduced by his stoned imagination, which can *conceive* of a trout stream sold by the board foot; which can make a pastoral in a junkyard. What I am finally hooked by is the sensibility which can create a lyrical space in our heads by play, by metaphor [Clayton].

Conversely, throughout *Trout Fishing in America,* Brautigan also creates a junkyard in the pastoral; he creates discordant spaces when the inclination is to be sweetly fishing. It is only in this junkyard chapter that the wilderness comes to town, so to speak. With these crosscurrents, Brautigan toys with our minds.

As for Brautigan's "stoned imagination," the word "stoned" evolved from the high of the booze and tranquilizer indulged '50s into being high on pot in the '60s. Interestingly, the author's daughter Ianthe Brautigan, in her 2000 memoir *You Can't Catch Death,* talked at length about her father's binge drinking and alcoholism, but when describing their home in rural Montana in 1975–76, she said that "drugs were everywhere, although I remained very protected. My father didn't do coke or smoke pot. He drank and occasionally took Valium to sleep" (99). She talks about a party at one of the neighbors there where everyone dropped acid, but she neglected to say whether her father participated. From what Brautigan's writer friend Keith Abbott said, there is no reason to believe that the author did. Brautigan's weakness was booze.

In her memoir, Ianthe Brautigan never labels her father as either a Beat or a hippie. Ianthe describes the modest apartment where her father lived in the late '60s after his sudden success:

> His apartment door had a small window, and my father had taped some interesting things against the glass. There was a Digger dollar and a feather. For a while in the sixties the Diggers had tried to present an alternative to capitalism. They opened a Free Store and created Digger dollars. They packed tables full of food under eucalyptus trees in Golden Gate Park, and my father had taken me there to eat with him [10].

The Diggers and Richard Brautigan were an integral part of the hip, new, San Francisco scene.

Clayton, a self-described citizen of the Woodstock Nation, goes on in his 1971 essay to articulate why Brautigan's work had such an impact on the hippie counterculture:

> The association with early America, the connection with the mountains, the simile becoming fantasy: I am also made to feel at home. [...] I want to live in the liberated mental space that Brautigan creates. I am aware, however, of the institutions that make it difficult for me to live there and that make it impossible for most people in the world. Brautigan's value is in giving us a pastoral vision which can water our spirits as we struggle—the happy knowledge that there is another place to breathe in; his danger, and the danger of the style of youth culture generally, is that we will forget the struggle [Clayton].

Such proclamations were common underground fare of the times, but a careful reading of *Trout Fishing* shows its juxtapositional tapestry to be more humorous than hopeful.

According to Janusz Buda, in addition to being too closely linked to the hippies, Brautigan also suffers from an "unwarranted" association of being too whimsical. He rightly points out that this is one of the strongest aspects of Brautigan's writing. There are many whimsical or fabulist precedents throughout history that are considered fine literature, such as Chaucer, Cervantes, Rabelais, Lewis Carroll, A.A. Milne, Kenneth Graham, Gertrude Stein, Italo Calvino and, not the least, Mark Twain. Brautigan's metaphorically rich work reflected the hippie sentiment, especially a countercultural sense of humor.

While Buda grossly minimizes the hippie phenomenon, his intent is laudable. The burying of Brautigan within this whimsical realm of "hippiedom" has obscured what Buda rightfully points out as Brautigan's "deeper levels of cabalistic symbolism and meaning" (20). What Buda misses is that cabalistic considerations—sometimes called, "the secret-forces-at-work-syndrome"—were at the reactive and creative core of hippie sentiment that extended far beyond San Francisco and a few months of time. As evident in Clayton's comment above, the hippies were suspicious of authority, of the mainstream, of the perceived conspiracies of "the man." Even more overtly than Brautigan's ironic symbolism, Chief Broom's "Combine" in *Cuckoo's Nest* and The Tristero conspiracy that Oedipa seems to be uncovering in *Lot 49* point to the growing cabalistic sentiment in America during the '60s. Recognizing this deep-seated suspicion of authority, helps explain the essence of how and why a counterculture, in all its diverse permutations, could take root so strongly in America.

In sum, Brautigan's metaphorically rich work not only reflected the hippie sentiment, but also offered a profoundly ironic look at the state of the pastoral American dream. Schneck, in 1967 articulated the sense of imaginative hope percolating in Brautigan's vision when he asserted that "[t]here is hope in Hell, and there is still some evidence of humanity in America. There are still American writers like Richard Brautigan who are perceptive enough to see the forest in spite of the absence of trees" (Ramparts, December 1967). Brautigan was an integral representative of this time period, of the changed American landscape. Those critics who dismiss Brautigan's writings along with the era, miss, not only the sociological impact of the phenomenon, but how innovative this particular author's successful style was in the transition to a style favored by contemporary literary postmodernists.

Act II

Narrative Interplay

6

Siddhartha (1922)
The Spiritual Quest

    Siddhartha and the other works by Herman Hesse, most notably *Steppenwolf,* entered the radar of the American literary landscape about 1957, at the peak of the Beat movement. *Siddhartha* offered a clear, narrative sense of the spiritual quest. As a narrative, this work stands out for its impact on the counterculture. Other religious texts, though not narrative works, also had profound impact in broadening the spiritual landscape beyond the Judeo-Christianity that thoroughly dominated American culture in the 1950's. Among these were the *I-Ching* of the Taoists, the Buddhist's *Tibetan Book of the Dead,* and the Hindu scriptures—the Upanishads and the *Bhagavad-Gita.* The eclecticism of the hippie spiritualists was not limited to the major religions, but also incorporated a fresh fascination with Native American cultural tradition as witnessed in the popularity of Frank Water's 1963 work, *Book of the Hopi,* the autobiography, *Black Elk Speaks,* published in 1932, and *The Teachings of Don Juan: A Yaqui Way of Knowledge,* published in 1968 and based on the dissertation of Carlos Casteñeda for his Ph.D. in anthropology. In the foreword to *Black Elk Speaks,* Native American author Vine Deloria, Jr., notes that "throughout the thirties, forties and fifties it drew a steady and devoted readership and served as a reliable expression of the substance that undergirded Plains Indian religious beliefs. Outside the Northern Plains, the Sioux tribe, and the western mindset, there were few people who knew the book or listened to its message. But crises mounted and, as we understood the implications of future shock, the silent spring, and the greening of America, people began to search for a universal expression of the larger, more cosmic truths which industrialism and progress had ignored and overwhelmed. In the 1960's interest began to focus on Indians and some of the spiritual realities they seemed to represent" (xiv).

    Future Shock, Silent Spring, and *The Greening of America* were among the most widely read non-fiction books of the countercultural era. Each, in different ways, fed the growing disaffection with the mainstream status quo. Like the religious texts, these works are worthy of mention here for the impact they had on the era, but are not narratives. *Future Shock* was published in 1970 and popularized the contention that too much technological change in too short a period of time was leaving people feeling disconnected and overwhelmed by the new pace of super-industrialized existence. Alvin Toffler, the author, coined the term "information overload" in this book. *Silent Spring* by Rachel Carson was published in 1962 and is recognized for triggering a new ecological awareness in mainstream America. The book describes with meticulous detail how DDT entered the foodchain and accumulated in the fatty tissues of animals, including raptors and human beings, and caused cancer and genetic damage. As a direct result of this well-reasoned, scientific challenge toward an established agricultural practice, DDT was banned. The current environmental movement in North America owes its start to the type of ecological awareness brought about by Carson's book. *The Greening of America* from 1970 by Charles Reich offers a sociological treatise on the new consciousness revolution that was taking root in the American corporate state. The author's heady optimism predicting that the new consciousness of the counterculture would prevail because of the vigor it had in 1970, is dated today. However, embedded in Reich's rhetoric are many systemic concerns and changed attitudes and values that are still with us. Reich failed to predict how thoroughly The Movement would be co-opted into the mainstream. Certain aspects such as a wider acceptance of recreational drugs never occurred, and others, such as the rock music, fashion, and alternative foods were fully commoditized within the conventional marketplace. All in all, these three works of nonfiction played key roles in shaking up the mindset of mainstream America during the '60s and '70s.

Siddhartha, by comparison, is a contemplative, sparse, yet richly evocative literary story. Swiss author Herman Hesse, with his protagonist Siddhartha, created a spiritual seeker at the time of Gotama, the Buddha. The story is the lifelong quest of this man who leaves his life of relative privilege as a member of the Brahmin caste. Along with his friend Govinda, the young men become ascetics.

After three materially impoverished years denying the inner Self, Siddhartha and Govinda hear word of the teachings of the Illustrious Buddha. They leave the ascetics and travel to find Buddha. Here Siddhartha, after his friend decides to become a monk and follower of Buddha, has a conversation with the divine teacher. He tells Buddha that he can worship no teachings, but must discover wisdom on his own. With only a hint of reluctance, Buddha blesses Siddhartha's decision and the young man leaves on his own.

Coming to a river, Siddhartha is tempted by a beautiful young woman, but resists her and crosses on the ferry. Still dressed as a poor ascetic, Siddhartha arrives at the edge of a city where he gazes up into the eyes of a wealthy courtesan at the gate of this beautiful woman's garden retreat. The next day when Siddhartha returns to the gate, his dirty beard and hair have been cut and the servants allow him in to see the courtesan. He tells her that he wishes to learn the art of love from her. She tells him that he will need fine clothes and jewels to learn such art from her. He tells her that compared to what he has endured this will be simple. When he composes a poem for the courtesan, she grants him a kiss, one that fully draws Siddhartha into this part of his quest. The courtesan introduces Siddhartha to a wealthy merchant in the city, and with him, Siddhartha learns the ways of money and trade and becomes quite wealthy.

From the courtesan he learns the art of lovemaking. Over the years, Siddhartha forgets the wisdom of his simple quest for truth and divinity and becomes enamored of finery, drink and gambling. The courtesan and Siddhartha each tells the other that, while she is so practiced in the art of love and he was her finest lover, neither is capable of loving anyone. One day after a disturbing dream, Siddhartha makes passionate love with her one last time and abandons his wealth and status and returns to the river. Here, his friend Govinda finds him sleeping soundly by a tree. Govinda doesn't recognize him as Siddhartha, but waits to protect the man from the dangers of the forest. When Siddhartha awakens, he recognizes his friend. Govinda, though a Buddhist monk for all these years, has not lost his anxiousness and is still urgently seeking enlightenment.

When the friends depart, Siddhartha decides to join the aging ferryman at the river, a man with a gift of listening, especially to the river. Siddhartha stays here for many years. Word comes to him that Buddha is about to die. The courtesan, who has long since given up her trade and donated her garden to the Buddhist monks, leaves the city to attend the funeral. A snake in the forest bites her while she is traveling there. She has with her the eleven-year-old son she conceived with Siddhartha just before he departed. She dies and Siddhartha is left to raise the boy.

Siddhartha is heartbroken when the boy, used to a wealthier life, wants no part of Siddhartha's simple existence and leaves. In his sorrow, Siddhartha learns what his own father learned when Siddhartha left to become an ascetic. Siddhartha witnesses the older ferryman die blissfully, in perfect peace. In time, after Buddha dies, Govinda comes to visit Siddhartha at the ferry. The story ends with a conversation about seeking and finding and with Govinda recognizing in Siddhartha the same perfection and peace that had drawn him to Buddha.

Hesse wrote *Siddhartha* at the end of World War I. As a writer, he was largely unknown in America until the late 1950's, despite the fact that he won the Nobel Prize for literature in 1946. In the mid–'60s, the author's popularity in the U.S. exploded. *Siddhartha* is an especially straightforward narration based on this seeker's quest for self and truth. Its mystical simplicity and archetypal symbolism appealed to many modern young Americans.

The quest of Siddhartha had many parallels with the life of Jesus Christ as depicted in the New Testament: leaving his family to embark on a spiritual journey, entering the wilderness as a form of asceticism, a rejection of the material belongings of the world, the "illustrious" years spreading the gospel (as Siddhartha witnesses in Govinda's discipleship to Buddha), the emphasis on love, and the attainment of heaven or Nirvana. As narrative, *Siddhartha* allows deceptively simple access into the spiritual essence of Eastern religious thought, one that encourages ready comparison to the essence of Christian belief. In Hesse's own childhood he experienced religion in two forms, as the child and grandchild of pious upright Protestants and as a reader of Indian revelations that honored the Upanishads, the *Bhagavad-Gita* and the sermons of Buddha. The author grew up with a sense of Indian and Christian spirituality—his parents served as missionaries in India. In his essay, "My Belief," Hesse says that "in my religious life Christianity plays by no means the only role, but nevertheless a commanding one, more a mystic Christianity than an ecclesiastical one, and it lives not without conflict but nevertheless without warfare beside a more Hindu-Asiatic-colored faith whose single dogma is the concept of unity" (180). Hesse was Swiss, and his native tongue was German. He struggled emotionally as a pacifist during the years of Nazi controlled Germany.

Siddhartha was Hesse's effort to reconcile, for himself, many aspects of Eastern and Western religious thought. Or, as Mark Boulby in *Hermann Hesse, His Mind and Art* says:

> Hess was throughout his life probably more influenced by Hinduism than by Buddhism; he apparently found that yoga better answered the needs and yearnings of himself and his contemporaries than did the Eightfold Path [of Buddha]. Yet *Siddhartha* differs in the end from all such faiths and systems by the extremism of its derogation of the intellect. Certainly, Siddhartha's experience leads him away from Buddhistic "pessimism"; it leads him away from ethical judgments to the total amoralism of chaos; while the doctrine of universal love points away from Indian teachings altogether toward that of St. Francis [137–8].

Also, *Siddhartha* articulated an underlying Eastern philosophy predicated on the oneness of everything, a notion heartily embraced by most adherents of the counterculture. Boulby notes that "Hesse's later novels [...] refer to the condition of faith, of chaos, of magical thinking, of perception of the One" (154). The works of Hesse had found its ideal audience in the mid–'60s shortly after the author died.

The writings reinforced, and, in fact, gave intellectual/spiritual credence to a sensory perception brought on, in part, by the experience of hallucinogenic drugs. At the end of *Siddhartha,* our hero is beyond seeking and has found his perfection and peace. This heightened and hallucinated sense of the interconnectedness of all experience is articulated when Govinda, always the seeker and follower, observes through Siddhartha the following:

> He no longer saw the face of Siddhartha. Instead he saw other faces, many faces, a long series, a continuous stream of faces—hundreds, thousands, which all came and disappeared and yet all seemed to be there at the same time, which all continually changed and renewed themselves and which were yet all Siddhartha. [...] He saw the face of a newborn child, red and full of wrinkles, ready to cry. He saw the face of a murderer, saw him plunge a knife into the body of a man; at the same moment he saw this criminal kneeling down, bound, and his head cut off by an executioner. He saw the naked bodies of men and women in postures and transports of passionate love. He saw corpses stretched out, still, cold, empty. He saw the heads of animals, boars, crocodiles, elephants, oxen, birds. He saw Krishna and Agni. He saw all these forms and faces in a thousand relationships to each other, all helping each other, loving, hating and destroying each other and become newly born. Each one was mortal, a passionate, painful example of all that is transitory. [...] And all these forms and faces rested, flowed, reproduced, swam past and merged into each other [...] And Govinda saw that this mask-like smile, this smile of unity over the flowing forms, this smile of simultaneousness over the thousands of births and deaths—this smile of Siddhartha—was exactly the same as the calm delicate, impenetrable, perhaps gracious, perhaps mocking, wise, thousand-fold smile of Gotama, the Buddha ... [Hesse, 152–3].

Hesse's depiction of a heightened, surreal sense of oneness, of becoming "newly born," and his clear articulation of interconnectedness and attainment of bliss reinforced the type of enhanced state that more and more people were experiencing in the Sixties. This narrative rendering of an individualistic Eastern seeker, who ultimately finds peace through meditative faith, resonated with these new Western spiritual seekers. Siddhartha in this regard was Christ-like, what Govinda calls, "a Perfect One." The possibility of such perfection seemed attainable in the narrative of Hesse, one that so simply and eloquently articulated a sense of "universal love" and "magical thinking."

Yet, at the time of this newfound adoration of Hesse, a healthy skepticism surfaced as well. In his 1968 article "Prophet of Youth: Hermann Hesse's *Narcissus and Goldmund,*" critic Stephen Koch is not comfortable with either Hesse's intellectual use of "habitual dualities" or the prospect of where this new sensibility of youthful discontent was leading:

But despite his faults, Hesse is a graceful and generally unpretentious artist. What can be said about his current bondage in the hands of the hippie philistines? A large part of Hesse's huge new audience reads nothing *but* Hesse, preferring nonliterary means for most of its Journeys to the East. It is an immense, energetic and ignorant audience with a wild capacity to co-opt the creative energy of high art [...]

   This capacity for cultural co-option scares the hell out of a lot of people, myself sometimes included. American culture is at the point of turning into a vast Children's Crusade, and Hesse is actually one of the best of its teachers. [...] And yet to turn to Orientalism and mysticism which Hesse feeds, though it is clearly dilettantish, naïve, and often damnably vulgar, I don't despair that some of the new *chinoiserie* may play some part in lifting the culture to a new stage of growth. [...]

   For the hippies are absolutely right: we are at a critical moment in the history of culture; we have been brought to a point of no return. But they don't see the intellectual challenge implicit in that fact, nor the prime fact that anyone can rise to it. I don't see any evidence that anyone can. Certainly, Hesse can't, and he is the most intelligent of the new doyens [88, 89].

At the time this article was published in 1968, the youthful tumult, in its many modes of manifestation, was gaining momentum and a foothold that threatened a spectrum of wholesale change, the nature of which no one could be certain. Spiritual, mind-expanding, wildly Dionysian, with a Beat-inspired erosion of the duality between high and low culture, those guardians of high culture such as Stephen Koch were, indeed, more scared than they were willing to admit. Koch was receptive to the hippies as a battering ram to change culture, but only if culture could be changed quite selectively and by battering only those doors approved by the likes of Koch. His ivory tower naïveté toward this thrust of change, especially a change in consciousness that was effectively leaderless, was typical of the time—treat the youthful changes in a guardedly derisive manner, backhanding to the enthusiasm of youth certain possibility for positive outcome.

   In retrospect, more than a generation later, the hippie phenomenon certainly made American culture more receptive to religious diversity. However, the sentiment described at that time as anti-materialistic met a different fate. Over the years came a mainstreaming of the most saleable commodities of the counterculture—its rock music, organic foods, fashion items, etc.—while the mainstream system of indulgent consumerism persists and expands in a manner that is less questioned than ever. What Koch in 1968 called "a point of no return" is now more global than ever with developing industrial nations like China and India feeding the insatiable consumption habits of the world with cheap goods and services. The hollow spirituality of this insatiable acquisitiveness practiced by individual human consumers remains as relevant today as ever, whether the hollowness is pointed out in The Holy Bible or by

Hermann Hesse in the quest of Siddhartha. Eugene Timpe, in his article, "Hermann Hesse in the United States" recognized this about Hesse's writing:

> The matter of a general appeal to youth is most obvious. It has always been the nature of the young to revolt against the weight of tradition, nowadays called "the establishment." [...] They can see themselves [...] subjected to "the system," forced into a mold, the spirit and intelligence crushed. [...]
>
> Not only has this rebellion been more intense of late by virtue of a high proportion of the population involved in it, but also it has differed somewhat from the usual youthful rebellion in ways which have made Hess seem almost to be its prophet. Few of his works fail to express antipathy toward bourgeois materialism, and the new generation heartily seconds his motion against the apotheosis of prosperity. It joins him also in his rejection of conventional morality [...] [141].

The significance of the counterculture in the evolution of American society since the last half of the 20th Century derives from its spiritual questioning. There has been no other collective voice since the counterculture, or at least none with a similar critical mass, to seriously question materialism and corporate fueled consumerism. The hippie phenomenon did so within the social confines of the world's greatest industrial machine. The quelling of this largely leaderless voice through ridicule, lampooning, oversimplification and derision is understandable considering the profit-motivated interests of the entities controlling the media, corporations and institutions benefiting from increased patterns of consumption.

The hippies were, indeed, the children of the ruling class. This made their rejection of the privileges of this class all the more momentous. *Siddhartha,* as narrative, provides a key to understanding the inner, spiritual disquiet that led so many hippies to reject the trappings of their affluence and to seek a higher peace.

7

Stranger in a Strange Land (1961)

The Ecstasy of Grokking

Winner of the Hugo Award for the best Science Fiction novel of 1962, Robert Heinlein's *Stranger in a Strange Land* did not have a second printing until 1968. In 1966 and '67, dog-eared copies of the first printing were being passed among the youthful participants of the burgeoning counterculture who used the story as a blueprint of sorts to experiment with communal relationships and religious practices. With this catalyst for renewed sales, the novel was on its sixtieth printing by 1983.

Stranger in a Strange Land tells the story of Valentine Michael "Mike" Smith, a human born on the planet Mars and raised by Martians after an interplanetary space exploration failed to return to Earth. The novel begins when this homo sapien with many Martian traits comes to earth with a crew of humans on a subsequent space voyage. World War III has caused the system of Nation-States to be reconfigured into one global federation. The story, which takes place in the former United States, traces Mike's development from a docile nestling to a dominant messiah. This premise serves Heinlein as a tendentious platform to wax philosophic about mankind's religious and sexual proclivities. The novel was one of the first of its genre to openly deal with the topic of sex. "Mike" is rescued from Bethesda Medical Hospital and is in danger of being assassinated by Federation officials. He's harbored by Jubal Harshaw, a retired physician, attorney, and author. Elderly, eccentric, individualistic, agnostic and not actively sexual, Jubal lives in a Playboy-style mansion with three attractive young women to serve him poolside. This character provides most of the narrative point of view throughout the novel and, in paternal fashion, is responsible for giving Mike his earthly education and protection.

The plot of this sprawling satire tracks Mike's use of his increasingly superhuman capabilities. Foremost among Martian concepts is "grokking" which starts out as an alien way of "understanding" something or someone. As the novel progresses, the reader sees that the word also implies an ability to intuit something. When Mike's sexuality evolves, "grok" develops the connotation of a biblical "'knowing." But that's not all:

> Mike looked faintly surprised. "'Grok' is drink."
>
> "But Mike would have agreed," Mahmoud went on, "if I had named a hundred other English words, words which we think of as different concepts, even antithetical concepts. 'Grok' means *all* of these. It means 'fear,' it means 'love,' it means 'hate' [...] you merge with it and it merges with you [...].
>
> "'Grok' means to understand so thoroughly that the observer becomes part of the observed—to merge, blend, intermarry, lose identity in group experience" [213–4].

Heinlein uses his sci-fi verb to evoke a transcendent, telepathic all-knowingness that his Martianized human comes to share with mankind. Valentine Michael Smith works to grok Earth and Earthlings. He communes with the worthy through the sharing of water. This water offering creates the ultimate commitment between Mike and those who drink with him. As the novel progresses, the stranger exhibits superhuman traits, notably a talent for heightened sexual bonding and the ability to make humans and objects disappear at will. Earth, as portrayed in *Stranger,* is synonymous with affluent North America. In *One Flew Over the Cuckoo's Nest,* Nurse Ratched serves as a metaphor for totalitarianism; the women in *Stranger* are literally subservient to the interests of the men. They are two-dimensional artifice for the story. Starting with one blonde, one brunette, and one redhead lounging by the pool, the reader finds only beautiful female specimens in this world of Heinlein's. Mike hides out here from the authorities until Jubal cleverly negotiates for the human-Martian's safety and freedom. Heinlein's women are shown to be bright and capable of far more than serving dinner and looking sexy, but they are always subservient.

The novel culminates with a new Martian-inspired church where there is grokking, water-sharing, and a communal oneness with a messianic Valentine Michael Smith. As with the betrayals experienced by Christ, Mike is ultimately stoned to death by the public.

Near the beginning of the novel Heinlein spoofs commercial television, when NWNW—New World Networks—broadcasts through stereophonic tanks to advertise the latest oral contraceptive: "The 3-D picture cut to a young woman, so sensuous, so mammalian, so seductive, as to make any male unsatisfied with local talent. She stretched and wiggled and said in a bedroom voice: '*I* always use Wise Girl '" (38). The use of "The Pill," noted here by Heinlein, was perhaps the single most significant pharmaceutical advance occurring at the time this novel was published (though it's never quite clear what future year it is when Mike lands on earth). While "The Pill" helped usher in a degree of sexual openness that extended far beyond the "Love Generation," the social role expected of professional women is palpably clear in Heinlein's novel. Jubal Harshaw was the story's old school patriarch, as witnessed here when served Scotch:

> "Here's yours, Boss."
> "You put water in it!"
> "Anne's orders. You're too tired to have it on the rocks."
> Jubal looked long-suffering. "See what I put up with, gentlemen? We should never have put shoes on 'em."
> [...] She patted him on the head. "Go ahead and have your tizzy, dear; you've earned it. We're proud of you."
> "Back to the kitchen, woman. Has everybody got a drink?" [210–211].

Heinlein made light of gender roles, but the entire cast of women in this novel is blatantly subservient.

Despite this, *Stranger in a Strange Land* offers an imaginative satire on the conventional religious and sexual outlook in America in 1960 through Heinlein's use of a Dionysian/Apollonian dichotomy in an alternative sci-fi reality. The authorial design in this regard was humorous and well conceived; Valentine Michael Smith provided the vehicle for Heinlein to explore the essence of religious and sexual expression at the time. The genre of Science Fiction allowed Heinlein to delve into a subject that would have been too controversial at that time had it been depicted via conventional realism.

As a model for the Martianized church that Mike eventually starts, Heinlein introduces his protagonist to the Church of the New Revelation founded by the Reverend Foster. In *Stranger,* Heinlein writes that Foster:

> had an instinct for the pulse of the times stronger than that of a skilled carnie sizing up a mark. The culture known as "America" had a split personality throughout its history. Its laws were puritanical; its covert behavior tended to be Rabelaisian; its major religions were Apollonian; its revivals were almost Dionysian. In the twentieth century (Terran Christian Era) nowhere on Earth was sex so vigorously suppressed—and nowhere was there such deep interest in it. [...]
> Foster [...] looked for men like himself and for women like his priestess-wives [...] potential satyrs and nymphs, as the secret church was that Dionysian cult that America had lacked and for which there was enormous potential market [289–90].

According to Bill Patterson, editor of *The Heinlein Journal,* after *Stranger in a Strange Land* exploded in popularity in the late Sixties, members of the counterculture would visit Heinlein's California home to see if the author might be willing to lead them in the communal pursuits outlined in the novel (Patterson, conference comments). Heinlein never intended the novel to be a religious directive, but in *Stranger,* he often used the voice of Jubal to ruminate on religious matters:

> Try reconciling the Old Testament with the New, or Buddhist doctrine with apocrypha. As morals, Fosterism is the Freudian ethic sugar-coated [...]. But he was in tune with his times, he tapped the Zeitgeist. Fear and guilt and loss of faith—How could he miss? [260].

Heinlein was amazed by the delayed interest in this novel he had written several years earlier, as well as in booming sales on a book that was out-of-print by the late '60s. With *Stranger in a Strange Land,* the politically conservative author, ironically, had tapped the Zeitgeist of an emerging counterculture.

In the book *Robert A. Heinlein,* author Leon Stover asserts that Valentine Michael Smith's water-sharing cult brought from Mars was not "taken by Heinlein as a serious model for the fixing of human brotherhood on Terra" (56). When discussing *Stranger,* he adds:

> Sincere communicants of Mike's cult are expected, in hippie language, "to dig" each other, to be able to communicate with a perfect mutual understanding beyond words. [...]
> In the event the novel became a how-to-do-it cult book among successors to Kerouac's beatniks, the hippies. In the Haight-Ashbury district of San Francisco and elsewhere these dope-taking dropouts of the so-called counterculture formed "nests" of free sexual sharing and group nudity. They did this, as they were wont to say, "by the book" out of Heinlein's book—much to the author's surprise [56].

In Stover's book on Heinlein, he routinely apologizes for the author's sexism and takes the common derogatory posture toward the hippies. Stover is also a cheerleader for Heinlein's literary ability.

In the world of Science Fiction writing, Heinlein won an unprecedented four Hugo Awards and was awarded the first Grand Master Nebula Award for Lifetime Achievement. *Stranger in a Strange Land* is considered his masterpiece, although in fairness, many of his staunchest fans are put off by this particular work. On the paperback cover it is called "the most famous science fiction novel ever written." Stover goes on to elevate Heinlein as the Mark Twain of his times:

> [*Stranger's*] range of opinions on things aesthetic, moral, political, economic, or whatever, is the most complete and compact consistent with orderly storytelling. [...] The majority of fans, witless hippies aside, sense what Heinlein is doing in his Twain-like watch over their country, as he takes its institutions to task when they make rags of its ideals [59].

Heinlein's storytelling here is certainly orderly, but not compelling. An orderly Martianized march toward a messianic climax fails to capture much in the way of moral dilemma for the key characters.

Despite the accolades Heinlein received for *Stranger,* the prose is blandly conversational and the narrative plods. The reader hears so much of Jubal Harshaw's viewpoints that the unfolding story suffers. The novel is sarcastic and predictable, and constantly explains its world rather than allowing the sensory details and immediacy of its dramatic scenes to do this work. The author ends up trying to think for the reader, rather than letting the reader draw conclusions for him or herself.

To its credit, *Stranger* demonstrates an imaginative conceit, an original platform for this author's didactic satire on religion and sex in the United States. However, to elevate this prose, or the quality of the satirical wit to that of Mark Twain—as Stover does—is patently absurd. Heinlein's repeated pontificating through the character of Jubal was often trite and now dated, and came at the expense of narrative momentum. Jubal, with his sexism and continual sarcasm, is often predictable and dull as a character. The last third of the novel is told at a distance, far from Mike. Consequently, the dramatic tension dissipates. Jubal's point of view becomes wearisome. Again, it is Heinlein's created universe that fascinates the reader.

If we are to listen to Stover and set the "witless hippies aside," then it's only fair, in a literary sense, to compare Heinlein to other writers of the '60s and early '70s who were much more witty. Authors Richard Brautigan, Kurt Vonnegut, and Tom Robbins all possessed a colloquial style full of clever twists that have an undeniable Twain-like tone and sensibility. Stylistically, all have been compared to Twain, and each of them is far more deserving of this comparison than Heinlein. Vonnegut and Robbins will be discussed in subsequent chapters.

Heinlein's book did offer Americans, through the veil of Science Fiction, an intriguing cultural look at themselves at their most hypersensitive, namely, on the subjects of religion and sex. The Dionysian/ Apollonian dichotomy explored by Heinlein is the novel's most compelling aspect. Stover states that with *Strangers,* in its open treatment of sex, "Heinlein jumped [...] to the Kerouac stage" (54). However, Stover failed to make the next logical connection. Namely, since Heinlein chose to write openly about sexuality—just as the Beats were doing in the late '50s—then it should have come as no surprise that those participating in the Beat-influenced, Dionysian upsurge of the mid–'60s would find fascination with the sexual and religious thematic possibilities delineated by Heinlein. Instead, Stover works too hard to justify Heinlein's sexism and political conservatism; he tries to elevate lyrically bland, heavily didactic prose to the stature of fine literature, yet feels justified in dismissing the hippie reaction to the book as a "witless" aberration.

Indeed, *Stranger in a Strange Land* charted a brave new world for the genre of science fiction, but not because this work represented literary writing. Moreover, it doesn't matter that the author could not foresee the cultural influence of his novel. Once an author creates a text, except for royalties, it belongs to the world. In this sense, beyond *Stranger's* veil of satire and genre, the book became a blueprint for unconventional religious and sexual exploration. Heinlein, though himself conventional, did create a novel that ritualized the spirit of human communing. His novel culminates in an odd Martian Love-In of sorts. Conceptually, *Stranger in a Strange Land* fed the tumult of America's unfolding Dionysian upsurge, and within this spirit of openness, the novel's new patterns of religious and sexual communing were explored.

Even though this novel was published in 1961, Heinlein's book was actually in the process of being written several years earlier. L. Ron Hubbard was another California-based Science Fiction writer who was well acquainted with Heinlein. In 1950 Hubbard wrote *Dianetics,* the seminal work for Scientology, the religion founded by Hubbard. Heinlein was clearly fascinated by the propensity in American culture to allow for the incubation and creation of new religions or cults—no matter how one distinguishes when a church is a cult, or vice versa. Heinlein was certainly aware of Scientology as one of these emerging religions. Considering how Jubal Harshaw served as Heinlein's viewpoint character throughout *Stranger,* then, from the way the novel ends with Jubal as the reluctant, albeit willing, designee as founding father of Mike's Church of All Worlds, the implication is that Heinlein, as an agnostic, reserved an open mind to the transcendent and telepathic spirituality and sexual oneness promised by Mike's church. The level of this author's autobiographical immersion within this text is not significant except to note the irony that the real-life Heinlein, similarly skeptical but ponderous, wanted minimal association with countercultural experimentations based on his "viewpoint" ideas in *Stranger.*

It's important to note that Heinlein, through Jubal, makes a clear distinction between the Dionysian and Apollonian practice of religion. In *Stranger,* Reverend Foster's Church of the New Revelation—the one Mike is exposed to before starting his own—is Dionysian, whereas the calmer, more controlled and less reactionary church started by Mike was Apollonian. Similarly, the Dionysian upsurge of the counterculture in 1967 demonstrated more Apollonian modes of expression as the era progressed. Near the end of *Stranger,* Jubal is talking to Ben, a secondary character, about Mike's new church:

> "[...] Jubal, you've seen Fosterites work themselves up—"
> "Too much, I'm sorry to say."
> "Well, this was not that sort of frenzy; this was quiet and easy, like dropping off to sleep. It was intense all right and got steadily more so, [...] it wasn't mild; it packed terrific wallop."

"The word is 'Apollonian.'"

"Huh?"

"As opposed to 'Dionysian.' People simplify 'Apollonian' into 'mild,' and 'calm,' and 'cool.' But 'Apollonian' and 'Dionysian' are two sides of one coin—a nun kneeling in her cell, holding perfectly still, can be in ecstasy more frenzied than any priestess of Pan Priapus celebrating the vernal equinox. Ecstasy is in the skull, not the setting up exercises." Jubal frowned. "Another error is to identify 'Apollonian' with 'good'—merely because our most respectable sects are Apollonian in ritual and precept. Mere prejudice [341–2].

Children of God, Hare Krishna, Brotherhood of the Source, Brotherhood of the Sun, Synanon, The Unification Church, the People's Temple led by Reverend Jim Jones, The Church of All Worlds (a direct derivative of *Stranger*), and the Love Family, are a few of the examples of communal religious and quasi-religious groups that began proliferating in the late 1960's in the U.S.

Unwittingly, Heinlein foreshadows this burst of non-conventional religions and his inadvertent model explains the interest in his novel roughly five years after it was published. Using the Jubal character as his mouthpiece, Heinlein also notes the fragility of such religious endeavors:

[...] this pattern has been offered to a naughty world many times—and the world has always crushed it. The Oneida Community was much like Mike's nest—it lasted a while, but out in the country, not many neighbors. Or take the early Christians—anarchy, communism, group marriage [...] [364].

In Mike's Martian-inspired church, like most, there are outer circles of believers and inner circles, with the most faithful followers aligned closest to the leadership. In the novel, the members of Mike's church greet one another with "Thou art God," implying a recognition of the divinity in one another.

In 1962 two people started a replica of Mike's Church of All Worlds. The small group incorporated as a religion in 1970 and still maintains several "nests" worldwide. The church practices water sharing. On its internet site one of the group's priests, Iacchus, describes the church as follows:

In 1962 CAW [Church of All Worlds] evolved from a group of friends and lovers who were in part inspired by the science fiction novel *Stranger in a Strange Land* by Robert Heinlein. This book suggested a spiritual and social way of life and was a metaphor expressing the awakening social consciousness of the times. Inspired by this awakening of consciousness and Heinlein's book, this group grew, evolved, became "water-kin" [...] The Church's organizing spiritual and social values include: a belief in immanent Divinity, a pluralistic perspective towards religion, living in harmony with Nature; self-actualization, deep friendship and positive sexuality. In time the church's spiritual and social concepts and values became recognized as Neo-Pagan. As CAW continued to develop, it both influenced and was affected by the broader Neo-Pagan movement.

CAW believes that the nature of our universe and planet is a manifestation of

Divine being. As such the nature of human being is an expression of Divine being. In recognition of this we greet and honor one another with the phrase "Thou art God" or "Thou art Goddess." [...] This [is] similar to the Hindu greeting of "Namaste" which means the "Divine in me greets the Divine in you." "May you never thirst" is spoken when the shared water is drunk. Since water is essential to all known life on this planet it is seen as being very precious. CAW envisions Water-sharing as a way of honoring this preciousness [Iacchus, *www.caw.org/articles/WhatIsCaw.html*].

Heinlein distilled a philosophy in his novel, much of it satirical, that challenged the conventional Christian model of the time—a model that was, indeed, highly Apollonian.

For example, the communalism articulated in *Stranger*—even in Jubal's Playboyesque mansion—was very radical compared to the single-family living pattern so vastly dominant in modern America.

When many countercultural communes formed in the 1960s and early '70s, such activities also flew in the face of an Apollonian society, in some ways even more so than the flourishing use of illegal drugs. The enforcement of zoning regulations and building codes were often used to thwart communal endeavors. Local laws favored single-family dwellings. Internal conflicts also arose when callow participants raised in a more individualistic, consumer society, discovered how much work was entailed in living with collectivist obligations. With internal and external pressures, the start-up hippie commune usually didn't survive for long. Moreover, such communal endeavors often took root in the most rural areas with the lowest level of land-use control. A shared religious bond was also a common denominator in most of the communes that stayed together for any significant period of time.

The Love Family, based in Western Washington, was one such hippie commune exhibiting the type of synergy articulated by Heinlein. The founders of the Love Family first met in the Haight-Ashbury district of San Francisco in the late '60s. Communal Jesus Freaks, they founded the Church of Armageddon and considered themselves part of the Tribe of Judah. About 350 strong at its peak in the early 1980's, this was not a large religious group, but consisted of longhaired hippies who desired to live simple, clean, communal lives by concentrating on the Bible. The leader of the commune went by Love Israel and those church elders closest to Love, none of whom were actually old, also went by virtue names such as Strength, Imagination, Serious, Royalty, Honesty, Simplicity, Logic, etc. The women were subservient. Those in the secondary circle of followers went by Hebrew names found in the Old Testament. The members believed themselves to be Israel, the children of God, and part of Judah as the ruling tribe of Israel, the Christ of Israel. Communally, all were required to concede that Love Israel was supreme.

Steve Allen, the first host of the *Tonight Show* and a musician and comedian, published *Beloved Son* in 1982 as a veiled plea to his son, Brian, who was then Logic Israel. Although the group never greeted one another with "thou art God," the founding philosophy of the Love Family was based on a similar sense of the divinity within all humans. Brian, while still Logic, wrote this to his father:

> An experience that *Love* Israel and I had (before the forming of the Family and before we had the names *Love* and *Logic*) is in many ways at the root of our community gathering together.
>
> Once while meditating, and on looking into each other's eyes [...] I became aware of a tug-o'-war of feelings within me. [...] It's important to note that at this time both of us were into Eastern, Zen-type thought and meditation as a way to higher consciousness. [...]
>
> Then as I looked I saw myself, like a reflection. It was a shock; I felt totally exposed. Then I saw the face of Jesus Christ. At first it was beautiful, then it was terrible because I was overwhelmed with guilt. [...]
>
> I felt at one with all mankind. It was judgment day and I was coming up guilty. Then I realized that *Love's* eyes were filled with love and compassion and forgiveness. I felt a terrific surge of relief, love and ecstasy. [...]
>
> As all the good feelings began to rush through me we began to melt together. We became one. We went to a place above You and Me, to the I AM of us all, pure light. [...]
>
> [I]t was totally clear that God is love, that we *are* One, that Jesus Christ *is* real, that the real part of me and you is loving, forgiving—which is to say Jesus Christ, that love *is* the answer to all problems, and that in this present moment is the only place we will ever find God. I knew then that the way to love God was to love each other. And I knew that it was fear that was keeping us all apart.
>
> The experience was the same for *Love*. To this day, when asked what woke him up, he tells a story of seeing Jesus Christ in me [76–77].

As hippie communes went, this group lasted an exceptionally long time. Most of the members, including Logic Israel, left in 1983. A smaller grouping of about fifty were still together as recently as 2001 when Love Israel declared bankruptcy. The Heinlein model as articulated in *Stranger*—the intuitive sense of 'grokking' one another, water-sharing as a type of communion, and the sense that thou art God and I am God— was a part of the hippie proclivity to connect with one another. The Love Family started from the Dionysian cauldron of the late '60s and was a commune modeled on the earliest Christian church described in the Book of Acts. The group required full immersion of its members. Like Mike's fictional church, it evolved into a more Apollonian religious community. The commune founded, for example, the Seattle food relief effort known as Second Harvest where fruit was gleaned from Eastern Washington orchards and distributed to the hungry in Western Washington.

Brian Allen was asked by this author in August 2003 how the members of the Love Family could believe their commune was at the epicenter of biblical importance; how could they believe in all of human history and place, that their group was the Tribe of Judah during the end time of Armageddon? Brian agreed that the Love Family considered itself to be that special, but he said that the inside joke with them was that every human is also that special, every person who believes is also "it." As to why the group broke up, he points not to *Stranger* or *The Bible,* but to Rudyard Kipling's short story, "The Man Who Would Be King," implying that what the group created was a special peaceful kingdom, but that the indulgences of Love Israel, their self-appointed "King," proved to be the group's downfall.

The tendency to dismiss the hippie as witless, as Stover does, has its humorous side. Brian Allen relayed the story that when the president of a large Northwest-based bank wanted to set up a meeting with the real estate company where Brian worked, he asked the bank vice presidents if they knew anyone over there. One vice president said that he knew Brian Allen, the son of Steve Allen. To this the bank president said: "Isn't it amazing that Steve Allen could have two sons, one the president of a major real estate firm and the other caught up in a cult?" To this the vice president replied: "and what's truly amazing is that this is the same person."

The Love Family evolved directly from the love and peace ethos of the '60s and was not without its controversies and eccentricities. Unlike Jim Jones's People's Temple, the adherents of the Love Family never attempted mass suicide, and like most hard-core hippies, its members sincerely tried to live lives of love and peace. In *Stranger,* Heinlein chose to have his Mike character sacrifice his life to serve the author's satire of the Christian passion play.

Again, the author of *Stranger* tapped into the religious Zeitgeist of his times, but never intended this book as an overt directive for any religious movement, least of all demonic. After the Sharon Tate murder in 1969, a rumor was started in an unsigned article in the San Francisco *Chronicle* that Charles Manson had used *Stranger* as a model for his demonic cult and murderous escapades. The Manson Family was an aberration of the hippie phenomenon, the antithesis of love and peace, yet frequently used by the media to discredit everything associated with the counterculture. According to Stover, Heinlein, through "his own lawyer, had discovered, by interviewing Charles Manson in jail, that Manson had never read *Stranger,* had never even heard of its author's name. Indeed, he turned out to be scarcely literate, a reader of no books at all" (Stover, 57). Heinlein's book, in this case, served as a pawn in a media campaign of derision to discredit everything associated with the hippie phenomenon. In having Manson interviewed, Heinlein was hoping to establish evidence for a libel suit, but the originator of the rumor was never identified.

In addition to religious exploration, *Stranger in a Strange Land* also fed a re-examination of basic sexual relationships. Author Kaaren Kitchell, a respected teacher in the application of ancient myth in our daily lives, lived in the Bay Area during the mid to late'60s. Her novel, *The Book of Twelve*, features a communal cast of characters caught up in a Valentine Michael Smith type of sexual permissiveness. In an interview, she gave her impression of Heinlein's vision in *Stranger* as follows:

> In some respects Heinlein's book was laughably patriarchal and unimaginative, yet in other ways quite radical. For instance, the way his male characters are condescending toward women is a mirror of 50's society. However, many of his articulations about communal, sexual and religious openness were quite radical for that time. In this way he wasn't conservative.
>
> Also, the sexual freedom he depicted was different for men and women, even as this played out in the late '60s. Though this is complex and shouldn't be overgeneralized, in spite of the thrill of the new erotic freedom for both men and women, by the end of the '60s, when that freedom had been taken to its limit, what emerged was that for men it worked magnificently on a surface level, and for most women, not so well.

Stranger served as a template for exploring sexual behavior in both communal living arrangements and when couples experimented with open relationships. Kitchell goes on to give her impression of the consequence of this transformative rejection of mainstream sexual mores:

> Those dozen or so marriages or committed relationships I was aware of where this was happening, simply failed. In the instances I knew of, the women who also experimented left for other committed relationships; the men they left, who usually initiated the multiple sexual play, ended up devastated. Men whose fantasy of having the steady partner at home and the unlimited play elsewhere, discovered that, without the central relationship, the play felt pretty shallow. Looking back, I believe that it is in the nature of passionate love to have a dimension of possessiveness. Heinlein's depiction of this open sexual play, which fascinated those in the early counterculture, is ultimately naïve. Yet, the book had a transformative effect on American sexual mores of the time. It is naïve because it ignores the natural pairing of passion and depth with its darker companions of possessiveness and jealousy.
>
> In certain respects, Heinlein recognizes the stultifying effect of '50s conformity and clannishness in this novel, and he creates a vision of a more vivid, inclusive, communal life where people could connect at all levels—sensual, intuitive, psychological, spiritual. There was a vibrant, exciting aspect to this experimental new way of living and relating, as well as a dangerous one. The danger was its unrecognized explosive effect on committed relationships. *Stranger in a Strange Land* had a fascinating double impact, both opening up and then shattering the lives of those it affected [Interview, 20 December 05].

So, unwittingly, Robert Heinlein with this sci-fi fantasy, tapped into an emerging new Zeitgeist where rebellion against '50s conformity, together with psychedelics, The Pill, and rock music created a Dionysian fervor.

His book managed to fascinate the first wave of hippies who took the satire more literally than the author ever envisioned possible.

The author's surprise over this reaction underscores the peculiarities in the triangular relationship of author, text, and reader. The author, once the text is published, has no control over the emotive and intellectual response of the readers. However, in this case, the sweeping response evoked from Heinlein's imagined world of words is irrefutable. This point is reinforced by Tom Wolfe in the next chapter on the "electricity" resulting from the literary techniques of social realism.

8

The Electric Kool-Aid Acid Test (1968)

Intersubjectivity

> I will miss your magnificent bullshit. I will miss the little Prankster smile at the corners of your mouth. I will miss your mythic stories and the life you led that was so rich in their production. I will miss the lean clarity of your words. No one of your generation wrote better than you.
>
> *–John Perry Barlow (Grateful Dead Lyricist), "Eulogy for Ken"*

Tom Wolfe's successes and shortfalls in the non-fiction narrative *The Electric Kool-Aid Acid Test* are linked to *intersubjectivity*—the ability to imagine being someone else, being able to put oneself in someone else's shoes. Ironically, intersubjectivity is at the core of both Wolfe's technique and at the thematic heart of his narrative which tracks the communal exploits of Ken Kesey and the Merry Pranksters from 1963 through 1966. The literary technique employed by Wolfe to portray the real-life characters of *The Electric Kool-Aid Acid Test* centered on the author's efforts to create the verisimilitude of being inside different characters' heads while telling the "true" story of what was happening to these actual individuals. The non-fictional narrative writing style required a melding of "objective" journalism with the "subjective" techniques of literature. Of course, when the "true" story of what happens involves actual people who are taking the potent hallucinogen—LSD—the difficulty factor of being inside the head of the characters increases considerably. But it's in this context that Wolfe introduces *intersubjectivity* as a primary concept for articulating what happened to this particular group when they lived together and regularly tripped on acid.

The Electric Kool-Aid Acid Test—as a hybrid of literature and journalism—is a formidable work of literary sociology by a Virginian with a Ph.D.

in American studies from Yale University. Published in 1968, the 369-page book was Tom Wolfe's breakout work as an author. Its importance was two-fold. First, the narrative gave mainstream America an insider's sense of the burgeoning hippie culture that, by '68, had exploded in California and several other urban areas in Western Europe and North America. Secondly, as a hybrid between non-fiction and fiction, this work was at the cutting edge of what came to be called, "The New Journalism."

Tom Wolfe described this style of writing in the insightful opening of an anthology called *The New Journalism* published in 1973. Wolfe and several other journalists from New York especially—Gay Talese, Jimmy Breslin, etc.—had been honing its technique since the early '60s. Wolfe says in his opening that "I wouldn't say the novel is dead. [...] It is only the prevailing fashions among novelists that are washed up" (35).

Wolfe's protagonist in *The Electric Kool-Aid Acid Test*, Ken Kesey, chose in 1964 to set aside his burgeoning career as a highly successful young author to create an expressive, largely communal, lifestyle that led him and his Merry Pranksters to become psychedelic provocateurs. The group's theatrical antics and parties served to help catalyze the Dionysian upsurge that enveloped San Francisco in 1966. Even though Wolfe's outsider's stripes do show through sometimes, and, as a literary work, the non-fictional details and circumspections intrude on the tone and dynamic of the narrative, *The Electric Kool-Aid Acid Test* provides the single best narrative for understanding the context of the West Coast sociological dynamic that led up to and launched the counterculture. He did so by seizing a territory in writing that had been largely abdicated by novelists. In *The New Journalism*, he states:

> The Sixties was one of the most extraordinary decades in American history[...] a decade when the manner and morals, styles of living, attitudes toward the world changed the country more crucially than any political events [...] when postwar American affluence finally blew the lid off—all this novelists simply turned away from, gave up by default [30].
>
> [...] I wrote *The Electric Kool-Aid Acid Test* and then waited for the novels that I was sure would come pouring out of the psychedelic experience. [...] I learned later that the publishers had been waiting, too. [...] [A]ll they got was the Prince of Alienation ... [31].

Wolfe wrote this in 1973 when Wolfe, Norman Mailer, Hunter S. Thompson, and Joan Didion, as New Journalists, in fact did have this vast turf of counterculture, with a few exceptions, all to themselves. Even postmodern author Thomas Pynchon, who tiptoed up to the edges of the new counterculture in his 1966 novel *The Crying of Lot 49*, wrote about the Second World War in *Gravity's Rainbow* (1973), but waited until *Vineland* in 1990 before he introduced a hippie protagonist. The books selected for this literary study were published more contemporaneously with the inception and evolution of the counterculture.

In *The New Journalism,* Wolfe describes the use of detailed realism in literature in the 18th century as the equivalent of bringing electricity to the machine. He notes how novelists in the 1960s were beginning to abandon realism. This, he said, was akin to abandoning electricity. "Fiction writers currently ['73] are busy running backward, skipping and screaming, into a begonia patch that I call Neo-Fabulism" (preface). Even though excerpts from Wolfe's work are often published in collections of postmodern literature, postmodernism in literature was a later term mostly applied to Neo-Fabulism, metafiction and deconstructionist literature. Richard Brautigan's *Trout Fishing in America* and Donald Barthelme's *Snow White* were examples of "Neo-Fabulist" works. By comparison, the New Journalism was drawing unabashedly from such unfashionable literary masters as Henry James. In *The New Journalism* Wolfe says that "I switched back and forth between point-of-view continually, and often abruptly [...] Sometimes I used point-of-view in the Jamesian sense in which fiction writers understand it, entering directly into the mind of a character, experiencing the world through his central nervous system throughout a given scene" (19).

This literary approach, when combined with journalistic methods that had always proclaimed to be delivering the "truth," could now be written with a heightened sense of realism. In other words, the New Journalism benefited by adhering to the primacy of the traditional narrative techniques which, among the reading population, had never ceased to go out of vogue. Wolfe stated that the New Journalists "had to gather all the material the conventional journalist was after—and then keep going [...] to get the dialogue, the gestures, the facial expressions, the details of the environment. The idea was to give the full objective description, plus something that readers had always had to go to novels and short stories for: namely the subjective and emotional life of the characters" (21).

The fact that Wolfe succeeded as well as he did in depicting the world of Ken Kesey and the Merry Pranksters was impressive. Wolfe was not an insider, never a hippie, and politely declined to drop acid. *The Electric Kool-Aid Acid Test* depicted a large number of characters, captured the essential aspects of the pioneering edge of the hippie counterculture, and managed to tell the Pranksters' meandering story. The book demonstrated Wolfe's superb reportorial skill, attention to detail, impressive command of language, and powers for sociological observation. For all of this, he was hampered by being an outsider to the Prankster scene and by the inherent limitations of trying to subjectively convey what he called the "mental atmosphere" of these real-life characters.

In *The New Journalism,* Wolfe expounds, with his ever-trenchant focus on class, on how in the hierarchy of writers, the lowest of the low—namely the journalists—were effectively employing the key techniques of realistic fiction and "dethroning the novel as the number one literary genre" (3). When journalists began to incorporate four primary devices of the novel—creating scene following scene, using realistic dialogue, finding wider applications for point-of-view, and depicting status life through concrete detail—Wolfe called this the "first new direction in American Literature in half a century" (3), and the journalists writing this way would never guess that their "journalism would ... read like a novel [...] [and] would wipe out the novel as literature's main event" (9).

The line between what is ethically non-fiction and fiction is still debated today, as is the future of the novel. Kesey turned away from the novel when he believed it wasn't the most relevant artistic form of his era. "I'd rather be a lightning rod than a seismograph"(8), Wolfe quotes Kesey as saying in *The Electric Kool-Aid Acid Test.* Unlike Kesey, who all but stopped writing, Wolfe instead championed this new non-fictional hybrid. He wasn't alone. Truman Capote's true story of two Kansas murderers was one of the first books to employ this technique when *In Cold Blood* was published in 1966. Capote didn't call his work New Journalism. He preferred to use an oxymoron, "the nonfiction novel." Hunter S. Thompson published *Hells Angels: A Strange and Terrible Saga* that same year. Norman Mailer's *The Armies of the Night: History as a Novel, the Novel as History* was published in 1968, the same year as *The Electric Kool-Aid Acid Test.*

The narrative structure of *The Electric Kool-Aid Acid Test* was fairly straightforward. Namely, the story starts with the first person narrator, Tom Wolfe, in October 1966 while he is observing a few of the Merry Pranksters in San Francisco as the group is preparing for the Acid Test Graduation Party. The narrator introduces the reader to Ken Kesey, who is back in California after hiding out in Mexico when he skipped out on two marijuana possession charges. Kesey, the story's protagonist, arrives on the scene fresh from a few days in the San Mateo County Jail after he has just been released on bail. From here the current story backtracks into exposition. This extended backstory makes up the bulk of the narrative; we are presented with the biography of Kesey, the man the Pranksters often call "Chief" after his character in *Cuckoo's Nest.* Once the reader learns about Kesey's background at Stanford and the success of *Cuckoo's Nest,* the story becomes immersed in the Prankster world of 1964, the year of the cross-country bus trip made famous by Wolfe's book. It isn't until very late in the book that Tom Wolfe is again the current story narrator and the tertiary character observing from the wings.

The effect of this narrative strategy is to create an illusion of third person omniscience, as though Wolfe's god-like eye is observing everything that happened. Wolfe points out in *The New Journalism* that, when writing *The Electric Kool-Aid Acid Test,* he often shifted intentionally from his narrator's omniscient voice into a stream of consciousness point-of-view from the minds of his other characters. The reason for this approach was simple. Prior to late 1966, Tom Wolfe was not present with the group, so even though he is telling the "true" story of the Pranksters in *The Electric Kool-Aid Acid Test,* he needed to create his verisimilitude second-hand. For example, when he recreated Kesey's state of mind while Kesey was on the lam in Mexico, Wolfe used letters written between Kesey and his friend, author Larry McMurtry.

In other words, to write the book, Wolfe relied heavily on the good graces of Ken Kesey and the other Pranksters and those close to the Prankster scene. Interestingly, many years after the fact, Kesey was asked whether Wolfe got it right, this story of the Pranksters. Kesey said that while Wolfe got it mostly right, he was "on the bus," but not "*on* the bus." This speaks to Wolfe's East Coast conservatism and perhaps the fact that the hippie movement was, as Kesey also noted, mostly a West Coast phe-nomenon. In fact, Wolfe was neither "on the bus" or "*on* the bus" accord-ing to Paul Perry in *On The Bus: The Complete Guide to the Legendary Trip of Ken Kesey and The Merry Pranksters and the Birth of the Counterculture.* Wolfe garnered much of his source material for *The Electric Kool-Aid Acid Test* while at Kesey's farm in Oregon, again, well after the 1964 bus trip was completed. (Perry, conversation)

Wolfe and many others in the late '60s were all but serving notice that the "New Journalism" would be the novel's logical successor form. Their techniques allowed the author to interpolate, to get into the subjects' heads. They included themselves in the stories as participant/ observers. When researching his biographies, Wolfe preferred the observer role more than being a participant. According to Perry, while at Kesey's farm, Wolfe was so much the omnipresent observer that Kesey finally told him to either "pitch hay or 'bale.'" Wolfe chose to leave.

One of the challenges in writing a non-fictional account of living people is the risk of libel, of course, and the danger—through a poor intersubjective rendering—of employing characterizations that don't cap-ture the personality or motivation of the person being depicted. Also, the level of access provided to Wolfe by the subjects varied. Some shared highly intimate details of their actions, thoughts, feelings, beliefs, while others were only minimally accessible. This had direct bearing on the interior depth Wolfe was able to create for these real people as charac-ters. For example, in the Author's Note at the end of the book, Wolfe states that one of the Prankster's, "Sandy Lehmann-Haupt told me about his Prankster days in especially full and penetrating detail" (371). It's not surprising then, that the sections of *The Electric Kool-Aid Acid Test* featuring Sandy offer a well-rendered depth of character.

Sandy's severe psychological problems while trying to adapt to the cross-country trip come across with riveting, realistic clarity. He is stricken with massive bouts of paranoia exacerbated by insomnia and LSD. Ken Kesey the non-navigator, non-leader, but "Chief" and underwriter of the bus trip, becomes the object of a psychotic power struggle in Sandy's mind. The power struggle erupts in several quirky outbursts depicted in the story. The reader is well able to understand the motivation behind the behavior. To again use the expression made famous by this book, Sandy vacillates from being "on the bus" to "off the bus." Because of this tendency, Kesey dubs him "dis–MOUNT." As was common with the later hippies, the Pranksters have nicknames. The story of Sandy's inner torment builds during the trip:

> The Pranksters now realized that Sandy was in a bad way. Kesey had a saying, "Feed the hungry bee." So the Pranksters set about showering ... Attention on Sandy, to try to give him a feeling of being at the cool center of the whole thing. But he kept misinterpreting their gestures. Why are they staring? [105].

Eventually, Sandy leaves the Pranksters to return to New York for mental help.

With non-imaginary characters, Wolfe was at the behest of his interviewees to develop a sense of interiority. For example, while the reader is given an excellent sense of the power struggle fomenting in Sandy's mind toward Kesey, there is never a similar sense of Kesey's own deeper motivations, even though he is the story's protagonist. In *Sometimes a Great Notion,* Ken Kesey's own inner conflict plays out with dramatic fullness when Hank and Lee Stamper are at odds with one another. As pointed out in that chapter, the divergent personalities of each brother are representative of a similar personality pull inside Kesey.

The level of access given by the subjects to Wolfe impacts the narrative depth, but there is also the question of an author's writing ability and intent while shaping the prose. Wolfe is an outstanding writer, but in a 2004 article by Tim Adams of *The Observer,* Adams points out that:

> I once asked Ken Kesey, hero of *The Electric Kool-Aid Acid Test,* what it was like to have Tom Wolfe write you into myth. "What you have to understand," Kesey said, "is that Tom Wolfe was never really writing about me, his writing has always mostly been concerned with itself" [*Sunday Observer,* October 31, 2004].

This comment by Kesey certainly opens questions of ethics and degrees of realism in this brand of creative nonfiction that claims, as Wolfe does, to capture the "mental atmosphere or subjective reality" (371) of the Prankster's story. In *The Electric Kool-Aid Acid Test* the situation is rife with underdeveloped dramatic potential. When real characters are adversely impacted by how the story is portrayed, this dampens how any nonfiction writer can ethically proceed.

For example, in *The Electric Kool-Aid Acid Test*, we learn that Kesey, who is married to Faye and has three kids with her, also becomes the father of Mountain Girl's baby, Sunshine. Kesey makes it with Sensuous X even though she got on the bus with Zonker when the Pranksters were in New York City. And, even though Kesey is our protagonist, we are told in passing about Zonker's unhappy initial reaction. Wolfe chooses not to create this intriguing moment as a developed literary scene. When Kesey is in Mexico, there are strong allusions that he takes up with Black Maria before the others travel down to Mazatlan, but Wolfe never probes the underlying aspects of this sexual openness. Either Wolfe was afraid to ask, or Kesey was too circumspect to share with Wolfe his feelings and attitudes toward these various women who are all important characters in the protagonist's life and in the Prankster scene. Considering how Kesey's behavior contrasted with the monogamous norm in American society, such surface treatment of Prankster sexual behavior is blaring by way of omission.

In a work of fiction, by comparison, the implications of events of this significance would be integral to the dramatic enactment. Wolfe's depiction of Kesey's wife is flattering—"Faye has long, sorrel brown hair and is one of the prettiest, most beatific-looking women I ever saw. She looks radiant, saintly" (23). However, unlike the interior view we are given of Sandy, the reader never gets close enough, whether directly or indirectly, to learn much of anything about Faye—about her feelings on her husband's philandering, or on the whole Prankster scene, etc. The Prankster children are all but ignored in this book, except as window dressing to various scenes. Had this been a fictionalized account of a commune, most readers would have felt shorted in not being told the emotional impact among those in the group when the main character has his fourth child with someone other than his wife.

In his opening to *The New Journalism*, Wolfe acknowledges the challenges and limitations inherent to respecting the privacy of real people. He points out that "there are certain areas of life that journalism still cannot move into easily, particularly for reasons of invasion of privacy, and it is in this margin that the novel will be able to grow in the future" (35). This is a highly important factor differentiating non-fiction and fiction, but it is only germane for those novels employing the techniques of literary realism ascribed to by Wolfe. "The reporter starts out by presuming upon someone's privacy, asking questions he has no right to expect an answer to [...] [reduced to] behavior that comes close to being servile or even beggarly" (44). Even though Wolfe has never acknowledged this with regard to writing *The Electric Kool-Aid Acid Test*, there were clearly limits to how closely he was able or willing to get with the Keseys.

Wolfe does not overtly impose his own opinions or political viewpoints on this story, but his tone and descriptions accrete over the course of the book. The overriding impact of this portrayal of the Pranksters is one of an LSD-fueled communal experience as colorful, but crazily out of control. Rightly or wrongly, one gets the veiled sense that Wolfe would like to relegate the psychedelic movement to the lunatic fringe of American cultural experience. Wolfe, in trying to "re-create the mental atmosphere or subjective reality," was limited by his own subjectivity, his own authorial word choice and descriptiveness. Wolfe's own perspective of what he witnessed or researched and chose to describe guided his prose. He had an intellectual agenda. This is what Kesey meant by Wolfe's writing being mostly "concerned with itself." This is how the "objective truth" inevitably wavers in even the most "old school" of "who-what-when-where-why" journalism.

Wolfe's creative literary techniques bring the events of this narrative to life by infusing bursts of thought and multiple points of view into the characters. This worked best with characters like Sandy, who allowed Wolfe to understand his motivations and mental disposition during the bus trip. When the technique is applied in the way it was with Sandy, then depictions of social realism function in the manner described in *The New Journalism:* "The most gifted writers are those who manipulate the memory sets of the reader in such a rich fashion that they create within the mind of the reader an entire world that resonates with the reader's own real emotions. The events are merely taking place on the page, in print, but the emotions are real. Hence the unique feeling when one is "absorbed" in a certain book, "lost" in it" (48).

To his credit, Wolfe took precautions not to overly speculate when portraying his character's inner thoughts. He states in his Author's Note to *The Electric Kool-Aid Acid Test* that "all the events, details and dialogue I have recorded are either what I saw and heard myself or were told to me by people who were there themselves or were recorded on tapes or film or in writing" (371). Being told things by people who were there is another tenuous matter related to secondhand subjectivity, but, as an ethical concern, Wolfe took the high road. He didn't guess, for example, what Faye Kesey might or might not have been thinking. Often it was the things left out by the author that were the most disconcerting. For example, Wolfe repeatedly pointed out the hard questions related to the communal social dynamic of the Pranksters as a whole, but he held back from delving into the messier aspects of the actual interrelationships. An example of this is found in this summative excerpt from the scene in Mexico:

Black Maria was going through a private hell. Namely, she was lonely as hell.
Lonely? [...] in the Prankster hierarchy.
   Prankster hierarchy? There wasn't supposed to be any Prankster hierarchy. Even
Kesey was supposed to be the non-navigator and non-teacher. Certainly everybody else was an equal in the brotherhood, for there was no competition, there
were no games. They had all left behind the straight world ... but ... call it a
game or what you will. Right now, among the women, Mountain Girl was first,
closest to Kesey, and Faye was second, or was it really vice versa, and Black Maria
was maybe third, but actually so remote it didn't matter. Among the men, there
was Babbs, always the favorite ... and *no games* ... but sometimes it seemed like
the old *personality* game ... looks, and all the old *aggressive, outgoing* charm, even
athletic ability—it won here, like everywhere else ... [295].

This is an example of Wolfe analyzing the group dynamic by looking for
a social hierarchy that may or may not have been present. Did the author
ever ask Mountain Girl, Faye, or Black Maria which one ranked where
vis-à-vis Kesey? Did he have the temerity to ask Kesey if he felt closer to
Mountain Girl than to his wife? Were there discussions with Kesey about
his sense of himself as the de facto leader? Wolfe poses fascinating questions, posits his sense of things, but then leaves the reader with impres-
sions of the situation that appear not to have been actually explored.
      In this respect, Augustus Owsley Stanley III, the underground
chemist who helped fund the Grateful Dead in the mid–'60s, was not
kind to Wolfe in a short interview from a 2005 issue of *Mojo Magazine.*
Owsley, the foremost manufacturer of a high quality LSD that was first
distributed in California during 1965, was a minor character in *The Electric Kool-Aid Acid Test.* In *Mojo* he was asked if his "freakout" in Muir Beach
was as profound as Wolfe described:

> Why would you think that Wolfe has the tiniest idea what was going on with us? I
> never spoke to the man. Wolfe is a stunningly talented, but bitter man, who is able
> to keenly report the personalities of people he interviews, but always tears any scene
> he writes about down. I always wondered why he hated the astronauts so much that
> he wanted to trash them in *The Right Stuff.* Of course, he made everything that we
> were doing seem like crap [Mojo Special Editions, February 2005, p.9].

In *The Electric Kool-Aid Acid Test* Wolfe introduces Owsley as: "A cocky little guy, short, with dark hair, dressed like an acid head, the usual Boho
gear, but with a strange wound up nasal voice" (186). When Wolfe describes
Owsley during the Prankster's third Acid Party held in Muir Beach at the
end of 1965, Owsley bursts in on the gathering at dawn yelling "survival"
and vowing never to allow Kesey to hold such a monstrous event again,
especially with his acid. Wolfe leads the reader to believe that Owsley thinks
Kesey's acid test is maniacal. Again, this underscores the delicacy of depicting the personalities and perceptions of real people in real situations,
especially when the author is developing the story second or third hand.
This application of authorial intersubjectivity underscores how the

technique is prone to intellectual dishonesty. By putting opinions into Owsley's head, Wolfe creates an opinion of the event for which Wolfe doesn't have to take ownership. If Owsley didn't actually feel this way or react as the author depicts, then the portrayal by Wolfe opens itself to serious ethical concerns. In *The New Journalism* Wolfe demonstrates that he is well aware of this difficulty of crossing such boundaries of privacy. Again, related to Wolfe's accreting subjective characterizations of scenes through points of view that were not the author's, Owsley is warranted in suggesting that Wolfe's depictions of what he and the Pranksters were doing, were being portrayed as "crap."

This leads to the challenge Wolfe must have faced in trying to depict the experience of being high on LSD, especially when he had never dropped acid. Wolfe attempts to accomplish this through a barrage of imagistic words and CLEVER::::::::PUNCTUATION:::::::::::OR::::::::: SURREAL LISTS:::::::::OR A BARRAGE OF::::::::PHRASES: "In fact, the trip back was a psychic Cadillac, a creamy groove machine, and they soon found themselves grooving in a group mind. Now they could leave behind all the mind-blown freaky binds and just keep going Furthur! on the bus. [...][T]he group mind take off that had begun, The Unspoken Thing, the all-in-one..." (97). Wolfe, in the book, undertakes the hard work of evoking concrete details, and in the case of portraying these acidheads, he strives for the sense of whimsy. Also, in conveying his theme of communal intersubjectivity, Wolfe chooses phrases such as *group mind, on the bus* and *all-in-one*ness.

In *The Electric Kool-Aid Acid Test,* Wolfe describes the Hell's Angels on LSD as strangely peaceful; he compares the experience on LSD as a long, serene trip whereas the hallucinogen, DMT, was like a rush of fragmented imagery and like "being shot out of a cannon." Yet, when the author chooses to evoke the ambiance of the Prankster scene, the words are like having buckshot fired onto the page from a cannon. Wolfe's many sections of disjointed imagery and wild punctuation do a better job of emulating what he describes as the effects of DMT than his own description of the effects of LSD.

Interestingly, the most serene emulation of the hallucinatory experience on LSD comes in the chapter called "The Electric Kool-Aid Acid Test." Here Wolfe inserted, virtually wholesale, the description that Clair Brush, from the Los Angeles *Free Press,* wrote for him of her inadvertent self-dosing at the Watts Acid Test in early 1966:

> I stood under the [black] light and drops of paint fell on my foot and sandal, and it was exquisite. I returned to this light frequently ... it was peaceful and beautiful beyond description. My skin had a depth and texture under the light ... a velvety purple. I remember wishing it could be that color always. (I still do) [246].

Interestingly, not only was the book named for Brush's experience in drinking the Kool-Aid, the quote that fills the back of the paperback edition is directly from this section. Wolfe didn't write it.

According to Adams in his *Sunday Observer* article, "Wolfe's real subject has always been class, that great taboo of egalitarian America, what he once called its statuspheres." This is apparent in *The Electric Kool-Aid Acid Test:*

> Most [hippies] were from middle-class backgrounds, not upper bourgeois, but more petit bourgeois, [120]

Or,

> They will broadcast on all frequencies, waving American flags, turning up the Day-Glo and the neon of 1960s electro pastel America, wired up and amplified, 327,000 horsepower, a fantasy bus in a science-fiction movie, welcoming all on board, no matter how unbelievably Truck Stop Low Rent or raunchy—[148].

When panning back from the trippy verbal barrages and into a sociological perspective, Wolfe is at his most intriguing. Yet, this is also where his highbrow tone is most discernable.

At its essence, this phenomenon he observed was an exploration of frontier. Wolfe's Ivy League education, gentried upbringing in Virginia, and observational distancing, did not make it easy for him to fully grasp the embodiment of a last gasp, Westward expansion into the frontier of the mind. The hippie phenomenon was mostly white, largely egalitarian, although sometimes susceptible to a hipper-than-thou form of censuring among its purely voluntary ranks. Of all regions in the United States, the West of the 1960s was the least elitist. On brains alone, more than connections or the prep school attended, kids in the western states could gain admission to the best colleges and universities in the region. The West was the most egalitarian area because its settlement was founded on the principle of a new start, a new beginning. This inclination, in part, explains the willingness of these experimental young people to forge new alliances, expand all manner of boundaries, and try to live wildly and fully in the face of nuclear annihilation or to defy the constraints of "the establishment." It was also, as exemplified by the Merry Pranksters, a newly formed lifestyle featuring play as power.

The rationale for calling this work "literary sociology," stems from the way Wolfe reports on events and often selects what to show in order to substantiate certain cultural hypotheses he has formulated. Wolfe has several such hypotheses coursing through *The Electric Kool-Aid Acid Test.* Above all, as sociology, *The Electric Kool-Aid Acid Test* is the story of how this lifestyle of disaffection and mind-expansion reached its critical mass. The Pranksters were one group of likeminded souls, experimenting with a communal lifestyle and taking a powerful hallucinogenic drug a few years before many people considered living in communes or knew about this drug. In *Acid Dreams: The Complete Social History of LSD: The CIA, The Sixties, and Beyond,* authors Lee and Shain discuss Kesey and the Prankster's attitude toward this new and powerful substance they had discovered:

> Kesey the psychedelic populist was attempting to broaden the very nature of the tripping experience by incorporating as many different scenes and viewpoints as possible. "When you've got something like we've got," he explained, "you can't just sit on it and possess it, you've got to move off of it and give it to other people. It only works if you bring other people into it" [125].

By 1966, the drug was on the street and discovered by enough people that a whole new phenomenon was born. It should be noted that marijuana was far more prevalent in the counterculture than LSD, but the difference in the drugs was like comparing a motor scooter to a racecar. In *Acid Dreams* it states that "[a]lthough acid and grass are both aesthetic enhancers, the strength of LSD put it in a whole other category. [...] Whereas pot is mild enough to be playful, acid is an intense and unremitting dose of bacchanalia. [...] The sheer duration of an LSD trip—eight to twelve hours and sometimes longer—requires a much greater commitment than smoking a "jay" (130).

The *Electric Kool-Aid Acid Test* may actually over embellish the impact of the Merry Pranksters in catalyzing this phenomenon. For example, the Merry Prankster's acid tests were by no means the only conduit, or even a major distribution point for LSD. The acid tests contributed, but Owsley and the other producers had begun wholesale street distribution while the drug was still legal in 1965. Millions of hits of this potent hallucinogen being sold on the streets had an incalculable impact on the disposition of the new youth culture. The easily transportable, miniscule hits of LSD certainly found receptive users in London and bohemian pockets in major cities across the Western world. Two or three bucks bought a multi-hour ticket to ride for the adventurous and this new drug was the psychoactive catalyst of the new psychedelia. In comparison to the covert underground hierarchy of drug dealing, the Merry Prankster's acid tests were quietly promoted to the hip. These parties, though very quickly promoted via underground channels, were also uncommonly public. This made the activity easier to write about, although widespread use of LSD and the era it ushered in, would have almost certainly occurred without the Pranksters. On the other hand, had the U.S. Government not opened this Pandora's Box with its widespread testing of this and similar drugs on civilian guinea pigs, then it's hard to imaging this psychedelic era coalescing with such fervor.

One of Wolfe's most intriguing sociological hypotheses is that Kesey and the Pranksters presented the prototype of a religious group in the making. The author points to the charisma of the leader, Kesey, and the core experience of all-in-oneness evoked when the group gathered and took acid. Wolfe also points to how this inner circle decided to spread its "gospel" by disseminating LSD through the public Acid Tests that Kesey chose to begin in 1965 after the bus trip was over. Prior to this, the group's use of acid was limited to private parties that started on Perry Lane in Palo Alto. When those bohemian cabins were torn down, the bohemian lifestyle and private parties resumed in La Honda where Kesey had bought some land in a redwood canyon with an austere home.

Wolfe differentiates between the ethical prophets, such as Jesus and Moses, and the exemplary prophets, such as Buddha. He describes the Prankster's "Unspoken Thing." There is the here-and-now experience of the holy with LSD as the group's vessel for the divine. "Kairos" is the supreme moment, something Wolfe intimates that the Pranksters have shared. Or maybe the author is being sarcastic. There is often the hint of flippancy in the run-on descriptiveness of Wolfe's prose. Ostensibly, the group tripping brings out the Prankster's intersubjectivity and oneness at its utmost. The author views this as the core experience. All the great religions began with such a core experience. Kesey, according to Wolfe, is the chief exemplary, and LSD is the Prankster's proselytizing agent.

There is strong indication that Kesey was the de facto leader of the Pranksters. He has said he wanted to share the enlightenment and consciousness expansion that he and his group were experiencing on acid. However, the hypothesis about the group emulating the origin of a new religious movement may be an instance where Wolfe tried to pigeonhole his protagonist a bit too conveniently. There is no indication from interviews, his books, or otherwise to indicate that Kesey was looking to be a religious leader of any sort. The Pranksters were selective about which individuals were allowed close to the inner circle of the group. They weren't looking to grow as a group, rather the group came into being out of living on Perry Lane, discovering these hallucinogenic drugs, and enjoying one another's company. New Pranksters stayed because, in various ways, they fit into the group dynamic. The communal arrangement was not planned. It evolved.

In *The Electric Kool-Aid Acid Test* Wolfe makes a major point of describing how Kesey and the Pranksters had moved beyond words, beyond the symbol and into the experience. Ironically, of course, Wolfe spends an entire book describing, with words, how the Pranksters had moved beyond words. In *The Road of Excess: A History of Writers on Drugs,* Marcus Boon has a chapter on "Psychedelics and Literature." In it he describes Aldus Huxley's work, *The Doors of Perception,* as one that proposes "an experiential model of the imagination and the imaginal realms that run counter to the symbolic, representational structures that had governed Western thought for centuries" (251). Boon goes on to say that "this shift was to have profound implications for art, politics, and religion that would begin to be realized in the 1960s. [...] [T]he new value and interest accorded to the psychedelics had everything to do with this broad shift away from an aesthetic of the symbol and toward one of experience" (251). Ken Kesey, by abandoning his literary writing, and the Merry Pranksters, by pushing the boundaries of collective experience and expression, were living this shift.

Later in Kesey's life he returned again to writing fiction. This idea of the experience taking primacy over the symbolic was a phenomenon that came full circle for Kesey. Stephen Tanner in his book, *Ken Kesey*, states that "if anything is demonstrated by Kesey's attempt to be a lightning rod, it is the primacy of the word. In the beginning was the word: and so at the end. Kesey tried to get beyond it, but the possibility proved illusory, and the attempt was in a way a betrayal of his highest talents"(102).

Kesey's creative focus had shifted from writing to making the great Prankster movie. He took the earnings from his first two novels and invested a significant sum at the time—about $70,000—on film and audio equipment to portray the Prankster experience. The hundreds of hours of amateurish footage was a mess, a well-documented failure, (but for the narrative Wolfe was writing, valuable source material). The goal for "The Movie" was to turn the world onto the group's high discoveries of enlightenment. Again, there is no sense that he ever wanted to become the center of a religious movement. When Kesey says that "we're not on a Christ Trip" (172), there is no reason to disbelieve him. What Wolfe was looking to describe in the Merry Pranksters with "Chief" Kesey at the pulpit, was the observation of a social dynamic that arises in many communal groups. A communal synergy and religious sense of shared ecstasy is common in communes with a spiritual centering. Many communes that were overtly religious with exactly the dynamic Wolfe describes, of course, did spring up during the counterculture. It would be interesting to learn when Wolfe first formulated this hypothesis—before, during the time, or after he was with the Pranksters.

Near the end of *The Electric Kool-Aid Acid Test* Wolfe speculates on what was then just burgeoning. He suggests that the psychedelic movement will head either one of two directions: "there's no earthly stopping this thing. [...] Right now there are two ways this thing can go in Haight-Ashbury. One is the Buddhist direction, the [Timothy] Leary thing. [...] a vessel of the *All* ... the *All-one* ...

"... as against the Kesey direction, which has become the prevailing lifestyle of Haight-Ashbury ... *beyond catastrophe* ... like picking up on everything that works and moves and [...] winding it up to some mystical extreme carrying to the westernmost edge of experience" (322, 323).

Again, Wolfe as sociologist very nearly hits the mark, except that he has created a false binary of East and West. Leary, the first tenured Harvard professor ever fired, is a Westerner out of same educational mold that produced Wolfe—elitist and East Coast American, but Western in the refined European sense of class and gentrified sensibility. LSD catapulted Leary into boldly proclaiming his discoveries with the drug, encouraging the world to turn on, and embracing in his new lifestyle the meditative elements of the Eastern Religious traditions. His life at Millbrook in upstate New York exhibited a more serene and meditative lifestyle without the playful wildness of lifestyle exhibited by the Pranksters.

Kesey was a true product of the West Coast, more specifically the Pacific Northwest, where the idea and cultural sense of wilderness and a self-reliant pioneering still existed in the '50s, '60s and '70s, despite the considerable encroachments of modernization. Kesey's reaction to LSD was to test the frontiers of personal freedom, of life, liberty and the pursuit of happiness. Arguably, America had never witnessed such a large-scale expression of personal freedom as that exhibited at the height of the counterculture. Kesey's sense of wilderness had moved beyond the institutionalized constraints of *Cuckoo's Nest* or the small logging town limitations in *Great Notion* toward a wildness of the mind seemingly free of mainstream edicts. LSD contributed toward a lifestyle where all existing propriety was called into question, where everything was examined anew. The imagination of possibilities prevailed, and the Wild West had never been wilder for those caught up in the realm of psychedelia. The West especially, seemed to have room to accommodate this lifestyle with its attendant notions of frontier expression. Leary's world was more intellectualized and subdued. Kesey's world was more robustly experimental on this "westernmost edge of experience," but no less smart. Wolfe, in his Author's Note, recognizes how fortunate he was "to get the help of many unusually talented and articulate people, most notably, Ken Kesey, himself" (371). Kesey, too, borrowed from Eastern Religion where it fit the collective Prankster "synch." Wolfe talks of the Prankster fascination of throwing the I-Ching coins and understanding this as part of the group's fascination with the *Now*. The Zen koan leading to a jolt of enlightenment was not unlike the merry prank. So, while Leary and Kesey differed in tone and approach, these were not the two directions of counterculture. Both responded to LSD in a Dionysian manner that radically changed their prior lives, and both were essentially apolitical people.

If a binary is to be constructed for the counterculture, then the apolitical and more Dionysian element could be differentiated from the politicized front of radicalism surrounding much of the growing anti-war effort. Yet, even this is not a clean delineation because political radicals began gravitating toward the Dionysian upsurge. By 1967, many politicos turned on to the same grass and LSD as the apolitical heads. With all this coalescing of disaffected energy, there was a palpable sense of major change in the air. For a period of time in 1967–68, the growing disaffection toward the Vietnam War created a common ground built on an amalgam of many movements. In the surge of disaffection, Black American discontent also found a limited measure of common ground with the white activists and hippies. Wolfe's perspective is noteworthy for how it captured the sociological sentiment of the more apolitical Dionysian upsurge. He recognized that the political radicalism of the era was only loosely aligned with those spearheading psychedelia. Leary, even more than Kesey, wanted nothing to do with the politicized left. Kesey opposed the Vietnam war, but mocked pacifist tactics for stopping it. The overlap of the political and apolitical elements of the counter-culture became more pronounced after 1967, when Wolfe was done writing *The Electric Kool-Aid Acid Test*.

While the varying depth of characterization in this book has already been called into question, Wolfe does present several interesting communal perspectives, especially in how the communal experiment so closely relates to the central elixir of the book. Even though Wolfe does not drop acid, he does approach the drug in an open and curious fashion. He gives a brief history of LSD. He tries his best to describe it. When he imagines this acid high, he creates a stylistic motif—the barrage of whimsical phrases, odd punctuation, and lists—and repeats the motif to create a tone throughout the book. Yet, even though the hip onslaught of words often gets in his way, there are moments in *The Electric Kool-Aid Acid Test* where Wolfe captures the transcendent potency of the drug. For example, Wolfe draws a parallel between the Pranksters and the communal church at the end of Heinlein's *Stranger in a Strange Land*. Heinlein's book is on Kesey's bookshelf at La Honda in 1965. In *The Electric Kool-Aid Acid Test* he links the group dynamic of the Pranksters with Valentine Michael Smith's new church and suggests that both share an acausal bond, the nest, the mystic brotherhood, the ability to transcend the materialistic, the Bacchanalia, the swapping, the communal spirit, the "thou-art-god" oneness.

Wolfe ascribed to the Pranksters the feeling of harmonics, synchronicity, and go with the flow brought on by the shared experience of LSD. He goes on to talk about the experience of the Other World, a higher level of reality that was being shared. The group had moved beyond a sense of cause and effect and into the supreme moment. And

it wasn't about words, it was about an indescribable experience where
the objective and subjective, the ego and non-ego, the I and the not-I
disappear. The more the Pranksters lived with one another and took
acid together, the more intuitive they became with one another, the more
their interactions transcended words into the intersubjective, the vibra-
tions of the higher realm. Even though it's never possible to be certain
in Wolfe's writing, due to his frequent "cool" affectations when attempting to capture the "mental atmosphere" and "subjective reality" of the
Prankster scene, there is no reason to believe that the author was being
facetious in his assessment of the communal oneness induced by LSD.

Clair Brush, whose description of her acid trip is used by Wolfe,
describes how she felt toward a man who guided her through the experience: "our bones merged, our skin was one skin, there was no place
where we could separate, where he stopped and I began. [...] I later read
about 'imprint' and that it was possible that we would continue to be
meaningful to each other no matter what the circumstances" (245–246).
Not only did Ken Kesey move with his wife and kids to the Eugene, Oregon area after his release from jail, but also several of the other
Pranksters took up residence near him. The network of friends, though
not living in one communal setting, remained strong for the rest of
Kesey's life. The Grateful Dead played at several of the acid tests, and
Kesey and the Pranksters continued to attend Dead concerts well after
the '60s. Mountain Girl and Jerry Garcia, the Dead's lead guitarist, were
together for several years after Kesey's place in La Honda was sold. Kesey
went to Egypt in the late '70s when The Dead played at the Great Pyra-
mids. Hugh Romney, better known as Wavy Gravy who announced breakfast in bed for four hundred thousand at Woodstock, came up with the
idea to spike Kool-Aid with LSD at the acid test in Watts, even though
some of the Pranksters questioned the ethics of making the drug available in a manner where some people might not know what they were
taking. Brush was one of those people. Wavy Gravy's commune was called
the Hog Farm and Black Maria went to live there when Kesey left California.

The communal experiment of the counterculture, of which the Merry
Pranksters were at the front edge, was widely considered to be a failure
because most communes broke up after a relatively short period of time.
It's doubtful that Kesey and the Pranksters, who were so into experiencing the moment, were thinking in terms of communal longevity as a measure of success or failure. The fact that most of these people remained
close friends for several decades is a testament to the heightened cama-
raderie they experienced together. They certainly "imprinted" with one
another. Group living of this sort, in a society that overwhelmingly favors
single-family privatization, works against a sustained communalism. Along

with this external pressure, there is also tension within the group when people raised in an individualistic society try living in larger groups on a day-to-day basis. Self-centeredness will inevitably work against a sustained cohesion. However, this level of interconnectedness seen over a period of decades among the Pranksters, though evolving away from a tight communalism, remained significantly stronger than what is typically sustained by the vast majority of Americans living standard, privatized lifestyles.

In *The Electric Kool-Aid Acid Test* Wolfe is fascinated by the tribal dynamic and, in line with his focus on class, he looked for natural tendencies in this group to establish hierarchy. He makes numerous references to Ken Kesey as the "non-navigator," "non-teacher" and unofficial leader of the Pranksters. Wolfe pounds this fact home when Kesey escapes to Mexico and Ken Babbs is unable to hold the group dynamic together. In *A Long Strange Trip: The Inside History of the Grateful Dead*, Dennis McNally states that:

> The media, for instance Tom Wolfe, whose *The Electric Acid Kool-Aid Test* was superior journalism but still the product of an outsider, would imagine that the scene centered on Ken Kesey. The Dead knew better. Disguised as a loony, mad-rapping speed freak, Neal Cassady was very possibly the most highly evolved personality they would ever meet, and was certainly among their most profound life influences other than the psychedelic experience itself. "He seemed to live in another dimension," [band member] Weir said, "and in that dimension time as we know it was transparent" [107–108].

However, not only would Cassady come and go as a Prankster, there is too much evidence outside of *The Electric Kool-Aid Acid Test* to consider him the leader of the Pranksters. Cassady came to the Pranksters as a Beat character of mythic proportions—as the real life model for Dean Moriarty in Jack Kerouac's *On the Road*—but this doesn't imply group leadership qualities. He and Kesey, both large robust men, took to one another immediately. Also, even though Cassady may have been a verbal virtuoso with amazing things to say, he was also a speed freak who talked incessantly. It was no disguise that he could go for days rambling on without sleep.

While this passage certainly attests that Cassady was a significant influence on the members of The Dead, among the Pranksters there was no evidence that Cassady tried to take charge, except with the driving. As a driver he had uncanny instincts, Weir continued: "Neal had his own art, his own medium, and it involved the way he moved through space" (108). Though Wolfe looked keenly for signs of assertion, leadership was seldom contentious for the Pranksters when Kesey was present, and, irrespective of where he fit on Wolfe's perceived sense of hierarchy, Cassady did fit in well with the group. The Pranksters didn't need an overt chain of command in order to function.

Wolfe was not off-base in diagnosing the dynamic of the Pranksters in the way he did. Virtually all human groups manifest into hierarchies of leadership and assumption of roles. Cassady, as mentioned, assumed the role of driver and drove Furthur most of the way across America. Kesey, by all accounts, led subtly; he had the natural interpersonal skills to keep the many Pranksters *on* the bus with him and involved in the group's many escapades. This was an organic hierarchy. Whether Mountain Girl or Faye was closer to Kesey was a question of Wolfe's but not something that he observed as a point of group contention. However, in retrospect, Faye, who didn't go on the cross-country bus trip, never left her husband and he never divorced her. Mountain Girl moved on with her daughter, Sunshine Kesey, to be with the Grateful Dead "family." Hierarchy in a communal dynamic is a fluid phenomenon and a rich area of study for understanding human behavior. It explains, in part, why the American public, not accustomed to communal living, was so fascinated with Wolf's account of the Merry Pranksters.

The Prankster's loose communalism, with the fluid flow of people coming in and out of the group, worked surprisingly well from the days at Perry Lane until Kesey's legal hassles prompted the sale of La Honda in 1967. The wild expressiveness had a carnival flavor as did the bus trip, though the Pranksters were not in the game of selling a carnie act. For all this wildness that was so far outside the norms of American society in the '60s, Kesey has been dubbed an American primitive.

At a surface level, living tribally, partying wildly, and expressing themselves with such reckless abandon, the Merry Pranksters were indeed primitives. They were thumbing their noses at "the system," at "the establishment," at "the machine." However, such rejection of the mainstream's materialistic rewards, was advanced, if advanced is measured by the edicts of the major religions which also encourage similar rejection of worldly things and concerns. The degree to which LSD contributed to this posture is speculative, but it was undeniably influential. The LSD-less Beats had a much less colorful tone. Suddenly, in a rush linked to this psychedelia, a distinct, kaleidoscopically day-glo fashion sense of paisley and swirls, black-light and fanciful lettering on clothing and in art appeared seemingly everywhere. There was also a heightened sense of spiritualism induced by LSD that multitudes of its users claimed helped reveal the potential of a new consciousness. It's not unreasonable to conclude that the drug itself contributed in a significant way to an array of behavioral responses. Certainly, Kesey and the Merry Pranksters were among the first to try to live out their responses to this drug that elicited more primal sensory exploration.

If material comfort is the sole standard separating the advanced from the primitive, then Kesey was indeed a primitive. If Kesey and the

Pranksters were advanced, however, they were striving for something higher than simply the modern trappings of comfort that society provided. Neither was Kesey adverse to technology, which was also not a primitive impulse. He and the Pranksters, like the hippies that followed, were simply selective as to which technology they would embrace. Kesey gave up the seemingly more primitive task of using word symbols to express himself. He invested a sizable sum in 1964 to create "The Movie" as a more immediate medium for expressing the new experience he and the Pranksters were creating. His intent was bold, but a man who was well mentored in the crafting of literature was not similarly trained in the techniques of filmmaking. None of the Pranksters were adept at filmmaking either. As mentioned, the result was amateurish and technically inept. Yet being in "The Movie" became a metaphor for the Pranksters and those who entered the Prankster world. Each individual was deemed to have his or her own movie, according to Wolfe. Kesey's personal movie was that of Randle McMurphy out on Edge City, goading and urging everyone to get into the present more, to "give themselves a little bigger movie" (132).

From a postmodernist perspective, the application of "The Movie" as an analogy for living life at its fullest is fascinating. Reality through "The Movie" becomes a simulacrum, a shadowy imitation of the actual thing, even though the Pranksters were fully immersed into living their movie. Perhaps this approach to living is related to how *Cuckoo's Nest* and *Great Notion* launched Kesey into the realm of a literary celebrity. With the Pranksters, the celebrity and attention were being reinvented into an experience that he thought would be better depicted through the immediacy of celluloid expression. The absurdity of living ones real life as though it were cinema at the edge of experience did not go unnoticed. Paul Perry in *On the Bus* suggests that The Beatle's *The Magical Mystery Tour* album and movie were inspired by the Prankster's bus trip across America. The Beatle's life in the fishbowl of global celebrity, not surprisingly, resulted in this expression of simulacrum where the band members starred as themselves in their own movie. The question becomes what is real and what is the imitation of what is real. LSD, in this regard, doesn't help matters.

A magical mystery tour is itself an expression of the type of spiritual inquiry brought on by LSD. Prior to 1966, the Beatles never exhibited the bright colors and flamboyance seen in the *Sergeant Pepper's Lonely Heart Club Band* album or with *The Magical Mystery Tour*. When John Lennon sang "I'd love to turn you on," and Paul McCartney was up fixing a hole to stop his mind from wandering, they were intimating what the Merry Pranksters were boldly sharing. The drug contributed significantly in changing the Beatles from I-wanna-hold-your-hand pop stars into serious artists who tested the limits of their own spiritual and artistic expressiveness. Their group was by no means alone in this. The song "25 or 6 to 4" by the group Chicago is a direct reference to LSD-25 and the sensations induced by the drug. Such oblique "underground" messages in the musical lyrics of the time were ubiquitous.

As humans—members of a species where every one of its cultures show the inclination to probe for higher truth and seek to explain the mysteries of what is not directly observable—it isn't hard to appreciate why these first proponents of LSD in the '60s felt that they were on the cusp of a consciousness changing revolution. The Prankster acid tests were not sinister attempts to overthrow anything except for a straightlaced staleness. The Beatles' song "Revolution" mocked Mao's little red book in a back-handed way to extol the revolution of consciousness expansion.

Valid arguments are made that some people respond very poorly to the effects of LSD. Unstable people jumping out of windows were well publicized, as was the misinformation that LSD would cause chromoso-mal damage in users. In *Acid Dreams,* which attempts to look at the soci-ological phenomenon of LSD use in the '60s in an objective light, the authors ask:

> How many people actually had bummers on LSD? More than many an acid buff would probably care to admit. In his paper "Social and Political Sources of Drug Effects: The Case of Bad Trips on Psychedelics," Richard Bunce, a research soci-ologist at the school of Public Health in Berkeley, California, cited statistics based on a survey he conducted in which nearly 50% of those questioned reported having a bad acid trip during the 1960s [155–156].

Likewise, it would be hard to imagine a functioning society if everyone came to work high on acid. Yet, it is equally valid to ask why this power-ful drug created so many positive responses such as the tendency of users to explore the essence of their own spiritual existence, to feel a greater connectedness to the cosmos, to want to interact more harmoniously with other people, to embrace a more colorful expressiveness in their own lives. Still, it was, irrefutably, a chemically induced sense of enlight-enment, which, depending on one's perspective, may or may not inval-idate such responses.

However, if the quest for truth is not to be spiritual, but simply intel-lectual, then isn't Marcus Boon correct in his "belief in the positive value of some of the psychedelics, for what they can teach us about the human mind" (15)? Yet, the same government that opened a Pandora's Box through its experimentations with LSD, chose to systematically criminal-ize and censure this drug starting in late 1966. Consequently, its "posi-tive value" likely will never be explored in full measure. Kesey referred to this Pandora's Box as the *Demon Box,* which he used in the title of the book he published in 1986.

The Electric Kool-Aid Acid Test shows how a critical mass of Prankster-like intrepid travelers called hippies came to explore this potent hallucinogen. Rarely have the cumulative consequences—positive and negative—of this widespread use of LSD in American society during the height of the counterculture been studied in a forthright manner. *Acid Dreams* is a notable exception. The authors assert that U.S. Government testing of the drug was still underway on foreign campuses as recently as 1991 suggesting that covert interest in the drug still persists in certain official circles. The impact of psychedelia on the shared cultural norms of American society and the shift of shared values and social expectations were dramatic. Wolfe's book lends important insight into the origins of this shift.

The end of this Prankster story in 1966 was described at the beginning of Wolfe's narrative: "[t]he cops now know the whole scene, even the costumes, the jesuschrist strung-out hair, Indian beads, Indian headbands, donkey beads, temple bells, amulets, mandalas, god's eyes, fluorescent vests" (2). This is an example of Wolfe at his descriptive best with:::::::SURREAL LISTS:::::::to detail the status life of his subjects. In this case, a particular status of "the rebellious youth" is created through a detailing of whimsical expressiveness being flaunted in the face of the authorities and to the world.

So even though *The Electric Kool-Aid Acid Test* suffered certain distortions due to Wolfe being an outsider and in the manner in which the prose held back from describing real-life interpersonal dynamics of a sensitive nature, Wolfe succeeds with a realistic rendering of an important story in America's cultural development. He is correct in noting that there are no prominent novels depicting this same era that came out just as the counterculture began to flourish.

It's also understandable that he holds to the conviction in *The New Journalism* that "[n]ovelists have made a disastrous miscalculation over the past twenty years about the nature of realism"(34). This, again, is the same realism from which Wolfe and others created the non-fictional writing style called "New Journalism."

Somewhere during the 1967–68 writing and publication of *The Electric Kool-Aid Acid Test* and Norman Mailer's *The Armies of the Night*, the United States of America—for lack of a better metaphor—had a massive orgasm of a cultural nature. The hippie narratives discussed thus far in this book have led up to this moment, and, in light of the ethereal nature of the event, it's not a simple matter to pinpoint the exact time of the emotional, spiritual, and physical eruption. The unrest was not limited to the United States. The socialist upheaval seen in the political New Left movement in America also erupted in an even more violent fashion in parts of Europe. Literary theory and criticism would be changed inalterably as a

result of this upheaval. Terry Eagleton in *Literary Theory: An Introduction*
states that:

> In 1968 the student movement had swept across Europe, striking against the
> authoritarianism of the educational institutions in France briefly threatening the
> capitalistic state itself. For a dramatic moment that state teetered on the brink of
> ruin. Unable to provide a coherent political leadership, plunged into a confused
> melée of socialism, anarchism and infantile behind baring, the student move-
> ment was rolled back and dissipated. [...]
>   Post-structuralism was a product of that blend of euphoria and disillusion-
> ment, liberation and dissipation, carnival and catastrophe, which was 1968.
> Unable to break the structures of state power, post-structuralism found it possi-
> ble instead to subvert the structures of language. [...]
>   The work of Derrida and others cast grave doubts upon the classical notions
> of truth, reality, meaning and knowledge, all of which could be exposed as rest-
> ing on a naively representational theory of language [141–3].

This leads neatly into the next chapter on *The Armies of the Night*, Norman Mailer's account of a massive anti-war protest that is written in the
New Journalistic mode of writing. The work, like *The Electric Kool-Aid Acid
Test*, employed literary techniques based on this "naively representational
theory of language." In *The New Journalism* Wolfe asserts that realism is
not just another device; the effects of such techniques on the emotions
of the reader is profound and thereby "real."

Whereas poststructuralism is a method of literary critique which deconstructs text down to the sign or signifier as the smallest linguistic unit, the
term is closely aligned in literature with postmodernism, an elusive
classification which relates, mostly, to the non-traditional narrative forms
that began to be published in the '60s. While *Cuckoo's Nest* and *Great Notion*
are examples of Late Modernism (and *Naked Lunch* and *Trout Fishing in
America* of postmodernism), when Ken Kesey gave up writing to live and
express a more directly experiential life, one could argue, in a generalized
sense, that he stepped into the postmodern. What the Merry Pranksters
had was "The Unspoken Thing. [...] If you label this, then it can't be" (112),
Kesey told the group repeatedly. The reader will note that in *The Electric
Kool-Aid Acid Test*, the term "hippie" as a textual sign and phrase of psychedelia was conspicuously absent through virtually all of Wolfe's book. The
reason is simple. Prior to 1966, the word was seldom used.

When Wolfe is present in the story in late 1966, he refers to Haight-
Ashbury as the "Home of the Hippies" (9). Then on page 335 in one of
his stanzas of prose poetry, Wolfe writes about "Ten thousand heads,
freaks, beats, hippy-dippies, teeny-boppers descending from the crest of
Haight Street." In the 326 or so pages in between, there is no use of the
term "hippie." Even though Wolfe implicates LSD use as the primary element differentiating the Beats from the hippies, he initially characterizes
Kesey as a glorified beatnik. Most of the time the Merry Pranksters are

portrayed as exactly that—eccentric pranksters, but sometimes the terms "head" or "freak" were used to describe the members. Neil Cassady had traversed the bridge from being a Beat icon to participating in whatever this thing was that Kesey and the Pranksters were doing. But Kesey was adamant not to label what they were doing.

In this sense, Kesey and the Pranksters may have been among the first to live in a truly postmodern niche where modernism with its rationality and absolute Truths, were supplanted by more illusory and provisional "truths." Brenda Marshall, in her attempt to define postmodernism in the literary sense in *Teaching the Postmodern*, states:

> One of the results of seeing the postmodern moment as an awareness of being-within a way of thinking is the recognition that such an awareness disallows the speaker (the subject) the comfort of absolutely naming the terms of that moment. Naming must occur from a position "outside" of a moment, and it is always an attempt to control. Crucial to an understanding of the postmodern moment is the recognition that there is no "outside" from which to "objectively" name the present. The postmodern moment is an awareness of being-within, first, a language, and second, a particular historical, social, cultural framework. [...] There can be no such thing as objectivity: all of our definitions and understanding of all that has come before us must pass through our historical, social, cultural being, as well as through our language—all of which precede us and constitute us, even as we insist on our own control [Foucault, 1970] [3].

The subjective framework being placed on the adherents of this growing bohemian subculture, came with the widespread media exposure of its San Francisco scene in late 1966 and '67. "Hippie" was the "outsider" term that stuck. From this time on, those in the psychedelic realm of the new counterculture, were constrained by a mostly pejorative label.

Hippie wasn't a label that applied to the Merry Pranksters during the time when Wolfe is depicting the group's story. Even though Wolfe does his "outsider" best to define, describe, and detail the world of the Merry Pranksters, he never labels them with one delimiting moniker of status. They were proto-hippies before the term hippie came into vogue. All across America in 1964, from California to Georgia to New York City and then back, the Merry Pranksters bamboozled the several cops who deigned to pull the bus over. The Pranksters simply kept filming and recording, while Cassady tripped the cop's mind with incessant chatter, eventually overwhelming the officer from wanting anything to do with being in "The Movie" with it's rush of carnie madness. The Pranksters were brightly clad eccentrics, theatrical carnie types, rolling through the countryside without a label.

But with the great flourishing orgasm of this psychedelic phenomenon in 1967 and '68, came the inevitable "outsider's" label. Sure, head and freak were well in use, but these monikers paled in comparison with the pervasive, pervading word that stuck. When the media descended like an invading army on Haight-Ashbury, it needed a label, the realism on which to ascribe all this surrealism. Of course, many in the midst of the phenomenon rejected the name. Perhaps, Kesey was correct. What they had couldn't be, if it was labeled. With the great flourish of 1967, with the sudden label, and with intensity and ecstatic craziness, the name itself heralded the beginning of a great dissipation. Psychedelia dispersed into the countryside, into the smaller towns and byways. Yet, with this dissipation, the mainstream powers-that-be also started into play a campaign to help contain all the freewheeling cacophony of high times and wildness. With the label, all the cops knew exactly what they were pulling over in those rigs converted from VW transporters, milk trucks, or old International Harvester school buses. In the intersubjective sense, the mainstream culture now had a name by which those in the youthful upsurge could be delimited, identified and, gradually, controlled.

Even though the cultural orgasm was huge and the dissipation slow, the phenomenon spread, not in intensity, but in volume, as the ranks started to swell away from a few urban centers. American youth everywhere began to yearn for a taste of the bacchanalian upsurge. Prior to 1966, a tiny psychedelic subculture floated under the mainstream radar screen. With the name "hippie" in late '66, the phenomenon was suddenly blinking brightly. Over time, Dionysus would be corralled, as this god usually is. He is never completely denied, but systematically, the Apollonian instincts push this urge to the shadows and subdue the bacchanalia.

By portraying the antics of the Merry Pranksters, Tom Wolfe was the first key outsider to fully textualize the phenomenon. His subjectiveness was more pronounced than even he appreciated, but it filled a yearned-for void in the reading public of mainstream America that was at once fascinated, shocked, and repulsed by what it read in this book. To his credit, Wolfe wasn't didactic and didn't argue against the Pranksters with opinionated edicts of absolute Truths, but neither was the portrait he painted with words in any way an endorsement of psychedelics or this new psychedelia. The author came as close as any outsider ever did to detailing the underground escapades leading up to this cultural climax. But from that point forward, everything in psychedelia was "hippie-dippy." The systematic lampooning and derision from mainstream America could begin in full force, but not before many, many more youth sampled from the "demon box."

In the next chapter, Norman Mailer looks at the period's unrest through the window of one event, an anti–Vietnam War protest in Washington D.C. in 1967. Ironically, with the traditional literary techniques of social realism, Wolfe and Mailer, in these two works, herald the postmodern era as a period concept. The upsurge was still climaxing in *The Armies of the Night*.

9

The Armies of the Night (1968)
Meta-Journalism, Insta-History

> In the fall of 1967 American society seemed to be coming unglued.
> Across the nation a massive "peace" movement was mounting against
> United States involvement in the Southeast Asia war. Antiwar protest-
> ers were burning their draft-cards, picketing draft-induction centers,
> clashing with police over the presence of military recruiters on col-
> lege campuses, and hiking prayerfully through suburban streets on
> long peace vigils [85].
>
> –*Philip Bufithis from* Norman Mailer

If *The Electric Kool-Aid Acid Test* can be called literary sociology, then
The Armies of the Night: History as a Novel, The Novel as History is socio-
political memoir structured as fiction. Both are products of "The New
Journalism." In the pages of a major daily newspaper, Tom Wolfe's book
would belong serialized in the Lifestyle section with bold warnings for
content, while Norman Mailer's work would be found on the National
Newspage with a disclaimer that the opinions expressed therein did not
necessarily represent those of the paper. Wolfe always made a concerted
effort not to bring his personal political views into his longer works, while
in this book, Mailer laid out his perception of the sense he had of his
own celebrity status, class awareness, attitudes toward women, race,
drugs, religion, literary ability, and political beliefs. All this came out in
the author's four-day account surrounding the March on the Pentagon
where he was arrested in October of 1967.

In *The New Journalism,* Wolfe discusses how autobiography fits into
this form, and how it was sometimes called "subjective" journalism. He
states that many writers, for technical ease, used the autobiographical
format, but believes that "[i]n fact, most of the best work in the form
has been done in third-person narration with the writer keeping himself absolutely invisible, such as the work of Capote, Talese, the early

Breslin [...]" (42). One consequence of this autobiographical tendency created public confusion between New Journalism and "advocacy journalism."

The Armies of the Night didn't help matters in this regard. The book was both "advocacy journalism," and "New Journalism" of the kind Wolfe espoused. Simply put, Mailer turned himself into a third-person narrator of his story and employed all the techniques of realistic fiction, specifically, those literary components outlined by Wolfe that distinguished the New Journalism from the old journalism. He crafted a literary narrative from his experience. The author used scene-by-scene construction, dialogue, and the details of his status life to create the narrative. It would be rare to find an "advocacy journalist" working this hard, or usually having the writing ability to create this greater sense of realism.

Mailer—the novelist as protagonist—went to Washington, D.C. as a well-known dissident to oppose the Vietnam War. Mailer-the-character, in the third-person limited point of view, allows the reader to view the many scenes through the four-day period. Mailer incorporates stanzas of rhetorical essay inside the form of a traditional novel by making those arguments part of the protagonist's point of view. In the book, Mailer-the-character admits disdain for the supposedly "objective" journalists who wrenched, garbled, "twisted and broke one's words and sentences until a good author always sounded like an incoherent overcharged idiot in newsprint. [...] Henry James would have come off in a modern interview like a hippie who had taken a correspondence course in forensics" (80). Such was the humorous bent of this cranky protagonist.

The Armies of the Night is a two-part book. Book One, *History as a Novel,* is Mailer's personal story of four days in Washington, on the celebrity frontline of the protest, marching, getting arrested, spending more time than he had anticipated in jail, and being released. Book Two, *The Novel as History,* is much shorter in length and takes a step back to render an organizational perspective on the event. This part of the work looks at the many groups involved, the planning, and the bigger media perspective. It has a decidedly different narrative arc, especially when the two "armies of the night"—one symbolic and one real—clash. This clash in the late reaches of the night occurs when Mailer is sequestered in his cell.

But is this history? On the same page where Mailer-the-character is presented as the narrative's "comic hero," there is acknowledgement from Mailer-the-author that "[t]he March on the Pentagon was an ambiguous event whose essential value or absurdity may not be established for ten or twenty years" (67). By deduction then, Mailer's account in Book Two is not a "history," but old-school journalism. It is also a different, more omniscient, narrative where Mailer-the-author must piece together the scenes and create a dramatic arc without benefit of first-hand experience. Because he's not there, the author recognizes that Book Two is more "novelistic" than Book One. Book One sets up Book Two. The personal ordeal of Mailer-the-author in Book One and his first-hand knowledge of the dynamic surrounding the event, create a palpable impression of authority that benefits the more global perspective in Book Two. Also, Mailer recognized, as Jean Bradford points out in *Norman Mailer: A Critical Study*, that "[h]istory, in a philosophical sense, is as much a fiction as is a novel. [...] [A] novelistic treatment within which the bias of the novelist and his beliefs is exposed as fully as possible, at least permits the subjective element to be understood and allowed for. [...] [A] historical approach to an event like the Pentagon march must always be 'exterior' whereas a novelistic treatment can deal with the interiority of the events and the people involved in them" (120). For these reasons, Mailer chose to call Book Two, *The Novel as History*. In fact, as a non-fictional and immediate rendering, it was neither.

In Book One—*History as a Novel: The Steps of the Pentagon*—the narrative unfolds as a realistic novel. During night one of the story, the reader joins Mailer at a liberal party where, despite his Leftist views and heavy drinking, the narrator expresses an elitism and admitted penchant for the parties of wealthy people instead of this one hosted by a professorial couple. This irony and mood set the stage for his appearance at a pre-demonstration rally being held that same evening at a nearby Washington theater. In other words, Mailer-the-author establishes that Mailer-the-character may not be altogether reliable for describing the protagonist's semi-besotted behavior on stage. In front of the crowd, Mailer-the-character talks of "their resistance to the war [as] some hopeless mélange, somehow firmed, of Pacifism and closet Communism. And their children—on a freak out from the suburbs to a love-in on the Pentagon wall" (47). From late 1967 into 1968, when Mailer wrote this book, open season on the "hippie" had been tacitly declared. Mailer is both brutally derisive in his lampooning of the hippies and "gloomily hopeful" in his assessment of the "mad middle-class children." Still, the hippies, for Mailer, are integral in his search for a human renaissance against the deadening corruption of the authorities. This comes despite his assessment on the effects that he feels this new "devil drug" LSD is having on these "drug-gutted flower children" (47). Mailer's fascination for the infusion of youthful energy into the dull reaches of Leftist rhetoric and cautious liberal dissent, also infuses *The Armies of the Night* with the book's most riveting prose and innovative perceptions.

The early development of himself as an unreliable character helps Mailer-the-author establish an underlying theme for the book that questions the ultimate reliability of any narrator or author. At the same time, the manner in which he reveals so much about his own petty biases and foibles, also establishes for the author a higher level of credibility and veracity. Mailer-the-author makes sure that Mailer-the-character is portrayed as very human—warts, brilliance, notoriety and all. Much of the humor in this work derives from Mailer's self-deprecating candor that calls into question such things as his well-publicized past behavior with ex-wives, or his exploits as an unruly celebrity. With Mailer-the-character's affectations and odd humility, Mailer-the-author is signaling the reader that he is doing his utmost to create an objective distancing in this work. This he does despite the admission that an objective rendering will never be fully possible.

Philip Bufithis in *Norman Mailer* also recognizes the charm and underlying intent of the author in this work:

> What makes this book so extraordinarily engaging is the characterization of the protagonist, Norman Mailer. Usually he refers to himself simply as "Mailer" or "he," but that he occasionally invokes other names as well—the Ruminant, the Beast, the Existentialist, the Historian, the Participant, the Novelist, the General, the Protagonist, Norman—attests to the marvelous diversity of his behavior, to the fact that all along he is at will improvising identities to accommodate himself to the multifariousness of American society. [...]
> He believes that the conflicts raging within him are raging within America. [...]
> The prismatic quality of his motivation is what gives the book its radiant psychological reality [...]
> Truly Mailer is a self-preserving rogue, a character of exorbitant disproportions, for always offsetting every sacrificial act of civil disobedience is some ludicrous vanity that would make us wince were it not so funny [88–93].

The author sets himself up as the "comic-hero" and a non-central character in the main event—the March on the Pentagon. In his third-person affectation, he allows that: "Mailer is a figure of monumental disproportions and so serves willy-nilly as the bridge [...] when a mass of citizenry [...] marched on a bastion which symbolized the military might of the Republic, marching not to capture it, but to wound it symbolically" (68). Rendering himself as a fallible character within the structural confines of a story that lasts four days, also allows Mailer-the-author the license to write overtly subjective, rhetorical and didactic prose. Ultimately, Mailer-the-author creates in Mailer-the-character, a metaphorical American.

Unlike Wolfe, who was an outsider to the Merry Pranksters, Mailer is a celebrated insider during the March on the Pentagon that took place on October 21, 1967. When at the March, Mailer describes with exceptional detail how so many different groups and types of people coalesced to take part. *The Armies of the Night* was published in December 1968, an exceedingly fast fourteen month turnaround for the writing, editing, and printing of a literary work. Mailer says in the book that he wrote faster than he ever had, "as if an accelerating history of the country forbade deliberation" (241). The social upheaval within the United States was at a level unseen since the Civil War. The book reading public was clamoring for insight into what was happening on the streets of America. In 1969, *The Armies of the Night* won both the National Book Award for arts and letters and the Pulitzer Prize in general non-fiction.

In section one of the book, Mailer's novelistic scenes serve as launching pads for overt socio-political analyses. Stylistically, the author is much more renowned for his long intellectualized sentences, than in possessing an ear for dialogue. Yet, this work is more than an Op-Ed diatribe, but rather an opportunity for Mailer-the-character to create a complex, insightful rumination on the state of American society and politics in late 1967 through the lens of one contentious demonstration. Consequently, the scope of Mailer's gaze extended well beyond the hippies, even though this phalanx of youthful rebels was of more fascination for the author/protagonist than were the other groups taking part in the March.

When Mailer describes these young people, he also defines a postmodern existentialism several years before the term, postmodern, came into vogue:

> The new generation believed in technology more than any before it, but the generation also believed in LSD, in witches, in tribal knowledge, in orgy, and revolution. [...] Their radicalism was in their hate for the authority—the authority was the manifest of evil to this generation. It was the authority who had covered the land with those suburbs where they stifled as children while watching the West in the movies, while looking at the guardians of dull genial celebrity on television; they had their minds jabbed and poked and twitched and probed and finally galvanized into surrealistic modes of response by commercials cutting into dramatic narratives, and parents flipping from network to network—they were forced willy-nilly to build their idea of the space-time continuum (and therefore their nervous system) on the jumps and cracks and leaps and breaks which every phenomenon from the media seemed to contain within it [103].

Mailer-the-character shows the reader, in reflective third-person, the gathering scene. The symbolic army gathers at the Lincoln Memorial in vivid detail, and none are described more vividly than the florid hippies who come dressed for the protest in every imaginable costume, or as Mailer says, "from all intersections between history and the comic books, between legend and television, the Biblical archetypes and the movies" (109). The costumes range from Sgt. Pepper's Lonely Hearts Club Band to confederate gray uniforms; the hippies come as Daniel Boone, Charlie Chaplin or Turkish shepherds. The descriptive list goes on and on. Mailer bemoans in the wearers of these costumes their fractured sense of past and present. Born in 1923, Mailer at age 44 during the March on the Pentagon, was old enough to be the father of most of these hippies, but as an astute observer of character, he described how they were products of "corporation-land" and its "sexo-technological variety of neofascism." But as barraged as these hippies were when nature's veil was ripped away, "that tissue of past history, whether traceable in the flesh, or merely palpable in the collective underworld of the dream, was nonetheless being bombed by the use of LSD as outrageously as the atoll of Eniwetok, Hiroshima, Nagasaki, and the scorched foliage of Vietnam. [...] Mailer's final allegiance, however, was with the villains who were hippies" (109–110).

Mailer, a World War II Veteran, calls Vietnam "Uncle Sam's Whorehouse War" (115), and "an obscene war, the worst war the nation had ever been in" (95). Those at the March included representatives from the old guard Left, Veterans Against the War in Vietnam, American Friends Service Committee, Women Strike for Peace, CORE, SCLC and others he collectively described as being "like rusty tin cans" (112). On the other hand, he had known immediately from just the name, that the Black Panther Party wouldn't be an insignificant phenomenon. Likewise, Mailer described the growing disaffection and detestation that the Black Left had toward the white antiwar movement by 1967 in the aftermath of the most strident period of the Civil Rights movement. After the speeches at the Lincoln Memorial, the Black activists chose to break apart from the main demonstration to protest elsewhere in Washington, D.C. on that day. The main body, with Mailer and the other celebrities leading, marched across a Potomac River bridge toward the Pentagon facility in Virginia.

Mailer-the-author was brazenly outspoken, and his attitudes toward women and Blacks were readily apparent in the book. In 1967, the term "Black" was just supplanting the term "Negro" as acceptable parlance. Yet when the March proceeds beneath an overpass as it nears the Pentagon, Mailer-the-character remarks on the "handsome young Negro carrying a placard. *No Vietnamese Ever Called Me A Nigger*" (134), it said. The protagonist is impressed and the other marchers cheer the man and his sign. Mailer-the-author-and-character, however well-intended, displays a backhanded affront when he says: "Was a mad genius buried in every Negro? How fantastic they were at their best—how dim at their worst" (134). When reading a racially delimiting remark such as this, it's not difficult to imagine the growing detestation of those in the Black Left toward the White Left in 1967. Mailer works to elevate himself from direct allegiances toward the groups in the cause, but he was arm-in-arm with the White Left on this day.

Mailer actually parses the issue of his affiliation with the American Left by claiming to be a "Left Conservative." He's resolutely critical of the unfettered technological development of the American landscape in the hands of the corporations and what this change has done to the American people. Yet, he also considers himself conservative, in that he feels some wars in the name of the Republic warrant fighting. In this respect, he is not so different from the hippie, not for his lack of pacifism, but in how they also opposed the dehumanizing impact of corporatization. The hippies were not anti-technology, but highly opposed to its abuses. Widespread psychedelic drug use was radical, but a reactionary traditionalism in the hippie movement would harken "The Movement" back to a more Jeffersonian focus on agrarian self-sufficiency. This occurred through a collectivist spirit that would attempt to re-establish a sense of extended family. Like Ken Kesey, many hippies had an affinity for the rugged individualism of the pioneer. The lifestyle alternatives just beginning to take hold among the hippies in 1967 differed radically from the mainstream sense of "progress" that in turn differed radically from the lifestyle of their grandparent's generation. The hippies wanted the best of what had been lost from their grandparent's world and what was deemed as "appropriate technology" from modern society. The fight against injustice, such as against a war in Indo-China that made no sense, or the blatant corporate pollution of the air and streams in the '60s was more often reactionary than Leftist. The hippie phenomenon was largely leaderless and voluntaristic, with adherents taking up any number of causes across a much wider spectrum of political and cultural concern than that represented by the New Left.

In *The Armies of the Night,* Mailer recognized that no group represented the hippies. He also distinguishes between the more visionary West Coast and the practical East Coast. Moreover, Mailer acknowledges that the troops are undoubtedly aware that these long-haired protesters were part of that "mysterious group of city Americans referred to first as hipsters, then beatniks, then hippies; now hearing that they are linked with those insidious infiltrators of America's psychic life, the Reds!" (285). The link is made when Mailer introduces the hippie wing of the Students for a Democratic Society (SDS) with its organizers such as Jerry Rubin and Abbie Hoffman. Rubin is a prime organizer of the March on the Pentagon.

In the book *Abbie Hoffman: American Rebel,* author Marty Jezer notes:

> Bearded, long-haired, guitar-strumming beatniks were a fixture at movement demonstrations, but many in the peace movement and on the left were embarrassed by their presence. [...] But the times were rapidly changing. By 1967 many activists—in SDS and pacifist circles—were looking and acting like hippies, smoking marijuana and experimenting with psychedelic drugs [97–98].

Even though figures such as Abbie Hoffman and Jerry Rubin are treated as iconic symbols for the hippie phenomenon, it was the politicized New

Left that gravitated toward the hippies, not the opposite. As constant media provocateurs, these two men, especially, became disproportionately associated with the whole of the hippie experience. The hippie wing of the New Left worked hard to appropriate the rebellious energy of the hippie phenomenon to its own ends. This explains how growing disdain and mobilization against the Vietnam War allowed a decidedly Leftist portrait to be painted by the mainstream media over the whole of the counterculture.

Mailer, too, oversimplifies the Leftist characterization of the hippie youth because the hippies at the March were obviously politicized. In the author's own binary of Left VS. Conservative, he adroitly reconciles seemingly irreconcilable contradictions. The counterculture, like Mailer's Left Conservatism, however, was more paradoxical than the author recognized. The old terminology for political labels no longer applied to the hippies, including the label of a New Leftism. The disaffection of the hippies was more broadly cultural and complex and the essence of its reactionary traditionalism decidedly more Dionysian than Marxist.

Paul Krassner in *Confessions of a Raving, Unconfined Nut: Misadventures in the Counter-Culture* published the exchange in a 1982 panel discussion featuring Abbie Hoffman and Timothy Leary who were discussing this issue of politics and culture:

> HOFFMAN: We saw in the sixties a great imbalance of power, and the only way that you could correct the imbalance was to organize people and fight for power. Power is not a dirty word. The concept of trying to win against social injustice is not a dirty kind of concept.[...]
>
> LEARY: Abbie, you [...] have much more faith in the political system's ability to change things, and I believe with William Burroughs that it's the culture that changes—you change the way men and women relate to each other, you change the way people's consciousness can be moved by themselves, you change their music and their dress, you change the way they relate to the land and to other forms of plants and animals, and you've got yourself a revolution—to use your word, a *fuckin'* revolution—that'll make the politicians and power-mad people ... it's gonna happen so fast they won't know it's gonna happen.
>
> HOFFMAN: [...] Tim, if you don't regard the four years you spent in prison as a political act, you took one trip too many. [...][I]t was a political act. So to separate what is cultural from political when we are talking about American society in the fifties and sixties is an absolutely hopeless and ridiculous task [319–321].

Hoffman's definition of politics is curiously broad in the manner that poststructural literary theorists will posit that all literature is political and all language rhetorical. In *The Armies of the Night* Mailer highlights the need within the Old Left and "good Socialist *Anti*-Communism" to employ a "sound-as-brickwork-logic-of-the-next-step" approach. By comparison, Mailer claims that the hippie branch of the New Left "had no respect whatsoever for the unassailable logic of the next step" [102–103].

According to Jezer: "What Abbie meant by dropping out was different from the Leary-Alpert definition. Abbie wanted people to drop out of their white collar lives and use their skills as doctors, scientists, teachers, technicians, as he was using his: to create an alternative society that would lead to revolution" (101). Emmett Grogan of the original San Francisco Diggers—though repulsed by Hoffman's and Rubin's media grabbing, self-aggrandizing stunts—admits to this same "logic-of-the-next-step" whereby an alternative society would lead toward a class-free society. Grogan in *Ringolevio* makes a strong case that the San Francisco Diggers were the architects of this strategy and Hoffman blatantly appropriated their lingo and anarchistic methods to grandstand, but didn't execute Digger tactics in a grass roots manner. Hoffman, Grogan and Rubin were certainly at the edge of change, but each one was caught up in the most fundamental miscalculation of the hippie era's Leftist politics. Namely, they were all superimposing a Marxist revolutionary model on a social phenomenon that was fundamentally Dionysian in its many cultural permutations.

Mailer didn't recognize the method to Rubin's and Hoffman's anarchistic antics as a first-step "deconstruction" of society. The hippies embraced "alternative" solutions to a host of societal and political ills, but, for most of them, the immediate political agenda was the goal, such as ending the war. Likewise, an alternative lifestyle was the end in-and-of-itself, rather than the overthrow of the democratic institutions in America. If anything, a cabalistic distrust of the big money interests controlling U.S. Government and society created a reactionary hope in most hippies that the institutions of the country might one day be more truly democratic again. In this, Timothy Leary's assertion that the culture would change is, in retrospect, what happened, though not to the extent that Leary, or certainly the New Leftists, envisioned.

By 1967, Hoffman and Rubin had embraced the hippie phenomenon. They employed a Merry Pranksterish and West Coast Digger style of theatricality and shock-effect. They were the vanguard of the politicized hippies. Their ploys established them as icons of the hippie epoch in a reductivist way that distorted for the mainstream the political and cultural breadth of the hippie phenomenon. The lifestyle changes invoked by the hippies were irrefutably radical, the disillusionment great, but only a portion of hippies were politicized activists in the manner of Rubin and Hoffman, or the San Francisco Diggers.

Raymond Mungo was representative of a hippie who in 1967 worked as an anti-war journalist in Washington, D.C., but by 1969 had moved back-to-the-land as a New Age communard in Vermont. In 1967, he helped found the Liberation News Service, a seat-of-the-pants "Associated Press" for the growing number of underground newspapers popping up in cities across the United States. The LNS got its start covering the same 1967 Pentagon war protest that Mailer wrote about in *Armies of the Night*. From 1967 to 1969, Mungo and his cohorts underwent the sort of transformation that was typical of many hippies of the era. In his memoir *Famous Long Ago: My Life and Hard Times with Liberation News Service* that was published in 1970, Mungo discusses this time:

> What we now call "the movement" is actually a thousand movements with a thousand inhibitions and restrictions and interpersonal hang-ups to it. (This doesn't mean, for example, that I am upset by Black Power as a separatist movement; to the contrary, I find it inspiring and necessary. But I am irrelevant to it.) What started as a small group of people (we could always tell, for example, who smoked pot among us, and we kept our secrets from the "straight" world), easily recognized, has become millions upon millions. [...]
>
> I do not seek to reconstruct the original movement, because I think we have all learned from our mistakes and I think our original optimism, our expectations for reform in the nation, would be hopelessly naive today. I seek to rediscover, however, the joy and purpose that movement held, and to apply them toward a revolution in life, [...] And the revolution is necessary, bloodful shit-spewing agonizing plastic saccharine shallow world that we live in makes it necessary for survival, for survival [114].

Outrage against the war fueled participation in the demonstrations as well as greater participation in the counterculture. In other words, the nature of most hippie activism was usually reactionary and specific. In terms of consciousness and lifestyle, however, this reaction was cultural and broadly immersive.

A few months after the March on the Pentagon, Hoffman, Rubin, Krassner and a couple others came up with the term "Yippie!" to signify a new Youth International Party. The intent was to rally the politicized hippies. According to Mungo, Rubin was always "anxious to be at the forefront of What's Happening, whether the Pentagon confrontation (of which he was "co-director"), the acid-youth culture, or the Democratic convention in Chicago. [...] But his actual power and constituency was and is very small, and when he announced that 500,000 Yippies would demonstrate in Chicago, only the federal government believed him" (59).

In *The Armies of the Night*, Abbie Hoffman's name comes up in association with the New York Diggers, his hippie group that provided food and water to the demonstrators on the night when Mailer was being detained in a nearby jail. Fred Goodman's book, *The Mansion on the Hill: Dylan, Young, Geffen, Springsteen, and the Head-On Collision of Rock and Commerce*, describes Grogan and another visiting Digger at the home of Bob Dylan's manager, Albert Grossman in Woodstock, New York:

"That scene around [Bob] Dylan was strange," says actor Peter Coyote. At the time, Coyote was a member of the Diggers, [...].

"We made a lot of shit happen," says Coyote, "but the truth was we were always broke. So when someone like Albert opening up his house to you, and giving you a car and serving you the best organic gourmet food and the best grass and hash and acid and introducing you to gorgeous women—y'know, it was great. And we paid for it by what we taught. Because that was the only commodity we had to trade. So Albert got to sit front-row-center at the wildest show in the world. This porcine, psychedelic Ben Franklin. And he knew if anything went down, Emmett [Grogan] and I were in front of him like a couple of dog soldiers. So he could play."[...]

"We had entrée because we were the hippest of the hip" [97–8].

The tactics of the Diggers and the "hippie-fied" New Left to unsettle public consciousness had an impact, but the realities of the Vietnam War—most directly its Selective Service Draft—created an unavoidable decision for those susceptible to its edicts. Apathy and disregard were not options for young draft-age men. They had to take a stance on the War. The first wave of "Baby Boomers" born between 1945 and 1949 were of draft age by 1967. Psychedelic drugs were prevalent by 1967. The Vietnam War was at its peak with a half-million soldiers serving in 1967. Rock music was harder, more vibrant and more unifying among the youth than ever before or after. For all these reasons, the floodgates had broken and the hippie phenomenon was suddenly omnipresent.

Mailer's Left/Conservative view in 1967 held that Asia would be best left to the Asians whether the continent were to turn to communism or not. Fear of communism was the prime rationale for US involvement in Southeast Asia. The author was convinced that the expansion of communism would be its own containment (211). Mailer's prescience as an insta-historian in these respects was "right on." In 1967, the U.S. had no diplomatic relations with "Red" China. Four decades later, capitalistic Hong Kong was absorbed into The People's Republic of China and the nation was the number one trading partner of the United States of America. Even the U.S.S.R., arch cold war enemy of America, had expanded into its own "containment" when glasnost and perestroika conditioned the dissolution of the union and the crumbling of the Iron Curtain in 1989.

Hippie theatrics plays into *The Armies of the Night* when Mailer describes how Abbie Hoffman proposes to the organizing group to have twelve hundred men encircle the Pentagon to "form a ring of exorcism sufficiently powerful to raise the Pentagon three hundred feet" (139). At this point the building would turn orange and vibrate until the evil was gone. In this way the Vietnam War would end. For the protest, a manifesto was written to abet this exorcism. In this declaration, the spirit of every deity imaginable is mentioned to help cast evil from the "pentacle of power." The Pentagon, it says, has "perverted its use to the need of the total machine and its child the hydrogen bomb and has suffered the people of the planet earth, the American people and creatures of the mountains, woods, streams, and oceans grievous mental and physical torture and the constant torment of the imminent threat of utter destruction" (140).

Mailer is impressed with the imaginative gesture and joins in when the crowd chants "out, demons, out" over and over. He then asks: "On which acidic journeys had the hippies met the witches and the devils and the cutting edge of primitive awe, the savage's sense of explosion [...]?" (142).

In Book Two, the author describes how in 1967 the Arab-Israeli war, together with Black riots in nearly a dozen city ghettos, had taken the thunder out of the early planning for the demonstration. But, according to Mailer, "the New Left was in a state of stimulation, and the hippies, dedicated to every turn of the unexpected, were obviously—as always—ready for anything" (251). The old guard recognized that "to call on Rubin was in effect to call on the most militant, unpredictable, creative—therefore dangerous—hippie-oriented leader available on the New Left" (251). Mailer believed in the potential of the New Left when he calls Rubin "a revolutionary mystic [...] [Rubin] believed that the chaos which followed disruption would force a crisis, force the government to overextend itself, and so would polarize the country and develop the strength of the Left who could build new values, new community, new power. [...] [B]ut it was not Rubin's apocalyptic vision alone [...]— it was the collective vision now of the drug-illumined and revolutionary young of the American middle class" (297). In this, Mailer was perhaps buying into the New Left party line. Disaffection against the War, and disaffection against perceived hypocrisy and corruption in the mainstream, and a widespread altering consciousness, beckoned loudly for change. The counterculture was astoundingly collectivist considering it was largely leaderless; change was being demanded on many fronts and this disaffection was reflected through a wholesale altering of lifestyle. When the government stopped drafting for Vietnam in 1972, the momentum of the New Left ground to a halt. This occurred sooner than most of the other countercultural permutations.

As literature, *The Armies of the Night* parodied the traditional novel in the fact that it was not a fictionalized account of the events. The natural sequence, and the way Mailer-the-author constructed Book One, evoked the emotional effect of a well-plotted novel where the reader sees the actualization of Mailer-the-character's potential through the drama of the situation. Like Wolfe, Mailer recognized the power of the story, the potency of narrative realism, and adapted his short memoir into its methodology. The work was grand narrative in the sense that the story had a rhetorical message summed up in Mailer's repeated articulation of his political stance and his hectoring of this War's immoral grounding. The narrative structure in both books were straightforward renderings of the March on the Pentagon; Book One from the personal vantage of Mailer-the-Character, Book Two from the overview of the entire orchestration of the event and its many diverse participants. By Book Two, the personal credibility of Book One's protagonist establishes the intellectual credibility of Mailer-the-author in Book Two. Book One sets the stage for Mailer to articulate the meaning of the event, something the historian routinely strives to accomplish.

The most salient postmodern features of the book are: (1) in its self-referential meta-narrative where Mailer-the-character tells the reader during the story the method in which the story is being constructed, (2) why it's being constructed in the manner that it is, and (3) how the objectivity of its rendering, and for that matter any rendered account of any event, should be greeted with the utmost suspicion. Such deconstructive irony, propels the narrative, characterizes the protagonist, earns the reader's trust with its level of refreshing candor, and becomes an intellectually engaging account of one man's dissent and its consequence. Book One is blatantly rhetorical, and a disarmingly effective display of storytelling, which is energeic and traditional in its rendering. Book Two is much shorter at seventy-five pages and comes across as a collection of the data surrounding the event that Mailer-the-character would have had no way of knowing at the time he was involved in the March and arrest. This part of the story is also written as an extended piece of feature journalism.

Book One, *History as a Novel* is, as Mailer addresses in one of his meta-narratives, a "history in the costume of a novel" (241). When he is done with Book One, then Book Two, *The Novel as History,* provides a journalistic account of the March that would serve as excellent source material for the writing of the history of the Vietnam era anti-war demonstrations. Yet, more compellingly, Book Two strives for the meaning of this specific larger event and captures the climactic essence of the story of the March on the Pentagon.

The Armies of the Night, as a title, serves double duty. It aptly characterizes both the brutality of the soldiers at the Pentagon after the media had left for the night, and it is indicative of the most resolute of the symbolic Army of protesters who braved the night to continue the occupation of the Mall at the Pentagon. Late in the night a wedge of soldiers moves through the protesters who are sitting around campfires in the Pentagon's outside Mall. The young hippie women, especially, were singled out for bludgeoning. The evocative writing here lacks any semblance of the self-satirizing tone found earlier. This is Mailer's climax scene. The author elevates the valor and resolve of the demonstrators who have stayed the night over his own predicament of being jailed elsewhere. Robert Merrill suggests in *Norman Mailer Revisited* that:

> What emerges is Mailer's interpretation of the march. In Mailer's view the demonstrators are visited with grace as they sit face to face with the soldiers [...][The symbolic Army] endure[s] a night that begins in "joy" but includes the terror of military attack. Those who remain to the end are subtly transformed. [...][T]hese flower children and fledgling revolutionaries are forever different in the morning from how they had been before the night. The particular experience of book 1 is generalized in book 2. The knot of nihilism is untied, if not "forever," then at least for the moment. This is the "mystery" Mailer discovers in the March on the Pentagon, first in his own experience and then in the collective experience of the demonstrators. Transcending the count of bodies, the tactical successes or failures of the demonstration, is the spiritual renewal attested to by the now-impersonal narrative voice of *Armies* [125–126].

Mailer found when he wrote Book Two that he had "delivered a discovery of what the March on the Pentagon had finally meant, and what had been won, and what had been lost, and so found himself ready at last to write a most concise Short History, [...] no, a Novel of History, to elucidate the mysterious character of that quintessentially American event" (241). Merrill calls it a subjective history, which differs from fiction in its attempt to find meaning in actual events, rather than, with fiction, trying to evoke the optimal dramatic emotion from within a situation.

Mailer's use of the term "novel" in both Book One and Two, underscores that the author recognizes the subjectivity in his accounting of this event. Mailer-the-author, with and without his monumental hubris, succeeds with a sense of verisimilitude in Book One that is often woefully lacking when biographies and autobiographies proclaim an objective truth. The reader may not like the protagonist, but the blunt honesty of Mailer-the-character comes with sharp hooks that lure the reader's empathy. The protagonist, whether one agrees with his beliefs or not, is a David against Goliath, the classic underdog. And, all the while, Mailer-the-character will stop the action to let the reader-as-empathizer in on, not only what is happening inside the protagonist's head, but what is going on inside Mailer-the-author's narrative bag-of-tricks, as well. *The Armies of the Night: History as a Novel, the Novel as History* is a fine example of the New Journalism, "advocacy" journalism, traditional narrative (Book One), old-school journalism and insta-history (Book Two), postmodern meta-narrative, and creative nonfiction. His take on the hippies, and the begrudging, reluctant hope he places on their concern and involvement in the future of the Republic, is also an integral part of the larger hippie narrative.

10

Slaughterhouse-Five (1969)

So It Goes

> For Kurt Vonnegut, there is a deep affinity with American life. His
> rise to popularity during the sixties was an event itself, taking its place
> alongside other milestones of popular history during those tumul-
> tuous times. Cultural historians already perceive those events as
> important episodes in the evolution of American culture. But Von-
> negut's importance is something more than as the spokesman of a
> counterculture. It is more like the authentic idiom of a whole cul-
> ture, with its contradictions, dissonances, and dreams as parts of the
> full orchestration. There has never been another writer quite like
> Vonnegut, just as there has never been another decade quite like the
> sixties [xii].
> —*From* Vonnegut in America, *Jerome Klinkowitz/Donald Lawler*

Kurt Vonnegut, Jr., was born in 1922 and published his short masterpiece, *Slaughterhouse-Five,* in 1969. In the novel, Vonnegut's protagonist, Billy Pilgrim, an American POW being detained in the cellar of a
Dresden, Germany slaughterhouse at the end of World War II, survives
a firebombing by a squadron of American planes that killed 135,000 German civilians living at ground level above the temporary prison. This
event actually happened. The author, as a young soldier, also survived
the same bombing raid. Billy's son in the novel became a Green Beret
in the Vietnam War. The author's son, Mark, was not drafted. In 1975,
Mark Vonnegut published a memoir called *The Eden Express* about dropping out and joining a hippie commune in British Columbia. It was the
father Kurt, despite being from the preceding generation, and not the
hippie son Mark, who was a hero of the counterculture.

Slaughterhouse-Five erupted on the literary landscape at the same time
that swelling numbers of Americans were seriously questioning the War
in Vietnam. This disenchantment extended well beyond the student protesters and those in the counterculture. Through this darkly funny work,

Vonnegut questioned human attitudes toward war and death in general. Vonnegut's absurdist sense of irony and experimental form is not unlike Richard Brautigan's in *Trout Fishing in America,* except that the central theme for Vonnegut is not the loss of the pastoral in the United States, but the supreme lack of coherence when it comes to when and why people will die or survive.

At every reference to death in the novel—over one hundred times—the author reflects on the occasion by stating: "so it goes." Initially, the phrase seems to imply that this is just the way it is. Over the course of the novel, the number of "so it goes" begin to mount like a death toll. The surface breeziness of the mantra sobers, philosophically, into an obtrusive emphasis on how we all must go; it's the when and why of our death that makes no sense in Vonnegut's cosmology. The hobo-soldier on the prisoners' boxcar, dies uncomplainingly. "So it goes." Robert Weary threatens revenge on Billy Pilgrim for his predicament. When captured with Billy, Weary was forced to wear wooden shoes. He dies of gangrene in his mangled feet. "So it goes." At age forty-four on the night after Billy's daughter's wedding, the champagne has gone dead. "So it goes."

Billy Pilgrim's life in the novel is beset, at every major juncture, with the question of why he seems singled out to survive when so many of his fellow soldiers in Germany, his fellow optometrists after a plane crash he is in, or his wife en route to Billy's hospital bed after the crash, all die. Most profoundly, the book hinges on the singular irony that Billy and the author were American POW's, part of the very few survivors in a city that was utterly and unnecessarily destroyed by American bombs. Dresden housed no industry related to war production; the bombing of civilian Germans there didn't impact the outcome of the war, and; the unconditional surrender of Germany took place a few weeks following the massive air raid. The facts surrounding this event were largely concealed from the American public until the publication of *Slaughterhouse-Five,* two-dozen years later.

Vonnegut asserts that this novel "is so short and jangled [...] because there is nothing intelligent to say about a massacre" (22). With his argument for compression and incomprehensibility, Vonnegut succeeds in setting the stakes of his novel exceedingly high. In its use of poignantly absurd imagery, *Slaughterhouse-Five* also succeeds masterfully.

Ken Kesey, in *Sometimes a Great Notion,* compressed time and had numerous narrative threads leading toward one culminating event. Yet, by comparison, *Great Notion* is a tome. Early on in *Slaughterhouse-Five,* Vonnegut informs the reader that: "*Billy Pilgrim has come 'unstuck in time'*" (25). Both novels are refractory, though *Slaughterhouse-Five* even more so than *Great Notion.* Vonnegut's book is a non-sequential portrait of one man's life, a barrage of the bits and pieces of Billy Pilgrim surviving war, domesticity, and alien abduction. The completed portrait offers a sense of this man, as well as a larger appreciation of how capriciously death affects every human. Billy Pilgrim is not an anti-hero or a fictional persona of Kurt Vonnegut, but, intentionally, an overtly innocent victim of the greater forces at work in the worst war mankind has ever witnessed. Billy, in this regard, was an unheroic hero. At Dresden, the author makes it known that nearly twice as many civilians were killed in this firebombing than were killed in the atomic blast over Nagasaki in Japan.

Kesey's novel employs parallel sequencing where many plot lines lead toward trying to make Hank Stamper give up. Even though there are numerous narrative threads in *Great Notion,* each one adheres to what John Gardner in *The Art of Fiction* refers to as the "uninterruptible fictional dream" (176) and, the result at the end of the novel, is a kaleidoscopic whole, and a full portrait. By comparison, *Slaughterhouse-Five* violates most semblances of an accruing narrative tension when Vonnegut tells the reader what will happen to each significant character and situation in the novel before he develops those scenes. We know from the author's snippets, for example, that Billy has survived the firebombing, that his wife dies in a car accident, that Billy will be the only surviving optometrist when a plane full of optometrists crashes.

Yet, even though narrative suspense is violated and Billy Pilgrim is "unstuck in time" in order to take the reader into many episodes in Billy's life—from childhood to mid-life back to being a man-child at war—Vonnegut deftly holds out the most incomprehensible scene of Billy's survival as the hook to keep the story propelling forward. In chapter one, the author as narrator, tells the reader that he, too, actually escaped the firebombing of Dresden; he mentions how he carried this story around in his head for years before he could begin to fathom the magnitude of it in a way that could be depicted with words. Finally, in the late '60s, Vonnegut discovered a narrative strategy.

In chapter one—conspicuously not a preface or foreword—Vonnegut-the-character goes to visit a fellow veteran who had also survived the massive firebombing. The veteran's wife has them sit in the kitchen at a sparse table to share their old stories. Vonnegut can tell she's not happy about this reunion of war survivors. Finally, when confronted on this, she declares that her husband and Vonnegut were just babies then. The world does not need more stories about babies pretending to be men, she tells them. To this, Vonnegut declares that he had probably written five thousand pages of this book and thrown them all away. He raises his right hand and promises that if it were ever to be made into a movie, it would not feature Frank Sinatra or John Wayne. Furthermore, it would be called *The Children's Crusade.* By doing this in the opening chapter of the novel, the author-as-autobiographer lets the reader know how difficult this topic had been for him to tackle. "As a trafficker in climaxes and thrills and characterization and wonderful dialogue and suspense and confrontations, I had outlined the Dresden story many times" (10).

Vonnegut kept his word to his friend's wife. The full title of the novel is *Slaughterhouse-Five, or The Children's Crusade: A Duty-Dance with Death* and this woman's name, Mary O'Hare, is in the dedication. The other name in the dedication is that of a former German soldier whom Vonnegut and his Vet friend met in the mid–1960's driving taxi on a return trip to Dresden shortly after that visit in the kitchen. Vonnegut is a German-American twenty-plus years after the war who empathizes with this German, his age. Due to forces out of their control, they happened to fight on opposite sides. The author humanizes the participants in this war. In 1968, unlike the young anti-war radicals such as Abbie Hoffman, Jerry Rubin or Paul Krassner, author Kurt Vonnegut was a middle-age, mainstream pacifist who had no interest in revolutionary change in America, except for the hope that Americans would embrace his humanist recognition that humans are their own worst enemy when it comes to matters of war, and only humans could do anything about the horror caused by warlike behavior. Mary O'Hare, the mainstream American housewife, was indicative of the growing members of the middle-class of America that, by 1967, shared a strong disdain toward a dubious war. This mainstream dovishness toward American involvement in Vietnam helped expand many countercultural sentiments far beyond the realm of hardcore hippies.

The memories Vonnegut shares with his friend were not very helpful to him as an author, but the perspective of the wife inspires the author to fashion a protagonist who would echo the sentiment of a Children's Crusade, an army of thirty-thousand European children who, in 1213, were recruited to march to Palestine to protect the holy land for Christianity. None of the children made it to Jerusalem, and most were exploited en route; many died or were sold into slavery.

Interestingly, when the hippie phenomenon has been lampooned, it is often by way of referring to it as a romantic Children's Crusade. To become a hippie was indeed a voluntaristic adaptation to drop out of the mainstream, but it wasn't orchestrated by some larger schemers, and at its most altruistic, there was a desire of its participants to better the world and to find alternative solutions to the institutional ailments of society. However, while the movement had its share of naivety, to characterize its many permutations as a crusade of innocent children is to denude the counterculture of its social potency. The dynamic of this phenomenon did change mainstream American culture. Of course, Kurt

Vonnegut's use of the Children's Crusade as a metaphor was not in reference to the counterculture. The author was making a global statement as to the propensity of man to kill his fellow man often without regard to the impact on innocent people or the price on the collective human psyche. As the embodiment of this damaged psyche, Billy Pilgrim is a schizophrenic man-child who survives war and several scrapes with death.

Vonnegut's approach to narrative structure in *Slaughterhouse-Five* is a literary technique that seems spatially configured rather than linear and sequential. Joseph Frank in his article, "Spatial Form in Modern Literature," written in 1945, theorizes that when culture is harmoniously adapted to the environment, novels reflect this by being organized chronologically. However, when men feel threatened by the environment, Frank holds that narratives adopt a more spatial structuring. Vonnegut used bits and pieces of the same set of scenes to create what is actually a temporal (not spatial) fracturing to capture the schizophrenic magnitude of war. One man, Billy Pilgrim, embodies the universal disharmony exacted by man on his fellow man. However, because the reader is taken to the same unstuck-in-time scenes again and again, conceptually, an illusion of spatial fracturing is created.

Throughout the narrative, the reader is told clearly at what point in Billy's life we are being taken during each of the fragments of storyline. The temporal narrative arc of Billy's life may be broken into bits and reordered for effect, and Billy may even be able to foretell his own future, but this man's schizophrenically rendered story eventually makes chronological sense to the reader. By the end of the book, a collage of the many fragments that comprise Billy Pilgrim's mind and experience manifest in a mosaic. The jigsaw puzzle is complete and Billy serves as a metaphor for a universal plight where mankind, by some schizophrenic fortuitousness, has only barely escaped its own self-induced annihilation.

Vonnegut, as a young Army scout, appears selectively throughout the novel. This presence helps dispel any thought that Billy Pilgrim was an autobiographical rendering of the actual author, although both are the same age and shared much of the same war experience, and, presumably, some similar perspectives. Like Vonnegut, Billy is twenty-one when he goes to Germany near the end of the War. Billy, however, is an ill-dressed, ill-prepared, funny-looking Chaplain's Assistant who survives the last major German offensive in Luxembourg. He hooks up with three other armed and well-dressed soldiers, but Billy barely survives the next few days of bitter winter cold. Ironically, Billy's life is spared when the Nazi soldiers discover them. Two of these American soldiers have already been shot when the Nazis find Billy. So it goes, says Vonnegut.

Vonnegut only ladles out portions of each scene in any one section. Billy Pilgrim is "spastic in time" (26). He can see into the future and the past. The reader travels with Billy on his abduction to the Planet Tralfamadore where he is forced to live in a pressurized atmospheric cage so the extraterrestrials can watch. The Tralfamadorians bring him Montana Wildhack, an earthling porno star so they can watch Billy mate with her. Billy moves forward and backwards in time. His father is killed in a hunting accident while Billy is in bootcamp. He meets the little-known Science Fiction writer, Kilgore Trout. Billy Pilgrim is one of Trout's only fans. Late in the book, in the display window of a Time Square porno shop in Manhattan, Billy finds a dusty copy of one of Trout's novels. In it, the main character is abducted to outer space and made to mate with a beautiful female earthling. Vonnegut establishes early in this novel that all moments—whether past, present, or future—have always existed and will always exist. The chaotic pieces of the puzzle that comprises Billy Pilgrim's mind gravitate through odd confrontations with a death that never quite kills Billy, yet impacts his fragmented psyche. From disaffection to disorientation to disengagement to disillusionment, Vonnegut paints, impressionistically, Billy's near escapes and the mounting toll that death and war extol on the human psyche. The author juxtaposes Billy's fragments of past, present and future experience for optimal irony.

Like *Trout Fishing in America,* the narrative structure of the novel is built on such juxtapositioning of absurdist irony. In this regard, Vonnegut's and Brautigan's works are Postmodernist, not Late Modernist. John Somer in his article "Geodesic Vonnegut; or, If Buckminster Fuller Wrote Novels," uses the geodesic dome as a conceptual device to describe the structure of *Slaughterhouse-Five.* The dome was a structure designed by the eccentric scientist Fuller. It met with great favor in the counter-culture because it used the least amount of material to create strong buildings with the most amount of space. This imaginative conceptual application would also apply to *Trout Fishing in America.* The fragments of prose are like the pentagonal units of construction creating a dome of narrative text. In the case of Billy, the temporally unstuck schizophrenia of his personality is a dome where the pentagonal units depict the many episodes of his passive survival; in the case of *Trout Fishing in America,* the dome is a man-made universe where each pentagon is one permutation of trout fishing in America. Taken as a textual whole, these absurd Trout Fishing in Americas have come to cover, like a surreal dome, the pastoral realities of actual trout fishing in a modernized America.

Somer refers to Vonnegut's geodesic narrative form in *Slaughterhouse-Five* in terms of man being his own salvation:

Billy weaves his way through time, creating a mosaic pattern in this spatial-form novel, moving artfully so that his movements create "an image of life that is beautiful and surprising and deep," moving carefully under the deft hand of Vonnegut, the narrator, [...] through the erratic corridors of Billy's schizophrenic passage through time. [...]

Billy's relationship to the narrator structures of this book [demonstrate] the technical significance of dynamic tension. *Slaughterhouse-Five* is a framed novel; that is, a story within a story—or more accurately, a fictive story within an autobiography. Consequently, this is not a mere framed story, but an innovation that strains the conventions of both the spatial and temporal-form traditions and even brings them together into a technical and structural relationship of dynamic tension [247].

Kurt Vonnegut, Richard Brautigan and Tom Robbins have been, likewise, compared to Mark Twain, not only for their colloquial tone and satirical wit, but in resemblance as well. Ample hair and big mustaches helped in this respect. These distinctly American writers all exhibited a highly imaginative wit. Conrad Festa in his article, "Vonnegut's Satire," reflects on how this author's humor is often treated as an aside when his works are studied critically. Yet, Festa contends that satire is central to the construction of Vonnegut's prose:

Vonnegut focuses our attention on evils in our society which make life unnecessarily painful, dangerous, and destructive—evils which, for the most part, can be corrected if only we would avoid our greatest folly: our tendency to escape unpleasant, threatening reality which demands corrective action, either by slipping into private dream worlds or by pretending that nothing can be done about it anyway.

Vonnegut's satires offer us hope, not despair—but not hope without action. [...] To a very large degree Vonnegut has accepted life as it is. But just as strongly as he has accepted life, he rejects the idea that we have no control over the evil in it that makes life unnecessarily painful. The tension between the two positions held simultaneously by Vonnegut creates not only the impulse toward satire but also the special tone of his satire [147–148].

Brautigan's juxtapositional imagery in *Trout Fishing* stays inside a private dream world where the modern world, more than individual men, are to be held accountable for the absurd state of our existence. Whereas Vonnegut inserts himself into the narrative of *Slaughterhouse-Five* with its focus on man's behavior toward fellow man, in *Trout Fishing* there is much less characterization occurring, simply a shifting conceptual lens toward what or who Trout Fishing in America is or might be construed to be. In many of the episodic fragments in *Trout Fishing*, the reader is given no reason to assume any separation between the author and the narrator. And, by the end of the book, the reader, presumably, will never look the same way again at trout fishing in America.

Vonnegut's focus as author is on developing Billy's character as a metaphor, not theme as metaphor as Brautigan does. Vonnegut creates a fully realized schizophrenic persona through the character of Billy Pilgrim. By the end of *Slaughterhouse-Five*, the reader, presumably, will never look at war in the same way again. Both books challenge the way in which the reader looks at the world by first fragmenting how the world is presented. The evocative power of these works, though, is in the impact of the completed assemblages, the textual whole of the narratives through the manner in which they have been constructed.

In a manner more similar to *The Electric Kool-Aid Acid Test*, Vonnegut begins with himself as the narrator, establishes the promise and parameters of this unstuck-in-time novel and then, once Billy Pilgrim takes over, the point-of-view shifts to omniscience, with the author entering the minds of any of the many characters at will. In the same way that Tom Wolfe maintains his presence throughout the narrative with the authorial "I", Vonnegut reappears on a few occasions throughout the novel, mostly to remind the reader that he is not one-and-the-same as Billy Pilgrim and that this book is only fictional on the surface. "That was I. That was me," he would say when making a cameo appearance. From the boxcar of the POW train entering the "intricate and voluptuous and enchanted and absurd" skyline of unbombed Dresden, the author-as-character sits behind Billy and describes the sight as "Oz" (133). At the opening of the last chapter, Vonnegut also surfaces to tell the reader that it is 1968 and Robert Kennedy was shot two nights earlier. "Martin Luther King was shot a month ago. He died, too. So it goes" (186).

The Electric Kool-Aid Acid Test treats the primary chronological narrative as an extended backstory to Wolfe's arrival on the scene, but the storyline never wavers from its chronological unfolding. The story starts in 1966 with Wolfe, moves back to Kesey's arrival in California in 1960 and progresses with the Merry Pranksters until the reader is back with Wolfe again in 1966 at the end of the novel. This reflects the traditional narrative form with the prime innovation being that the story took the reader into the subjective minds of real-life characters. Billy Pilgrim is a fictional construct modeled by Vonnegut on an apathetic, real-life private who survived the Dresden firebombing only to refuse to eat. While a fictional Billy survived the war, this soldier died of self-induced starvation in Dresden, just days before the war ended.

Vonnegut's own appearance in his novel also allows for its metafictional attributes, meaning that the novel draws attention to its own structure and telling. Similar to Norman Mailer making himself a character in *The Armies of the Night*, Vonnegut uses his own real-life experience in surviving the Dresden bombing to establish authorial legitimacy. Like Mailer, he can talk about why he was writing this book and the difficulties involved. When Vonnegut appears as a character, the reader believes in the plausibility of the framed, fictive story within this autobiography; the delusional reactions of a Billy Pilgrim are not flights of fancy as much as realistic adaptations of a man who is justifiably disturbed. *Slaughterhouse-Five* is, consequently, a fascinating blend of creative nonfiction and postmodernist fiction.

The fictional aspects of the novel allow the author to establish his absurdist ironies with greater definition than had this been strictly autobiographical. Billy Pilgrim is an innocent at war, a man-boy entering the war at the holiest and lowest rank afforded by military establishments. Billy is a chaplain's assistant. This lends weight to the idea of the war as a "Children's Crusade." Billy is one moment at war, the next time-traveling. He fixates on a gruesome crucifix that his mother had bought while on a trip across the American West. In constructing his Postmodern simulacra, Vonnegut describes Billy's mother, "like so many Americans,[...] trying to construct a life that made sense from things she found in gift shops" (39). The crucifix was one such item. Like a giftshop facsimile, death for Billy is always just one step removed, always surreal and absurd, an imitation of the given finality that we all will die. "So it goes," says Vonnegut.

When Vonnegut describes Tralfamadorian writing as clumps of symbols with urgent but brief messages, he is outlining, in part, his own narrative design in *Slaughterhouse-Five:*

> There isn't any particular relationship between all the messages, except that the author has chosen them carefully, so that, when seen all at once, they produce an image of life that is beautiful and surprising and deep. There is no beginning, no middle, no end, no suspense, no moral, no causes, no effects. What we love in our books are the depths of many marvelous moments seen all at one time [82].

Vonnegut's assemblage of reoccurring imagery presents a non-linear mosaic of Billy Pilgrim's life (and the author's war experience). Yet, due to the linearity of the written form, the author's curtain can only gradually reveal its patterns of thematic and scenic fragments. There is, also, deftness in the placement, and suspense in wanting to know all that happened to Billy and how, causally, it happened. The reader is told one-third of the way into the novel that "Billy [age 44] was guided by dread and lack of dread. Dread told him when to stop. Lack of it told him when to move again" (68–9). Ultimately, Billy's paradoxical blend of numbness and luck yield for Vonnegut a deep probing of mankind's often senseless behavior as relates to warfare. The author, in the context of man's warfare, repeatedly asks just what sort of creature we human beings are. The element of science fiction in the novel, allows this question to be posed humorously, but in a profoundly metaphorical way, too.

Perhaps one of the primary reasons this novel resonated with the growing anti-war sentiment of 1969, was in the manner Vonnegut successfully juxtaposed the oddly successful life of a quietly disaffected optometrist in 1968 with the horrors of a distant war. Of course, at the time Vietnam was distant and being fought by 500,000 American soldiers while the home front in America was, for the most part, complacent in its affluence. World War II impacted the American domestic calm much more directly. In 1967, the Second World War was historical and distant, but still haunting the memories of the many living participants. Vonnegut refuses to glorify or ennoble a war that was typically glorified and ennobled: "World War Two had certainly made everybody very tough. [...] The nicest veterans in Schenectady, I thought, the kindest and funniest ones, the ones who hated the war the most, were the ones who'd really fought" (15). When Vonnegut, as his own character, states this early in the novel, his credibility with those questioning the war in Vietnam was immediately enhanced. Also, *Slaughterhouse-Five* was notable in that unsympathetic representations of World War II were not commonplace.

When Billy Pilgrim is abducted by the flying saucer, he asks, "Why me?" (72) When an American P.O.W. is pulled out of line for talking and an English-speaking German soldier knocks his teeth out with the butt of his rifle, the American wonders, "Why me?"

"The guard shoved him back into ranks. 'Vy you? Vy anybody?' he said" (85).

Most of Vonnegut's earlier works were more overtly sci-fi. With the many fragments of Billy's time-travel to the Planet Tralfamadore, *Slaughterhouse-Five* employed science fiction fantasy as a metaphorical device to illustrate how tenuously any human being's hold on sanity actually is. When Billy Pilgrim is in a Tralfamadorian cage and mates with a fellow earthling, Vonnegut doesn't strive for verisimilitude, but an absurdist sense of pathos. Billy's flights of fantasy grow increasingly understandable as a human survival mechanism. There is a traditional narrative cause and effect at work here. The man's amazing fortuitousness for barely surviving takes an increasing toll on his mental equilibrium. The reader comes to empathize with Billy and his quirky ways.

Billy, in his World War II dress, is also unwittingly theatrical, not unlike a Merry Prankster. When he is the recipient of a greatly undersized overcoat off of a tiny man who had just died, his skinny arms protrude outward giving him the appearance of a stork. He finds silver painted boots to wear that are left behind from the British P.O.W.'s production of Cinderella. From the makeshift stage he appropriates an azure curtain to drape over his body in the manner of a toga. The curtain is Billy's bedding and his warmth. As an outfit, this appearance gives him the look of a buffoon. The German captors laugh hysterically at the sight of this gangly boy-soldier so attired. In Dresden, prior to the bombing, a German surgeon confronts Billy on the street. In English he asks if Billy thinks the war was funny, something to mock. Billy, in his typical disoriented mode of detachment, doesn't answer the doctor, but instead pulls from the seam of the tiny overcoat a large diamond and a partial denture he had found lodged there to show the German. After the war Billy has the diamond mounted and gives it as an engagement ring to his wife-to-be. She is the daughter of a wealthy optometrist who helps Billy become affluent. The odd luck of this odd young man created a comically captivating protagonist.

Interspersed with the absurdist humor are the author's constant reminders of the philosophical depth at the cusps of life, and the inequality of our human fates. Vonnegut refers to life as liquid, and death as stone in his weave of domestic life, wartime life, and outerspace life. However, foremost in *Slaughterhouse-Five,* the young men were off fighting—like a Children's Crusade, and: "Most of the privates on Billy's car were very young—at the end of childhood" (65).

At the beginning of the decade, Joseph Heller in *Catch-22,* wrote an absurdist satire about the Air Force in World War II where the commanders were all bumbling incompetents and the protagonist, Yossarian, was always scheming to be sent home. However, Yossarian was caught in the "Catch-22" where the leadership could keep him there at the base off the coast of Italy flying bombing missions for as long as they pleased, despite the fact that the protagonist had met his quota of bombing missions. The novel was written in the late '50s, but its anti-establishment tone did not come out of the Beat literary movement. It was, however, like *Slaughterhouse-Five* and the Beat writings, a part of the underground literature that typified an anti-authoritarian upsurge of expression that grew common by the late '60s.

Stanley Schatt in *Kurt Vonnegut, Jr.,* addresses the similarities in the protagonists of both novels, particularly how the absurdist tone in each book leads to climactic resolutions filled with mental dissonance:

> Yossarian is compelled to think about Snowden's death yet finds it too painful and tries to avoid the memory, so too is a reluctant Billy Pilgrim forced to return again and again to the fire-bombing of Dresden. Only when Yossarian and Billy Pilgrim learn to cope with mankind's inhumanity and the horrors of war are they able to describe the atrocities they have repressed. Billy consistently retreats from Dresden just before the atrocity is to take place until he hears a group of optometrists singing, for the barbershop quartet reminds him of the group of German soldiers who shared the protection of Slaughterhouse-five with the American prisoners during the bombing. [...] [H]is observation or recall of the past incident represents the climax of Vonnegut's novel since it is only after Billy has faced the past that he is able to return to Dresden and live through the holocaust once more. Vonnegut himself had blotted out his memories of the actual fire-bombing of Dresden... [82–83].

This underscores the earlier point that *Slaughterhouse-Five* offers the illusion of being built solely on random juxtaposed images and fragmented scenes that render a spatial meaninglessness. Actually, the repetition of these fragments build and accrete toward this culminating confrontation with the horror of death that is seemingly not deterministic, but atrocious beyond the mind's comprehension. In this sense, *Slaughterhouse-Five*, though overwhelmingly juxtapositional, builds slyly toward an energeic climax, the traditional narrative form where dramatic actualization is rendered through the potential of character and situation. Just as Vonnegut must confront his inability to articulate the horror of Dresden, so must Billy, always so passively surreal, confront in a climactic fashion, Dresden's reality as well. This novel is, ultimately, the story of confronting the horrors in one's own life as well as an imploring cry that mankind must address its own complicity in the horrors of war.

In terms of anti-war sentiment, *Catch-22* and *Slaughterhouse-Five* served as bookends of the decade. *Catch-22* was widely advertised when first published in 1961, but, while initial sales were slow; its popularity grew steadily over the next few years due to word-of-mouth, and the unpopularity of the latest war in Vietnam. According to Heller's 1994 foreword to the novel: "in late summer of 1962, Raymond Walters, on the bestseller page of the Sunday *Times* [...] reported that the underground book New Yorkers seemed to be talking about most was *Catch-22*. (The novel probably was more heavily advertised than any other that year, but it was still underground)" (11).

The term "underground" applies to every book being examined in *The Hippie Narrative*. Even *Stranger in a Strange Land*, though not intended to be a template for communal religion and relationships, became part of the underground scene when its satire on the mainstream churches and sexual mores of the time began to be taken seriously by the earliest hippies. By this point, the book's messages were self-contained and divorced from the sentiments of its conservative author, Robert Heinlein. The term "underground" is often misunderstood to mean clandestine or non-commercial in nature. However, in the '60s an underground press, the underground rock music, or underground rebelliousness meant simply a posture of anti-authoritarian disaffection with the mainstream culture. Rock groups were often phenomenally successful financially, but still part of the underground.

Again, as cited in the opening chapter in *The Beat Generation and the Popular Novel in the United States, 1945–1970*, Thomas Newhouse describes the underground narrative as "the literary response in fiction to the spiritual malaise that grew from dark cold war realities affecting artists and intellectuals immediately after the Second World War, a response that reached its fullest expression in the counterculture of the 1960s" (4). *One Flew Over the Cuckoo's Nest, Sometimes a Great Notion, Been Down So Long It Looks Like Up to Me, Trout Fishing in America, Armies of the Night,* and *Slaughterhouse-Five* are all direct propagators of this specific literary response.

Jess Ritter was a teacher at San Francisco State College University and a frequent contributor to *Rolling Stone Magazine* at the height of Kurt Vonnegut's popularity. Few American campuses witnessed more student turmoil during the Vietnam War era than S.F. State. In his article, "Teaching Kurt Vonnegut on the Firing Line," Ritter points out how: "somewhere in the late 1960's Kurt Vonnegut, Ken Kesey, and Joseph Heller took a generation's consciousness on a sharp left turn down the crooked road to the absurd. Yet it was a recognition of the absurd that was not a surrender to meaninglessness but a wholehearted, raucous Bronx cheer for the false pieties and Aesopean language of rampant technology and the cold war" (35). In this lack of surrender, Ritter points out the structural discontinuities, radical juxtapositions and ironies which surfaced in Vonnegut's fiction through what Ritter calls social surrealism. "Much as William Faulkner created his mythical Yoknapatawpha Country, so Kurt Vonnegut is creating a mythical modern universe. [...] The Planet Tralfamadore suggests technology gone awry, time turned inside out" (38).

Ironically, for this 1973 article, Ritter—in the autobiographical mode of the New Journalism—uses literary realism to establish his case for Vonnegut's social surrealism:

> "Hey, man." Victor has already taken a chair. "Space Daisy tells me you dig Vonnegut, man, you really read all his books? Fahr out!"
>
> "Space Daisy?" I had been reading literary criticism for an evening class.
>
> "Yeah, my old woman. She's in your whatchacallit, 'Language of the '70s' class, man, I been reading the booklist, all that Heller and Southern and Vonnegut and Barthelme. How come you don't have Hesse in there? You gotta get into Hesse's head trips. You ever read *The Sirens of Titan* on acid, man? Wow! [...]

Ritter's hippie character goes on to inform Ritter that he and Space Daisy live in a commune up the hill from the Haight where it's cool, except for a couple dudes snorting coke or shooting meth, but that they are going to split for far northern California in the summer to avoid all the dope and the bad vibes from the city. Even though Ritter, as a hip contributor to *Rolling Stone Magazine,* has a countercultural sensibility, he mocks the anti-intellectual lingo and flakiness of this hippie sitting in his office. At the same time, Ritter captures the back-to-the-land sentiment that was pronounced when he wrote this article in the early '70s. He also lets the reader of his article know that the intelligence and concerns of these hippies was not to be underestimated:

I hear from the Midwest and East Coast that literature people worry: "The young don't read." I don't know what "young" they're talking about. The young I know read—maybe not freshman anthologies or *Silas Marner* or *Harper's*, but Heller, Vonnegut, Hesse, R. Crumb and *Snatch Comix*, McCluhan, Pynchon, Kesey, *The Whole Earth Catalog*, Brautigan, and *Rolling Stone*. In fact they read too much for their Peace of Mind [32–33].

Vonnegut, in the opening of his novel, speaks about his own unsettled mind as an author trying to write *Slaughterhouse-Five*:

I would hate to tell you what this lousy little book cost me in money and anxiety and time. When I got home from the Second World War twenty-three years ago, I thought it would be easy for me to write about the destruction of Dresden, since all I would have to do would be to report what I had seen. And I thought, too, that it would be a masterpiece or at least make me a lot of money since the subject was so big.

But not many words about Dresden came from my mind then—not enough of them to make a book, anyway [8].

Perhaps it took until the arrival of the children's crusade into Vonnegut's imagination before the author could confidently sculpt this masterpiece. Perhaps it took until 1969 and the height of American involvement in the Vietnam War before it would fully resonate with a reading public. As "unstuck in time" as *Slaughterhouse-Five* was, the novel was very much a product of its time at the peak of anti-war unrest in 1969. There was an audience of young people, questioning one war and receptive to hearing a compatible and freshly disturbing take on a war that was almost always treated as good and justly heroic. In this sense, Vonnegut deconstructed the prevailing American disposition toward World War II. This literary work experimented boldly and convincingly to find an alternative narrative form for expressing the absurdities of war and death. From an authorial perspective, this assemblage of the schizophrenic fragments of multiple narratives was not deconstructivist on Vonnegut's part, but brilliantly constructivist—an alternative geodesic vision. He not only tore apart the status quo vision of itself as noble and just, but, more importantly, moved beyond iconoclasm to create a more humane vision in its place.

The real-world story of the hippie phenomenon in 1969 could be said to have reached the peak of its cultural allure. This was the point where the counterculture shifted from its own iconoclastic approach toward the system, toward a more serious vision of creating sustainable alternatives. The Woodstock Music Festival took place in September to several days of peace and love and mud. At Altamont in California in December, a Hell's Angel bludgeoned a man to death as the Rolling Stones played. The demonic communal cult of Charles Manson was responsible for the murder of Sharon Tate. In many respects the hippie phenomenon was seemingly "deconstructing." However, at the same time, many in the counterculture, such as the young hippie talking with Jess Ritter, were earnestly seeking alternative lifestyle solutions. Altamont and Charles Manson were viewed as isolated aberrations to those many hippies who sought out lives anchored in living more peacefully, creatively, and lovingly. For the hardcore, their immediate lives were being wholeheartedly committed to this endeavor.

As the movement diffused into the cultural seams of America, signs of its own fracturing into different spiritual persuasions and lifestyle choices grew more evident. From Tiny Tim to the Hippie Dippy Weatherman, the countercultural phenomenon became easy to lampoon and spoof, a victim, in part, of its own colorful theatricality, but also because its multifaceted dissidence always faced significant mainstream opposition. A hawkish hostility continued to greet the radical anti-war activism. The Weather Underground (or Weathermen), a small group that resorted to bombings to confront the system, was an example of the most extreme manifestation of this activism. Opposition to the war from the growing middle-class, however, including the likes of Vonnegut, precipitated a painfully slow exit policy from Vietnam that ended the draft in 1972, resulted in the peace accords in 1973, but wasn't complete until North Vietnam violated those accords and successfully invaded Saigon in 1975 and forced the U.S. to evacuate its embassy.

On the fringe of American culture, the hardcore hippies ignored the increasingly systematic derision from the mainstream media. And, despite the growing countercultural ire toward the government's seeming intractability on withdrawing from Vietnam, there was also a deliberate transition by many hippies into a more "constructivist" mode. As the 1970's took shape, "The Movement" began to diffuse into multiple movements from New Age to environmentalism to organic to any number of spiritual affiliations. In the early '70s, the hippies were by no means extinct, but actually still growing in numbers. Key aspects of the counterculture—longhair, amplified music and a host of rebellious attitudes— were not only less shocking to the mainstream sensibility, but being assimilated by the larger culture. This process of assimilation is notable in the works of literature examined in the final section of *The Hippie Narrative*.

Act III

Narrative Afterplay

11

Divine Right's Trip (1971)

The Last Whole Earth

We are as gods, and might as well get good at it.
　　　　　　　　−Stewart Brand, The Whole Earth Catalog

Divine Right's Trip is the authentic hippie cross-country bus adventure that Tom Wolfe, with his outsider's vantage in *The Electric Kool-Aid Acid Test*, couldn't quite nail. The limitations of real-life kept Wolfe's creative nonfiction at arm's length from his main characters, Ken Kesey and the Merry Pranksters. Largely, he failed to render them as three-dimensional characters. Gurney Norman, the author of *Divine Right's Trip*, was an insider to the hippie scene and part of the outer circle surrounding Kesey and the Pranksters. Even the Kool-Aid shows up at the end of the *Trip*. Norman's treatment of drugs in his novel, however, is a way to get deeper into his main characters and their journey. Wolfe focuses on the surface flash of LSD and a parade of celebrities when Kesey, Jack Kerouac, Allen Ginsberg, Timothy Leary, The Grateful Dead, The Hell's Angels, Hunter S. Thompson, etc., parade through *The Electric Kool-Aid Acid Test*. In contrast, *Divine Right's Trip* is not the story of celebrity, though Kesey and the Pranksters and other fellow authors from the writer's program at Stanford make cameo appearances near the end of this picaresque hero's quest. This episodic and roguish "folk tale"— Norman's term—is the updated hippie rendition of Jack Kerouac's picaresque beatnik tale, *On the Road*. Except, in *Divine Right's Trip*, the journey moves west to east from California to the Cumberland Mountains of Kentucky instead of primarily from New York to California.

Authors, such as Kesey, Fariña, Brautigan, Heinlein, Wolfe, Mailer, Thompson, Robbins, and Didion, who were born before the "baby boom" period, wrote most of the narratives included in this study. The bulk of hippies were born from 1940 to 1957. Gurney Norman, born in 1937, was no exception to these authors, except that in *Divine Right's Trip* he features a protagonist, D.R. "David Ray" or "Divine Right" Davenport, who is born, roughly, in 1949. The novel takes place in 1970 when D.R. is twenty-one.

The prose exhibits an understated believability and powerful verisimilitude. The fictional narrative is not without touches of absurdity, whimsy, irony and humor, but the palpable vulnerability of the protagonist and his hippie girlfriend, Estelle, give *Divine Right's Trip* its place as the single most accurate narrative rendition of the hippie lifestyle and ethos ever widely published. The key to the "truthful" aura surrounding this novel is in its low-key realism.

In contrast to *Trout Fishing in America* or *Slaughterhouse-Five* with their juxtapositional structures, Norman doesn't stray from the traditionally energeic narrative form with its continuously vivid dream and actualization of the potential of its main characters. The novel is built around the situation of this couple traveling in a wildly painted Volkswagen bus most of the way across North America. Although there are many episodes where the potential for more ramped-up confrontation is established, this never materializes in the way the reader might expect. Such avoidance of dramatic flare-ups helps to heighten the core dynamic—that of the relationship between D.R. and Estelle who are being tested by the fatigue of constant travel, drug use, spiritual diversions, and a youthful unwillingness to openly commit to one another. Norman's deft characterizations of D.R. and Estelle, and of those they encounter, is the strength of this unflashy, but immersive book.

Near the end of the novel, D.R. finds a mangled copy of *The Whole Earth Catalog* and Estelle's book, *Stranger in a Strange Land,* in the back of Urge, his VW bus. The self-referential (postmodernist) humor stems from how the full text of *Divine Right's Trip* was first included inside the *The Last Whole Earth Catalog,* an oversized (11 × 14 inch) publication that came out in 1971. The narrative of *Divine Right's Trip* sprawled along the right hand outer edges of the hefty catalogue. When Norman originally approached publisher Stewart Brand about the idea of incorporating his novel in this way, they had discussed how the narrative could mention the items in the catalogue.

The Whole Earth Catalog was first published by Brand in 1968 as an outgrowth of him selling hip hardware out of the back of a truck to the communes springing up in the outskirts of the Bay Area. The 1971 issue, in which *Divine Right's Trip* was included, was widely distributed. Unlike a catalog of consumer wares only, it highlighted tools it deemed as "appropriate technology" for man to better co-exist on the planet in a non-destructive and more ecologically harmonious manner. There were also ideas for self-education, personal empowerment and a host of suggestions on alternatives to conventional religion, education, business and health care. No other single publication better summed up or promulgated the countercultural attitudes in North America in the late 1960's and '70s. *The Last Whole Earth Catalog*, in which *Divine Right's Trip* was included, sold 1.5 million copies and won the National Book Award for contemporary affairs in 1972.

Norman and Brand were both friends with Kesey and the Pranksters from about 1960 on, and they were an active part of the burgeoning alternative scene that was reaching its height of participation when the 1970's began. Although Norman decided not to risk compromising his narrative with direct plugs for the hip items of commerce in the catalogue, he captured the essence of the hippie counterculture in this narrative. As *Divine Right's Trip* unfolds, the story greatly complements the spirit of *The Last Whole Earth Catalog*, especially at the end of the novel when D.R. discovers his own small direction for "changing the world." The catalogue steered a growing and interested public toward specific ways to embrace the alternative lifestyle. *Divine Right's Trip* took its readers deep inside the lives and minds of two young hippies trying to navigate a "righteous" path that might best honor this alternative approach.

In a 2001 interview with a Kentucky television station, Gurney Norman talked about how the public's sense of the hippie phenomenon is distorted:

> [W]hen the media wants to treat the 1960s, the cultural revolution and the antiwar movements and so forth, it has a list—the media has a list of about 12 iconic figures who did stuff and got themselves registered by the media, in the media. They got in a database of some kind. And so when we think of the '60s, we're always shown pictures of Joan Baez and Abbie Hoffman, and others—you know, familiar people. And yet those guys don't represent the '60s counterculture and social ferment at all. They just are not representative. They only are available to an impatient media that no longer even goes out and tries to report on anything. It all has to, like, stream across the computer now. And those are the images from the '60s that are in the computer. But the '60s were not about that at all. And I could go on. [...]I think of the 1960s as when massive waves of young, earnest people set out to try to find something about themselves and to go join something. And the unknown ones ... You see them; they're in the background of some ... of some of the movies. But I'm kind of against icons because I think that the message is ... stuck. It's not revealing of truth [KET Interview, November 28, 2001].

Divine Right's Trip, however, is intimately revealing of the earnestness of those "massive waves of young" out searching for alternative possibilities. The iconic "peace and love" of the Woodstock Music Festival in upstate New York in September 1969 segued into the Altamont Rock Festival in December of '69 when the Hell's Angels killed a man while the Rolling Stones played. Gurney Norman chooses to establish his narrative in the direct aftermath of this second festival gone awry. Early in

Divine Right's Trip: "Exhaustion had been catching up with them for a long time now. In a way their whole experience since Altamont had been a steady descent into exhaustion, a drop that gained momentum as they went along, like falling" (28). The novel in this way traces the loss of "hippie" innocence through D.R.'s and Estelle's fall and recovery.

Norman's novel captures the internal and external manifestations of this quest by allowing the personal to represent the universal. The story of D.R. is illustrative of a larger social transition in the youth of that time from a reactionary iconoclasm to an alternative constructivism. The larger hippie narrative moved beyond the Bacchanalia with its explosion of psychedelia toward finding a way to engage and change the world as individuals. The novel traces, through its characters, this social reaction to the shortfalls and constraints of mainstream America. The story of D.R. and Estelle evolves into the belief that something tangible, by way of personal lifestyle and adaptation, could be done to improve on the modern insanity of nuclear destruction, environmental rape, and spiritual complacency. To get there, D.R. must cope with his own sanity, his own spiritual struggle for identity when both David Ray and Divine Right stake claim to his essence. This is his most serious "trip," and a heavy dose of LSD precipitates the inner conflict, especially when his inner turmoil and floundering spirit contribute to Estelle's decision to split from him after they arrive in Cincinnati.

Social and cultural historians of the 1960s and '70s can draw superb insight from *Divine Right's Trip.* The fluidity of travel, communication and human networking in the period helped the hippie phenomenon root itself nationwide and diffuse across the country. More than this, the book demonstrates, through its period nuances and the interior perspective of the characters, the profound drive of individual hippies to create an "alternative" way to adapt to American society. This appeal extended beyond the use and abuse of drugs, even though hallucinogens helped facilitate an inner quest for change and contraband was an integral part of the currency of the subculture. Just as significantly, this novel gets at the heart of the societal dynamic whereby the reactionary phenomenon of the hippie was gradually absorbed into the mainstream culture when the best of its ideas and expressiveness were co-opted or commoditized. This is shown in an immediate way when D.R. is accepted into a traditional backwoods community in the Cumberland Mountains. This mainstreaming shows how the counterculture also began to change the dominant culture when many of its values were absorbed.

Gurney Norman only mentions Vietnam in passing, and doesn't let his novel become sidetracked into political, religious or social rants about the ills of the mainstream world, a didactic tendency that was commonplace in countercultural writing from the time. Rather, he stays focused on D.R.'s and Estelle's immediate adventure of "hip" engagement with the "straight" world. Even when D.R. finds his grounding at the end of the journey, this new mission is a culmination of the long quest and a logical outgrowth of the realistic travails of the protagonist's story. Yet, neither does Norman shy away from a realistic portrayal of the surrealism induced by drug use or in depicting an extreme situation of environmental rape that becomes the purpose and "salvation" following D.R.'s metaphorical resurrection.

Like Norman, who grew up in Kentucky, went to California, and then returned, D.R. returns with his hippie bus, after Estelle has left him, to help a dying uncle who lives on the old family farm in the coal country of Appalachia. When confronted with the strip mining practices of the 1960's, he finds them to be even more appalling to the hillbillies and miners he meets there than to his aggrieved hippie sensibility. When D.R. gives a lift to a local miner, the miner describes the devastation:

> Got cows, good garden and a spring, man can live good there if he's willing to work. But they's this outfit owns the coal rights underneath, and they're on their way to get it. Eighty miles long, that bench is. Reminds me of a big sarpent sneaking through the hills, big old eighty mile long snake killing everything in its path. It's that way everywhere around here. Some folks call it the end of time but me, I just call it a bunch of goddamn criminals out tearing up the world [193].

This sets the stage for D.R. to find a purpose in life, but only well into the novel, long after Norman has earned the reader's empathy for this floundering protagonist. Every character Norman introduces along the way is tightly drawn and introduced into the novel for a purpose that relates to the quest of our "alternative" hero.

At the start of the journey, D.R. picks up a hitchhiker late at night in the rain in California. The young man refuses to enter into any sort of conversation. Estelle is asleep in the back of the VW. After a few miles, D.R. gets miffed and tells the mute hitchhiker to get out. As he's getting out, the hitchhiker asks D.R. if he's ever heard of St. George and the Dragon. When D.R. tells him that he hasn't, the guy says that it was far out shit and started walking on the highway back toward where he had started. In this brief scene, the author has established this story as a hero's quest with a beckoning of strange adventures to come.

D.R. loses his temper when he can't find his dope after scrounging for the stash hidden in the chaos of clothes and bags in the back of the bus beside where Estelle is sleeping. Drugs are introduced as part of their adventurous scene.

At Eagle Rock Campground, these hippies unwind. D.R. climbs toward Estelle who is naked and sunning herself on the flat surface of a large boulder in the nearby creek. In this passage, Norman characterizes

D.R.'s attitude toward Estelle, a sentiment that establishes the depth of
their relationship and further develops his character as a hippie:

> [A]s D.R. climbed he thought: climbing for Estelle is climbing for the sun.
> [...] Her skin was naturally dark, a sort of pale olive. [...] Estelle's hips and her
> thighs were too thick for anyone ever to call her figure "beautiful." And her face
> was too much the face of the average girl in a crowd [...]. And yet Estelle was a
> truly beautiful girl. She had dark hair and very large, dark brown eyes. Her
> breasts weren't especially big, or little, or round, or pointy or any of those
> magazine-writer tit-fetish clichés. They were just nice boobs on a nice woman,
> absolutely real like everything else about her. Goddamn, D.R. thought. Tears
> came into his eyes [26–27].

When D.R. approaches Estelle, the author establishes how genuine
his attraction is for her. There is an early feminist sensibility in how he
doesn't objectify her or buy into the "plastic" treatment of women that
typified the era. Compared to the early '60s and the way Kesey wrote
about the women in *One Flew Over the Cuckoo's Nest* and *Sometimes A Great
Notion,* this scene demonstrates how perceptions of women by many men
were undergoing significant change by the beginning of the 1970s.

While the two make love, the Lone Outdoorsman, depicted as an
ultraconservative redneck and self-appointed protector of the campground, spies on them. He calculates how he might ambush these kids.
The author has set the stage for a confrontation. The Lone Outdoorsman waits until the youngsters are back at their bus and goes over to
them. Instead of accosting them, he invites them over for barbequed
steaks. The hippies, hungry, readily accept.

The scene is believably rendered, yet it violates the expectation of
the type of food a hippie will eat, or what happens when rednecks and
hippies meet (such as in the movie, *Easy Rider*). Despite his powerful
recreational toys and militaristic outlook, the Lone Outdoorsman is
shown to be a generous and lonely individual who comes to like these
kids, even though he has no idea that they've shown up to dinner stoned.
The believable manner in which the author breaks through the perceived wall between the straight world and the hip world, is at the essence
of this novel's effectiveness. This motif is repeated throughout the novel.

When D.R. enters a comatose state after taking a heavy dose of acid,
Estelle drives. She pulls over, but, exhausted, can't drive any more toward
their destination in St. Louis where they are to meet Eddie who owes
D.R. some money. At the gas station she meets the Greek, a spiritual
guru who only eats walnuts and acidophilus milk and believes that mucus
is the primary enemy of Western man. Against her better judgment, she
offers the Greek and his girlfriend a ride so that she can sleep while the
man drives. In the bus, the Greek talks non-stop making it hard for
Estelle to sleep in back. The talking wakes up D.R. who is still so far gone

on LSD that he literally can't talk, though he is mesmerized by the stream of philosophy coming from this strange new driver's mouth.

In this segment, the author introduces the monumental explosion of spiritual openness that typified the counterculture:

> The thing that particularly bugged Estelle was the way Divine Right was zapping on the stupid Greek. There he'd been in a stupor for eight hours, sometimes huddled in her arms like a baby, and as soon as he comes out of it what does he do but fall in love with the first wise man to come along and lay a heavy trip on him. [...]
>
> When he was clear and cool and up and unhassled, D.R.'s mind was as beautiful to see in operation as anybody's that she knew. [...] As far as Estelle could see there were at least twice as many wisdom pushers as dope dealers in the world, so how come the cops never got uptight about them [70–71].

Estelle had seen D.R. like this so many times before. This trait of D.R.'s not to trust his own instincts, and to fly off wildly into the spiritual hinterlands, is established as the essence of the conflict facing this young couple. The paradox of how open the two could be to the wildness of the counterculture yet so circumspect in communicating their feelings toward each other is both highly realistic and ironic. At the same time, Norman has let the reader know how good Estelle and D.R. are for one another and, to his credit, he doesn't fall prey to sensationalizing their conflict. This is the understated aspect of this novel that works so well to propel the narrative forward in a way that generates empathy for the characters.

At one point, Estelle gets so tired of the man's rap, which is always pushing the edges of sanity, that she forces him to pull over at a rest area. The Greek repulses her. At the rest area, even the Greek's girlfriend takes off with another family that had stopped there. The Greek is unfazed. The Greek believes that people should strive to lose the name given them at birth, to completely forget it. This concept of one's name will play into D.R.'s looming identity crisis that stretches between him thinking of himself as the hippie, Divine Right, or by his family name, David Ray. Angrily, Estelle takes some downers and crashes in back while the Greek and D.R. are in front. The Greek gets out of the V.W. at his destination in Oklahoma.

The author effectively grounds the story inside D.R.'s quest, but, laudably, doesn't attempt to address all the spiritual diversity of the counterculture. Norman's characterization of the Greek is enough to sufficiently portray this openness to all things metaphysical and outside the realm of traditional Judeo-Christian theology. When D.R. hooks up with his family in Kentucky, the author comes back to this motif by showing how the eastern and western approaches to spirituality are not as irreconcilable as they might seem to be. From the Bible's Book of James he quotes: "a double-minded man is unstable in all his ways," and from the Book of Tao, "the surest test if a man be sane is if he accepts life whole as it is" (302). This duality of wholeness or double-mindedness—not the acid—is the essence of Divine Right's uncoiling trip.

In the section of the book immediately following the departure of the Greek, the scene opens in St. Louis. Eddie, the friend who they are traveling across the U.S. to meet because he owes money to D.R., is dead. Something about a shootout in an alley, cops and a bust, but the author doesn't digress into the specifics. D.R. and Estelle are in the corner of the living room with several of the drug dealers in St. Louis present. D.R. has gone from mute to barely stuttering his words now; Estelle still feels distanced from him. Everyone is grieving Eddie's death and sharing hits from a nitrous oxide canister and watching three televisions at once including the picture only of the evangelist Billy Graham on the big color screen with a voice on meditation blasting from the smaller black & white set. The juxtaposition fills the room in comic overdub. When D.R. goes into the bedroom to talk with Eddie's girlfriend, they embrace, consolingly, and lie down on the mattress to kiss, but don't have sex. With Estelle in the other room, this seems like it might be a plot development, the potential for significant conflict. But, the author violates expectations again. Estelle remains aloof and seemingly unaware of this bedroom event. The author seems to want to show the love-the-one-you're-with openness of the hippies, but chooses not to test this proclivity on the relationship between D.R. and Estelle, despite the opportunity presented here. The point of the scene has more to do with D.R.'s distance from his own instincts and feelings than it does with how Estelle might react.

When Norman decides to begin the St. Louis episode in this scene with the local dealers mourning Eddie's passing, he keeps the focus on D.R.'s and Estelle's newfound estrangement. D.R. is still not recovered from his heavy LSD trip. The author shows a tension between rival dealers when one of them hogs the nitrous gas. The scene in the alley when Eddie dies was gruesome, but no one talks about it. The dozen or so people gathered there are cool, but no one talks much about the cops or the bust or the obvious risks of their trade. Eddie's death is simply a bummer, part of the risk. Norman shows how widespread the drug trafficking network is—Eddie was planning to go to Mexico to score some bricks of grass before he was killed. The author portrays how integral drugs were to the underground of the counterculture.

The author doesn't go into any significant detail, but hints that the main reason D.R. bought the V.W. Bus was to transport drugs. The author uses this one immediate scene in Eddie's apartment to paint the druggie world, the omnipresent paranoia, the turf rivalry, the covert discreetness, the surrealism of the highs, yet he doesn't pass judgment or mock the scene. He lets the scene unfold with concrete details and realistic nuances. This is key to D.R.'s trip, the part where his Bacchanalia and need for financial sustenance coalesce, and where his life, as it has been, begins to unravel.

From the standpoint of crafting this hero's quest, this scene is pivotal. Norman allows it to pool in one place. Leading into the scene, there is a palpable sense that D.R. and Estelle are placing too much significance in meeting up with Eddie and collecting the money he owes D.R. The reader's expectation is that something will go wrong and they won't get the money, but seemingly because Eddie will stiff them rather than pay up. Instead, we have an insurmountable reason why D.R. and Estelle are left broke. This impels D.R. to contact his family. This is where he transitions from counterculture to the mainstream, where Divine Right must confront David Ray. He is able to get money wired to him from his sister in Cincinnati. As one question of inconsistency in the novel, it's logical to wonder why D.R. didn't bother to contact Eddie to have him wire the money he owed to California without them having to drive to St. Louis to get it in person. On the other hand, the sojourn of a hippie was not always rational.

In any event, D.R. and Estelle leave St. Louis for Cincinnati. D.R.'s voice gradually returns without the stutter, but Estelle still won't talk with him. She is detached, but doesn't seem bothered when D.R. asks her to wait at the bus depot while he goes to visit his sister's family. They talk again by phone in the afternoon and she still doesn't seem bothered. He goes to eat dinner at his sister's. When he shows up that evening at the bus depot, the whole day has passed and Estelle is nowhere to be found. Despondent, D.R. returns to his sister's house and sleeps for a full day. Estelle has split. Over halfway through the novel, this is when D.R., with his sister and family gone to church, takes the call:

> [T]he phone rang and woke him up and when it turned out to be God Himself calling to summon D.R. to Kentucky, alertness spread through him like a rush.
>
> God was calling in the guise of Mrs. Godsey, Uncle Emmit's neighbor down in Finley County, but Divine Right had no doubt who it really was [171].

At this point in the novel, the author has set up the conflict and dynamic at multiple levels: D.R. in inner turmoil, Estelle gone, the promise of something intangible in Kentucky on the horizon.

Interestingly, one might also expect D.R.'s straitlaced family to be a source of new conflict. We come to learn that D.R.'s mother remarried after his father's death, but is also dead. D.R. is very close to his sister and brother-in-law who are a few years older. They are both born-again Christians, but assume that whatever D.R. was into was just the type of "youthful outlawry" that had been a phase for the brother-in-law in the '50s.

On the way to the family homestead in Kentucky, D.R. reminisces about going there as a young kid with his father every weekend. He gives a ride to a miner as he nears his destination. The miner gives him a brief recent history of the area, including the recent strip mining. Before the strip mining, the men had been out of work. With the people hungry, big roving gangs of men had been stopping traffic, and shootings were commonplace: "now you take this Happy Pappy program. Take all this welfare stuff. It ain't nothing but sop to keep the people from acting up" (191).

When D.R. arrives at Mrs. Godsey's store near where his uncle lives, he is also greeted warmly, even though the elderly woman later says to another woman in her store that, "[y]ou'd think he was one of them hipeyes on television to look at him" (217).

Anne Caudill in an Eastern Kentucky University website article on Gurney Norman, quotes from two Kentucky book review articles that came out shortly following the publication of *Divine Right's Trip:*

> Jim Wayne Miller had this to say about it in the July 31, 1972, issue of *The Courier Journal*: "The amazing thing is how this unlikely mix of California freaks and East Kentucky mountain people inhabit the same book without destroying its credibility ... It works because Gurney Norman may be the only person on the planet who genuinely belongs to both scenes."

And,

> In an interview with Shirley Williams in *The Courier Journal & Times* in 1972, Norman calls Divine Right "a modern frontiersman." Gurney Norman was a frontiersman himself. He was the first to combine the trends of the 60's with the steadfast heritage of the mountains of eastern Kentucky. *Divine Right's Trip* is unique because it dares to blend two opposing forces and make them real to both worlds.

With his insider's pulse on the nature of the hippie phenomenon, the author of *Divine Right's Trip* was indeed a participant in both the hippie scene as well as a part of the East Kentucky hill people scene where he grew up. Yet, his ability to reconcile the two stemmed from his astute observations that play out through the novel, that the two worlds were not as opposite as it might first appear. At the website for Appalachianbooks.com, there is a description of why the forces alluded to in above the review were not so oppositional.

> Many of the characters in *Divine Right's Trip* are stoned much of the time, and they swear constantly. Deep down, however, they have the greatest respect for the old-fashioned rural life style of their forbearers of previous generations. They are rebelling against their parents' generation but not against their grandparents. They want America to skip the generation which brought the world the atomic bomb, the multi-national corporation and the substitution of formula for breast milk. They want their country to get back to a way of life which cares more about the land and people and less about technology and profits. [http://www.appalachianbooks.com/Authors/Gurney%20Norman.htm].

So, if Norman Mailer can consider himself a Left Conservative in *The Armies of the Night*, then the hippie phenomenon, in its back-to-the-land manifestation especially, was similarly one of a, seemingly contradictory, radical traditionalism. This description, more than Leftism, can be viewed as the more accurate common denominator of hippies.

The bulk of hippies were not New Leftist, but certainly reactionary when protesting the war or other failings of the establishment. The hippies embraced the concept of personal freedom as vibrantly as any Americans had ever before. This went along with the distrust of authority in a system that they believed had allowed its technology and military to run amok, a direction well noted by Mailer in *The Armies of the Night* when he talks about technology-land and corporation-land controlling contemporary America.

The radical traditionalism of the hardcore hippies, with a freewheeling impetus that rolled across the moral high ground of the late '60s, best explains the era's great and terrible vitality. This was a Dionysian phenomenon filled with drug-taking and conspiratorial suspicions of the corporate and government leadership. And the hippies were also filled with an expressive hopefulness. With the liberties allowed in America, the revolution was not against the structure of its democracy. This radical traditionalism was linked to a revolution of consciousness in how a person should engage his or her own mind, spirit, body, family, community, and environment. In this, the hippie sincerely believed in the possibility of creating a more harmonious way to live.

Drug use was the most radical feature of the hippie counterculture. Communalism was arguably the most traditional in how it harkened back to the extended family and away from the contemporary patterns of privatized, single-family living arrangements. Illicit drugs were usually rationalized by contrasting such consumption with the straight-world indulgences in alcohol, nicotine, caffeine, prescription uppers, downers and opiates. The hippie wondered why these were acceptable when their preferred drugs were not. The dissidence of the hippie stemmed from this and other hypocrisies of "the system." The traditionalism of the hippie was rooted in a love of personal liberty and a respect for a more caring way of life when things weren't so technocratic or institutionalized.

Gurney Norman appreciated this, and, after D.R. arrives to help his Uncle during the man's last days, D.R. must inveigh himself to the constraints of a community that was very traditionalist. Yet, there is still the question of inner demons. After his first meeting with Mrs. Godsey, Divine Right runs ahead of David Ray on the path to his uncle's house. At this point in the novel, such a blatant depiction of schizophrenia has been earned through the narrative buildup of D.R.'s inner tension and confusion. The author has gradually taken the reader to this moment of reckoning where the surrealistic depictions legitimately reflect D.R.'s interior chaos.

Divine Right disappears inside an abandoned mine and engages in vicious combat with the dragon deep inside. Norman allows D.R.'s schizophrenic manifestation to take over this short portion of the novel. This part of the hero's quest is the shedding of the scales and a spiritual rebirth. Below the bridge, "both streams were yellow now, and acid filled, and rusty from the mining that had killed the hills and the waters all around" (202). D.R. runs ahead of David and into an old house. David then chases D.R. into an old mine shaft where the two battle:

> There is David, lurking in the shadows of the ledge. [...] My stomach turns, my hair feels wild, but my adoration of the light remains serene. It's only David's eyes, and lower forehead. The rest is monster, the mouth of dragon teeth, [...] He's the monster guardian of the light [207].

Then the two battle into the depths:

> He stabbed again,[...]. Black blood spurted and darkened the churning water as D.R.'s own mind darkened into sleep. In his death throes the dragon plunged, carrying D.R.'s body and its own down through endless fathoms of the deep [209].

This is D.R.'s climactic moment, his born-again resurrection that allows him, as the hero, to find his home and his peace.

From this point in the novel, there is no more mention in the novel of D.R. getting high, except naturally. The neighbor, Leonard Godsey, teaches him how to work with his hands, how to take care of the rabbits that D.R.'s uncle left him. D.R. learns how to swing a hammer and build. D.R. becomes neither Divine Right or David Ray, but, seemingly, the best of both personas. His dissociated selves have been reconciled. And, here on the devastated remnants of a family farm, the revelation comes to him. D.R. decides to take over a strategy started by his longhaired hillbilly uncle who is dying. He will finish Emmit's project to reclaim garden soil by raising rabbits for manure and with worms to help this process.

Appalachia is a land of moonshiners and bible-toters. In Kentucky, D.R. seems to have gravitated beyond an abuse of drugs. He is also still open to the spiritual mysteries of life. He finds common ground in discussing religious mysteries with Mrs. Godsey. The neighborly helpfulness and sense of extended family he finds in this rural mountain community were what D.R. was lacking in his life:

> And he walked with Leonard leading the horse up Trace Creek, the others coming behind, not the old folks, not Mrs. Godsey nor Mr. Olney, just those who could make it in the sun over the broken road, and then across the broken hillside and up the rugged slope past yellow, yellow earth of churned up land.
> He helped them lower the coffin down into the grave [247].

Emmit has died. D.R. was there as a survivor, as one of these people to help carry on. The prosperity and progress enjoyed by most of that generation of World War II with its sense of technological invincibility had all but by-passed the mountain folk of Eastern Kentucky. "Environmentalism" as a term was only beginning to have currency in the mainstream lexicon in 1971, but a growing concern over not polluting the skies, poisoning the water, or desecrating the land went far beyond a hippie sentiment. The "fathoms of burden" bulldozed from the mountaintops of these Cumberland hills fouled the creeks and leveled the dales. This grotesque treatment of the land was not viewed by the locals as modern man's divine right. D.R. shared the outrage with his newfound kin. But, even if modern technology had despoiled the beloved mountain landscape, D.R., through his uncle's vision to create a garden patch on what little area was left unscathed on the original eighty acres, found a reason to be hopeful, a conviction for his life.

He had found his place, now he wanted Estelle back; she was worthy now to welcome into his family, if only she would come. The picaresque wanderings of this rogue were over. David Ray and Divine Right had joined. D.R. is neither, but both, like a dialectically synthesized new man. The Magic Rabbit enterprise was about to begin.

Even though reclaiming garden-sized plots of soil was an infinitesimal contribution when compared to ravages of the strip-mining, the nurturing rather than exploitative philosophy had a contagious effect. In subsequent years, coalmining operations were required to restore topsoil and vegetation after strip mining and to prepare environmental impact assessments before extracting the subsurface minerals. The political battle between extractive and ecological interests, of course, is showing no signs of abating, but an environmental sensibility began to surface as a significant movement in around 1970, which was also the year of the first Earth Day. The radical traditionalism of the hippies, as seen with D.R., was integral to this shift in a broader cultural attitude toward the environment.

As literature, *Divine Right's Trip* is traditional, not radically experimental; even the surrealism surrounding D.R.'s drug taking and psychic schism served to move the traditional plot forward. The author doesn't interrupt the continuous and vivid fictional dream, except near the end when Gurney Norman interjects himself into the story to tell the reader that it is he, the author, who goes up to the commune near San Francisco to find Estelle and gets her to a phone to talk to D.R. in Kentucky. In this way Norman is having fun with the New Journalism that was growing so prevalent. While slightly distracting, it also enhances the verisimilitude of the story by making the reader wonder if D.R. and Estelle are real people. Whether the characters are based on real individuals or composite characterizations from real people or completely fabricated, the omniscient manner in which the author enters the minds of D.R. and Estelle, renders their treatment as fictional. Even if loosely based on actual people, Norman's authorial projections are crafted to serve a larger purpose, to portray, through the experiences and perspectives of these individuals, the grander phenomenon of the hippie experience.

The author also pays homage to his own countercultural friends when his Kentucky characters are named after Norman's fellow Kentuckians who had also gone to California to write in the Stanford Program. Two-thirds of the way into the novel, at the small community store, Norman introduces Wendell Hall and Barry Berry, named after poet James Baker Hall and environmental writer Wendell Berry; Old Mr. Callahan is from Ed Callahan, another member of the Merry Prankster circle of friends. On the same page he talks about "promotional material from the Stewart Kesey Soap Company" (213), perhaps as a way to fulfill, in part, his original agreement with *Whole Earth Catalog* publisher Stewart Brand, and to get his friend Ken into the story, as well. "Ken and Faye and Babbs and Gretch and Hassler and Paula and Zodiac and Sky and Hagen" of the Pranksters make a cameo appearance at the end of the story as well.

Divine Right's Trip is a novel with fully actualized fictional characters that serve, metaphorically, the much larger countercultural scene. These young hippies are more representative of the wider hippie phenomenon than the higher profile people mentioned in the paragraph above. Norman, as an author who was well trained at Stanford in the rudiments of literary craft, selected his secondary characters carefully to create a rounded portrait of the workings of the counterculture. For example, the hitchhiking scenes were particularly representative of the fluidity and movement of the hippies. It was relatively easy to move about the country with little cash, at least significantly easier in 1970 than in recent years where the fear of harm has greatly limited this mode of travel. Even when Estelle leaves D.R., she hitchhikes as a lone female back to Oregon and California.

The Lone Outdoorsman establishes these hippies against the backdrop of a redneck world, and surprises the reader with the common ground he creates there. This foreshadows the treatment D.R. will receive in Kentucky. Ironically, the Greek, who is quite hippie, stirs up a cauldron of tension in the relationship between Estelle and D.R. This again violates the expectation of such an encounter among peaceniks. In the section of the novel when D.R. and Estelle are in St. Louis, the reader sees that Gurney Norman is not writing a travelogue. The author knows how to make his dramatic situations adhere to the development of his main characters, and keeps them from getting sidetracked.

Later, it is never explained why a wealthy Anaheim Flash is so willing to front D.R. a gas credit card or a hundred dollars a month. Norman mentions Owsley County in the novel. Augustus Owsley Stanley III, the most famous LSD manufacturer of the '60s, had a Kentucky grandfather who was a U.S. Senator. This county is named after his family. Anaheim Flash is tightly linked to D.R., but while the author wants it to seem like benevolence, The Flash is tightly connected with D.R. in past dealings. Was D.R. a mule for the Flash's acid, or was this man simply a wealthy eccentric who relished the psychedelic scene of friends? Late in the book at D.R.'s new home in Kentucky, Anaheim Flash shows up from California in a silver space-age outfit driving a Lotus sports car.

At D.R.'s party, "the Captain, an utter freak in purple velvet and long mustache and a conductor's hat too small for his shaggy head held a tape recorder mike in front of their mouths and [...] recorded [...] at the Kool-Aid table [...] Elmer the mailman rapping with a leather and denim freak from San Diego" (297). This is part of the novel's denouement that raises many interesting questions about what had seemingly been a simple life led by D.R. As a whole though, Norman keeps his novel very well reined in and doesn't allow the narrative to diverge from D.R.'s core story. Author John Updike, in a review of *Divine Right's Trip* for *The New Yorker* magazine, called the book "a fictional explication of the hopeful new consciousness come to birth" (www.edmcclanahan.com).

Divine Right/David Ray finds a home in Kentucky. He's a widely connected hippie with Appalachian roots that craves an inner centering and a communal network of friends and family, both conventional and countercultural. In *Divine Right's Trip,* the author earns this sense of completion, and this integration of worlds, both psychically and socially. As a snapshot of the counterculture circa 1970, this traditionally crafted novel shows, as well as any, how the hippie phenomenon, with its values and sentiments, was diffusing into the rural enclaves of America. As a genuine hippie narrative, the realism of this novel is unsurpassed.

12

Fear and Loathing in Las Vegas (1971)

Going "Gonzo"

Hunter S. Thompson was a fixture of the counterculture as a writer and self-described drug dilettante, but arguably never a hippie. Thompson's jaded and blunt sense of the ironic in *Fear and Loathing in Las Vegas: A Savage Journey to the Heart of the American Dream* portrays the drug culture in a separate light from the utopianism and spiritual seeking that also helped define the era. The author exposes a taboo indulgence in illicit substances to comic effect and portrays himself and his sidekick/ attorney in the book as wasted druggies out to get one over on Sin City, a place that is simultaneously a bastion of law and order and the American capital of sex shows, plentiful booze, quick marriage, easy divorce, and legal gambling. In 1971, Thompson and his attorney aren't outlaws, but crazed heads on a bona fide journalistic mission in a town that loathed this type of drugged-out sin. The loathing, over the course of the book, is reciprocated.

This narrative also pushed the boundaries of the New Journalism beyond what Capote, Wolfe, Mailer or Thompson himself wrote in the late '60s. In *Fear and Loathing in Las Vegas,* the author filters the story through his drug-addled mind. Unlike Wolfe's or Mailer's accounts of the counterculture, Thompson was fully immersed in the '60s drug scene and offers a first person rendition of himself as a jaded druggie/journalist. The neon world of Vegas and America-at-large are strangely illuminated when viewed through the prism of his substance-altered brain. Unlike *The Armies of the Night* or *The Electric Kool-Aid Acid Test,* where the narratives stick to the "journalistic" assignment of a war protest or a series of acid pranks, *Fear and Loathing* has little to do with reporting on the Mint "400" off-road race or the conference on drug enforcement which Thompson has been hired to cover. In this crazed journalism, we never come to learn who won the race or very much of what occurred at the Conference. The story is much more about Hunter S. Thompson's drug-warped attempts to make sense of his assignment via the American dream of Vegas, which turns into both an indictment of his own sanity and that of the broader culture. James Stull in his chapter on Hunter S. Thompson in the book, *Literary Selves,* notes that:

> While Thompson's journalistic and metaphorical selves teeter on the brink of absorption by mainstream culture, he also defines himself as a countercultural model, an emblematic figure who endorses and gives life to a repertoire of unorthodox practices and beliefs [...]. Thompson thrives in this marginal area that exists between civilization and anarchy. Thompson, as a romantic, feels most alive when the self exists precariously between ecstasy and annihilation, when he takes his body to the "Edge" as he calls it, through taking drugs or driving ... [94].

While it can be argued that Thompson was too cynical to ever be a romantic, it's never clear when Thompson, a.k.a. Raoul Duke, is telling us objective details or embellishing events and perspectives for comic and surrealistic effect. In his never-can-be-certain world between delusional paranoia and bliss, or hung-over crankiness, Thompson coins his style of writing, "Gonzo Journalism," a self-delineated genre of one, since it is made up of only his own bizarre and unrestrained work.

Blitzed on a spectrum of illegal substances, midway into the book Thompson and his equally stoned attorney cover the National District Attorneys Conference on Narcotics and Dangerous Drugs. Playing off this hilarious paradox, the author's eye is both absurdist and acerbic as he constantly mines the American landscape for veins of political and social hypocrisy. Equally jaundiced is his lack of personal responsibility for rental cars, hotel rooms, and the publisher's expense account that are royally abused in the wake of the good, crazed fun. Or as the author was quoted to say: "We took enough speed to keep Hitler awake in the bunker for fifty days and enough acid to make him think he was in the Austrian Alps" (Perry, 158). Thompson's narrative is replete with such comic terror and his penchant for outlandish, original and on-the-mark imagery is the strength of his prose. A story may be in its telling, but after this Gonzo-soaked ride, it's tough to stomach Thompson's assertion that the cops and businesses and magazine publishers and politicians are the only "swine," and not these two drugged-out hedonists. But such is the edgy, damning, self-implicating humor of Hunter S. Thompson.

Along for the ride with Thompson is his 300-pound "Samoan" attorney, who in real life was Oscar Zeta Acosta, a 250-pound Chicano activist/lawyer and fellow drug-indulged counterculturalist. The relationship is far from sacrosanct, but becomes a vehicle for Thompson to expose the entrenched racism of the era. As active participants in the counterculture, Thompson harkens back to that short window of time in the Bay Area before psychedelia was discovered by the huge influx of kids who would be dubbed "hippies." His "golden period" extended from about 1963 to 1966 when a hip assortment of drugs had supplanted the booze and tranquilizers of the '50s era. LSD was not yet illegal. In *Fear and Loathing* Thompson says "[t]here was madness in any direction, at any hour" (67), and he was in with the biggest partiers, such as the Merry Pranksters or the Hell's Angels. Thompson even arranged a party at Kesey's place that included these two very different rebellious groups. The author wrote about it in *Hell's Angels: A Strange and Terrible Saga,* published in 1967.

Hell's Angels, along with Truman Capote's *In Cold Blood,* was one of the first full books to employ what would be called "The New Journalism." Tom Wolfe borrowed Thompson's tapes and notes about this biker/acidhead party of Kesey's so he could write his own chapter on it in *The Electric Kool-Aid Acid Test,* published in 1968. But compared to Wolfe, who wrote as though he were a fly on the wall, Thompson was fully immersed in his subject matter. His text, even though the drugs and comic caricatures had him straying from the factual, was autobiographical.

In *Fear and Loathing in Las Vegas,* Thompson also acknowledges that this book marks the end of an era. He talks about a sense of sparks flying, about how what they were doing was right and that they were winning:

> And that, I think, was the handle—that sense of inevitable victory over the forces of Old and Evil. Not in any mean or military sense; we didn't need that. Our energy would simply *prevail.* [...] We had all the momentum; we were riding the crest of a high and beautiful wave ...
> So now, less than five years later, you can go up on a steep hill in Las Vegas and look West, and with the right kind of eyes you can *see* the high-water mark— that place where the wave finally broke and rolled back [68].

Discussing something as amorphous as "culture" is challenging, but the use of the tide as metaphor is largely apt. In the case of the counterculture though, it could be said that a maelstrom of multiple currents ripped and changed the waters of American society unlike any typical ebb and flow. Also, the water that flowed onto the beachhead in those years was not the same as the water that rolled back out.

Hunter S. Thompson has a keen eye for spoofing specific aspects of the mainstream culture that are contradictory or "Evil." Within this narrative he occasionally picks up the newspaper and reads. The articles serve to provide a satirical context to his sanity-testing sojourn through Vegas. There is Nixon's invasion of Laos; a report on all the G.I. drug deaths in Vietnam; an article on the torturing of "slopes" (or Asians) in the war, which is deemed as being justified in the mind of the torturer because they are "slopes"; or Muhammad Ali being sentenced to five years by the US Supreme Court for "*refusing* to kill 'slopes'" (74). These examples of the world-at-large are juxtaposed with a protagonist who is loaded to the gills, paranoid, in possession of an unregistered .357 magnum handgun, and the renter of a red convertible still packed full of drugs.

Thompson is keenly aware of the risk of trying to pull off a '60s style drug trip in this city. The Nevada billboard at the edge of town warns of 20 years for possession of marijuana, or life in prison for selling it. Thompson tells the reader that he doesn't expect any mercy as a "criminal freak" on The Strip. He compares Las Vegas to the Army: "the shark ethic prevails—eat the wounded. In a closed society where everybody's guilty, the only crime is getting caught. In a world of thieves, the only final sin is stupidity" (72).

Again, his assignments as a journalist are tangential to Thompson's recurrence of paranoia about getting busted. This establishes the core tension sustaining the narrative. His prevailing ethic seems to be that if the whole world is corrupt, then he's going to have a higher time than all these fools as he wades through this sea of corruption. This is an example of how the drug scene of the period exacerbated the "us vs. them" gulf between those in the counterculture and those in the mainstream. The author, who is as much an expert as any on the drug scene, points out how the cops were several years behind the times in their war on drugs. "These poor bastards didn't know mescaline from macaroni" (143). Thompson also states how the cops of 1970 were woefully unaware of drug trends: "the popularity of psychedelics has fallen off so drastically that most volume dealers no longer even handle quality acid or mescaline except as a favor to special customers: mainly jaded, over-thirty drug dilettantes—like me, and my attorney" (201).

Thompson's comic use of exaggerated, drug-riddled prose is impressively sustained, but reading *Fear and Loathing in Las Vegas* shows that the official approach to the "drug problem" never substantially changed through the '60s and beyond, but worked to catch up with an exploding problem. Kesey and Leary were both sent to jail for marijuana in the mid–'60s. Joan Didion in her 1967 article "Slouching Toward Bethlehem" calls the young hippies in the Haight, "the probation generation" because of all the busts there. LSD was only legal because it was too new to be criminalized. In a 1970 article from *Rolling Stone*, Thompson describes how he lived a block away from Haight Street for a couple of years until "the end of '66 [when] the whole neighborhood had become a cop-magnet and a bad sideshow" ("The Battle of Aspen," *Rolling Stone* October 1, 1970). This compared with 1964 where, in a different article, Thompson described how there were so many heads in Haight-Ashbury that drug use was ignored. He describes the Haight as a magical forty-block neighborhood from '64 to '66. ("The 'Hashbury' Is the Capital of the Hippies," *New York Times Magazine*, May 14, 1967). What Thompson calls the "Great San Francisco Acid Wave" swelled before the authorities could see it coming and it crested when law enforcement was struggling to react.

In the '70s some state and local governments did come to decriminalize marijuana, or tacitly avoid prosecuting its growing use, but, over time, the official trend with drugs was to engage in a "war" on its domestic use, with only slight differentiation between the "soft" drug of marijuana or the "hard" stuff, such as speed, cocaine, opiates or LSD. The drug scene at the domestic enforcement level and in global drug trafficking was fraught with selective prosecution and heinous government corruption, something the author would be quick to point out, but the debauchery exemplified in *Fear and Loathing in Las Vegas* by Thompson and his attorney argues more for criminalization than otherwise.

Thompson's style, however, is to take salvos at the mainstream, while cloaking his personal behavior in high risk but comic exoneration. It scares him to the core, but he is willing to face punishment for exercising his personal freedom to take any drug he pleases ... though he has no intention of getting caught. He is so outrageously upfront about his drug indulgences that the reader believes Thompson when he relentlessly attacks hypocrisy, especially the fascist tendencies he sees in American big government and law enforcement. The author, as journalist, wields a politico's sense of a political answer to keep the corruption of "the system" at bay. In this, he is motivated not so much to win, but to not completely lose. He asserts that America owes it to its children to move beyond a "crippled self-image as something better than a nation of panicked sheep" (213). Paul Perry in *Fear and Loathing: The Strange and Terrible Saga of Hunter S. Thompson* states that, "Thompson's theme, the Death of the American Dream, began in the sixties and it is serious, political, and personal, a prophet's cry. To the extent that it is political, it is about the decay of liberal hopes" (xii).

Despite Thompson's disaffection and anti-authoritarian posture, he is too cynical and jaded to have ever bought into the utopianism of the '60s. He relishes having been a part of the "Great San Francisco Acid Wave" and believed it reasonable that "the energy of a whole generation [would come] to a head in a long fine flash" (65, 67). However, he's not sure whether or not it meant anything on a grander scale. It was something, he says, that was hard to understand at the time and doesn't actually explain what happened. Yet, the experience was potent for the individual and the culture. Moreover, Thompson and his attorney "have never been able to accept the notion—often espoused by reformed drug abusers and especially popular among those on probation—that you can get a lot higher without drugs than with them" (63). This is a fair question, but there is little indication that Thompson, with his fixation on guns and speed and induced euphoria, ever delved—drug-free or deeply—into spiritual or meditative realms to be in a drug-free position to diligently test this hypothesis through his own experience.

Instead, this narrative features a protagonist at the cutting edge of the drug scene who comes to Vegas with his attorney and a trunk full of grass, mescaline, blotter acid, cocaine, a galaxy of pills, tequila, rum, Budweiser, ether and amyls. Drug expert that he is, Thompson claims that "consciousness expansion went out with LBJ" (202). He skewers Timothy Leary's trip for having taken too many others down with him:

> All those pathetically eager acid freaks who thought they could buy Peace and Understanding for three bucks a hit. But their loss and failure is ours, too. What Leary took down with him was the central illusion of a whole life-style that he helped create ... a generation of permanent cripples, failed seekers, who never understood the essential old-mystic fallacy of the Acid Culture: the desperate assumption that somebody—or at least some *force*—is tending that Light at the end of the tunnel [178–179].

What Thompson calls a "desperate assumption" is at the essence of most religious belief, certainly in no way limited to the Acid Culture. Clearly, this is where Thompson parts company with most hippies, the spiritual manifestations of the counterculture, and all those who believe in a higher realm or "Light."

Perhaps the central illusion was not *if there is or isn't a higher force*, but that most of the fellow humans in the same American society in the mid–'60s, would refuse to condone a new array of drugs, one in particular—LSD—that purported to offer a shortcut to enlightenment. Moreover, it was precisely the sort of delusional and destructive behavior exemplified by Thompson and his attorney in the hotels of Vegas—when witnessed by the powers-that-be on a much larger scale—that contributed to continued prohibitions on drugs. Opposing this perspective were hosts of unrepentant drug users in the '60s who railed at the hypocrisy of a system that tolerated excessive drinking, smoking or anything the doctor might prescribe, but treated every other substance as societal threats to be prosecuted with prison sentences. Many heads openly endorsed the drugs they enjoyed. This was the most visible impasse between the straight and hip culture and the one that, to this day, frames the lasting perception of a countercultural phenomenon that was much more encompassing.

The psychedelics of the '60s, which were safe enough for the government to test on citizens in formal laboratory environments, were then subjected to an orchestrated smear and fear campaign by the same government warning of heinous consequences if consumed. Tactics such

as these only exacerbated in youth the sense that official pronouncements couldn't be trusted, and that these drugs were hip and cool to
use. However, if the overriding objective of the government was to main-
tain order, then, despite governmental hypocrisy, it can be argued that
establishing order is a prerogative of all governing powers everywhere,
and what was done as a reaction to the explosion of drug use in the '60s,
made sense as official policy. Despite official actions by the American government that contributed to psychedelic drug use and this drug culture,
it's difficult to imagine any government, left, liberal or conservative, con-
doning an ongoing bacchanal on a mass scale of the psychedelia that
was overflowing from the hip centers of California, New York City, and
London in and around 1967.

As for Hunter S. Thompson, he created a narrative that probes this
social rift caused by drug use when he questions the essence of the American dream. He uses himself and his attorney to make a point about the
nature of how the real and the surreal are often indistinguishable, how
our ideals of free expression have been greatly compromised, and how
the garish extremes of modern culture have become a form of hallucination. Thompson is also an astute observer of his cultural surroundings and very aware of the role he was playing in the larger medium of
publication. Or, as Stull points out:

> Thompson plays the trickster figure who intentionally—and at times uninten-
> tionally—disrupts the social order or shows his disdain for certain persons while
> he underscores his role as deviant or putative outsider. Thompson thus enacts
> much of the playful and passive-aggressive posturing that characterized the
> behavior of the counterculture [...] Thompson not only plays the trickster, but
> tacitly acknowledges his awareness of the role he is playing. [...] For Thompson,
> the quester's experience is not so much the means by which self-discovery takes
> place, in which identity is created or confirmed, as it is a means by which the
> personal and metaphorical selves are obviated or destroyed by a punitive and
> destructive social order [96, 99].

The counterculture in which he participated was, indeed, a brief period
of time when many diverse and disaffected elements of society coalesced
with this "energy" to rebel against a hypocritical authority structure. It
was a bacchanalian energy, and within this upsurge there were many factions with many differing motives and visions. In *Fear and Loathing in Las
Vegas* Thompson paints a story of himself and his attorney indulging in
one last binge to honor the retreating counterculture, and brazenly or
foolishly risking imprisonment, or even death.

In the book, Thompson refers to the unfortunate inability of Kesey
and Allen Ginsberg to unite the Greasers and the Longhairs in a sustained way. However, as an amalgam of diverse "movements," the aims
and adaptations of groups within the counterculture were irreconcilable

and never had any chance of being sustained. For example, the Hell's Angels were not against the war in Vietnam and were fervently anticommunist, a position diametrically at odds with the goals of those in the New Left. At the same time, this biker gang was very much a part of the underground drug scene. Angels mingled with hippies, but detested the intellectual radicals, even though the student rebels were becoming more and more "hippie" in dress, drug use, and in the way they were detaching from the mainstream. Despite the shift toward a hippie sensibility, the New Left was fraught with inner dissention and differing views on how to mobilize. Within the counterculture, spiritual paths began diverging into Sufi, Zen, Krishna, Jesus Freaking, Transcendental Meditation, or, the like. What galvanized the "energy" across this spectrum of dissent, was an anti-establishment spirit coupled with all these new drugs.

The Movement, with its amalgam of rebelliousness, was destined to collapse, and as things dispersed, a significant back-to-the-land movement developed. At this same time, the beastly side of the bacchanalia produced an icon when the Hell's Angels—being used for crowd control—tarnished the California rock festival at Altamont Speedway by killing a spectator while the Rolling Stones played. As Thompson points out: "The orgy of violence at Altamont merely *dramatized* the problem. [...] [T]he energies of The Movement were long since aggressively dissipated by the rush to self-preservation" (179–180).

This "rush to self-preservation" was not mainly a reaction to drug prosecutions or the failure of The Movement to render appreciable change in the political system, though these were factors. Drugs certainly took many casualties during the era, and, in light of the Democratic convention in Chicago in 1968 with all the police brutality, Thompson says "there is no point in kidding ourselves, now, about Who Has the Power" (213).

More significantly, the primary catalyst for the waning of the counterculture was a fundamental need of individuals to make a living and support themselves. Few businesses would hire a longhair in the late '60s and early '70s. For a host of reasons, most young people in the counterculture gravitated beyond using drugs, but the impetus was individual and mostly economic to cut one's hair and go clean. The more resolute adherents of the counterculture, however, persevered in trying to create alternatives to the mainstream way of doing business and engaging the world. Raymond Mungo includes a letter written in 1968 from Verandah to Nel in *Famous Long Ago*. It expresses a back-to-the-land sentiment and a desire to leave the riots and political upheavals of the Nation's capital, which Mungo, Verandah and their closest cohorts did a year later when they set up a commune on a farm in Vermont:

1. We are all of us city folk and, therefore, while being slaves to the hustle and bustle, we are susceptible to bucolic myth.

2. Raymond, Marty (you don't know him yet), and I are all political freaks trying to be relevant, helpful, moral, revolutionary, forward-looking, virtuous, self-sacrificing, etc. (you know the scene). [...]

[B]ehold there is a New Age of humanity bursting forth with cries of Oh Wow, Dies Irae, and FAR OUT! Space creatures, artsy-crafties, people who take themselves lightly and seriously, [...] It has a lot to do with post-psychedelic ethics—simply caring for your neighbors because there is such a tremendous universe to be lost in. It is acid consciousness but it has little to do with drugs. It's where your mind is at. But I am rambling far afield. Turn on, tune in, drop into Vermont [136–137].

This is an example of the idealistic shift from iconoclasm to constructivism, the part of the legacy of the counterculture that would, as the mainstream began to embrace or reject different elements of the disaffection and lifestyle, change society in many ways for the better. In this idealism, the hippie had for a brief time seized the moral high ground in America, through the battles against the war, discrimination, poverty, and environmental degradation. However, to those on the front lines at the time, "The Establishment" seemed impervious to the protests for change. Or as Mungo says in 1970: "The combination of the LNS [Liberation New Service] and Washington had pushed us to something drastic; [...] Vermont, where God will give us an asparagus or a cow instead of merely raising rhetorical dust" (108). This is the sort of callow hopefulness from the era that Hunter S. Thompson disregards in this book. He favors a satirical focus on his last great binge of the drug culture in 1971. Yet, as will be discussed, Thompson, too, at the end of the '60s had moved back-to-the-land.

Drug trafficking was and is, of course, one way to survive economically, but fraught with peril. No one wants to get arrested, as a dealer or a user. Thompson depicts the druggie paranoia in lurid, turbulent detail in *Fear and Loathing in Las Vegas* during those frequent freak-outs when he fears getting busted. Self-medication has always been a part of mankind's *modus operandi*. Las Vegas itself, as Thompson illustrates, is a drug rush of boozy winners coupled with the odds-on bummer for far more hung-over losers. Today's drug culture in America is one aspect of the counterculture that has persisted as a sub-cultural and black market phenomenon. However, unlike the now desiccated counterculture, the drug culture continues outside any broader impetus for social change, and, as with alcoholism, substance abuse problems still continue as a significant societal issue.

In one scene where Thompson is "zombie drunk" on sleeplessness, booze, drugs and adrenalin reserves, he is not looking for sympathy from the devil or elsewhere:

> Buy the ticket, take the ride ... and if it occasionally gets a little heavier than
> what you had in mind, well ... maybe chalk it off to forced *consciousness expansion:*
> Tune in, freak out, get beaten. It's all in Kesey's Bible ... The Far Side of Reality.
> And so much for bad gibberish; not even Kesey can help me now [89].

In this passage, Thompson takes ownership of the potential impact of
his decision to indulge in these drugs. He alludes to the artificiality of
his higher state. In this, he is also setting the stage for his nontheistic
posture toward drugs and countercultural enlightenment. The author
keeps his drug sensations—even the most bizarre hallucinations—as cor-
poreal or cerebral rather than depicting them as spiritual experiences.
He mocks the notion of a spiritual authority. Thompson views "blind
faith in some higher and wiser 'authority,' The Pope, The General, The
Prime Minister ... all the way up to 'God'" (179) as a hypocritical hoax
perpetrated on mankind. So, it's logical that Thompson would also
eschew the spiritual dimension of the counterculture. Thompson is enti-
tled to his subjective belief on spiritual matters, even though, more objectively, this does impact the tone and content of his psychedelic
expression.

In *The Road of Excess: A History of Writers on Drugs,* Marcus Boon points
out how Thompson projects his subjective interior perceptions onto the
world of Las Vegas. In *Fear and Loathing in Las Vegas,* Boone states that
"the neon-saturated night of Las Vegas is just as much a hallucination,
a myth, a product of the imagination, as any triggered by LSD[...]" (266).
This potent theme, created from a thread of drug-filtered revelations on
modern American society, is perhaps Thompson's most insightful observation of all. Who is to say who has a more legitimate vantage on "reality" if our man-made constructs are as surreal as our induced states of
consciousness?

Boon goes on to point out how the manner in which Thompson
describes his hallucinated states is related to the author's orientation
toward the sacred context, which is to say that it is not sacred at all, but
profane:

> Psychedelics amplified the crisis that modernism found itself in with regard to
> the question of literary form. So long as psychedelics were experienced within
> an atheistic worldview, they produced convoluted, fragmentary, chaotic snakes of
> text. When Huxley [in *Doors of Perception*] took mescaline in a sacred context,
> this apparent disorder subsided into a kind of lucid clarity [...] But later nonthe-
> istic explorations of the psychedelic realms, such as Burroughs' and Hunter
> Thompson's, returned to textual turbulence, suggesting that it too cannot be
> wished away so easily [274].

Thompson's text is certainly turbulent and his philosophy nontheistic.
Intriguingly, this causal connection by Boon presupposes a larger observation with regard to those in the counterculture. Those inclined toward

the spiritual with its sacred context—if Boon's premise holds—would be more likely to find, while high on hallucinogens, a lucid clarity in their belief in a higher force. Thompson, by comparison, uses textual turbulence as a literary device to help him depict the fractured nature of the drugged state in a way that emulates the chaos and destructiveness of the modern American State. He is not seeking spiritual enlightenment or lucidity, and doesn't find it. His textual turbulence, while rendered in the context of a traditional narrative structure, is also fractured in a postmodernist sense.

Beyond any belief in a higher force, Thompson's text also begs the question of individual responsibility within the modern American State. When Thompson dishes out his satirical indictments, he begs for his own behavior to be subject to indictment as well. Certainly, Hunter S. Thompson was at the bravest end of a spectrum of journalists and authors when it came to confessing his personal proclivities for drugs. However, burned mattresses, crashed rental cars, or grossly abused expense accounts completely fly in the face of any notion of personal ethics and responsibility. Stull argues that Thompson "too readily asserts, or suggests, that American culture is merely a harsh and punitive one, based on and perverted by a predatory capitalist system. Thompson's deficiency as a cultural critic centers on his refusal to adequately discuss the causes of his personal behavior" (93). Thompson's exaggerated humor toward his madcap binge seems to ask that it be dismissed as good, wild fun. This notwithstanding, the only justification for these actions must stem from the belief that two wrongs make a right. In other words, big business and big government are so corrupt that the abuse of their property in this random way is legitimized. The behavior of Thompson and his attorney also dismisses any argument for decriminalizing drugs through the suggestion that taking drugs is a personal choice and doesn't harm anyone else. The author smashes that argument along with the hotel room. During one stoned-out blitz that he describes to the reader, the destruction has happened a night or two before. Thompson shows that he can't remember when or how it happened. When such behavior is viewed as a backdrop to a slow-witted law enforcement establishment and the broader hypocrisies of big American government, it is hardly an inducement for changing the drug laws. The absurdity of Thompson's extended rants had many humorous moments, but as a tool for pointing out political and spiritual hypocrisy, he succeeded just as pointedly in highlighting how pathetically little his excessive drug culture offers the society it lampoons.

This leads to the most disturbing aspect of Thompson's work. Certainly, his connection to the counterculture was as legitimate as anyone's, but only at its crudest level. Masterfully derisive, Thompson could point out the many problems with the dominant culture, and, thoroughly hedonistic, he could lay claim to having fully relished the highest of highs. In this book, which he describes as an epitaph for the counter-cultural era, there was no recognition of the ample hopefulness of his times. Also, Thompson, like so many caught up in the growing chaos of the inner city scene, chose to move to the country at the end of the '60s decade. He bought a spread near Aspen, Colorado in 1970 where he could shoot his guns in peace. Or as Stull points out, "on a social level, Thompson's escape from society, [...] coincides with the counterculture's rural retreat in the early 1970s" (99). So, while *Fear and Loathing in Las Vegas* may have been an epitaph for the great bacchanalia of the counterculture, the "rural retreat" of the counterculture shifted from a reactionary to a more constructivist mode of trying to change the world. In his inimitable style, Thompson took part in this shift, as well. In a political statement against unfettered land development and a more tolerant attitude toward individual drug use, Thompson waged a campaign to be elected county sheriff after he moved to Colorado. He ran under the banner of the Freak Power Party. Though he lost, he garnered enough votes and his statement was made loudly enough to unnerve the local establishment. His first books following *Fear and Loathing in Las Vegas* also dealt with the political system, particularly as regards presidential election campaigning. Thompson was too jaded to be a back-to-the-land utopian, but he was a civil libertarian willing to rail more openly than most about the hypocrisy he saw in the American political system.

Kurt Vonnegut, like Thompson, doesn't put man's salvation in the hands of God in *Slaughterhouse-Five*. In that novel, Vonnegut shows much more cause for obliterating human hopefulness than Thompson does in *Fear and Loathing in Las Vegas*. However, Vonnegut is a humanist who places full responsibility on man to treat his fellow man mercifully. In this narrative, Thompson holds everyone else to account without being culpable or responsible himself. His "Gonzo" journalism that followed *Fear and Loathing in Las Vegas* began to show a bit higher level of social responsibility to accompany his acerbic and irreverent observations. He was certainly a major voice of the counterculture, but, again, not the hippie voice. His was the voice of a cynical civil libertarian, a jaded left-leaning journalist, and an unapologetic denizen of the drug culture.

How, then, should *Fear and Loathing in Las Vegas* be judged as literature? Certainly, it exhibits sustained originality, vitality of pace and surreal imagination. It is highly deserving of recognition as being among the finest examples of the New Journalism. However, in the same spirit that Tom Wolfe is not comfortable with the accuracy of this label, Thompson's work was a druggie's version of autobiography that doubled as a spoof on the journalistic approach to storytelling. Its accuracy was toward conveying a spirit of truth rather than the letter of what happened. In this aspect, the narrative was an autobiographical fiction. For example, Perry documents that the visit to Vegas for the Mint "400" off-road race occurred many weeks before the trip to visit the drug enforcement conference. This raises the question of whether Thompson was ever pulled over by a California cop while going over 100 miles-per-hour. In this story, he is only part of the way back to Los Angeles before turning back to this second assignment. However, the accuracy of such details doesn't matter when Thompson's intent is, in part, to obliterate a factual pseudo-objectivity of traditional journalism. It makes the librarian's job of classifying this book as fiction or nonfiction problematic, but much of his narrative is clearly fictionalized for greater literary effect. More importantly as literature, the narrative is a genuine reflection of the underground drug culture in America in the late '60s and early '70s. In this, Thompson succeeds in taking the reader deep inside his own drug-addled sensibility and experience with superbly rendered comic absurdness and irony.

In terms of literary style, *Fear and Loathing in Las Vegas* comes at the reader as a frenetic hallucination sobered up with passages of paranoia and occasional op-ed reflections on the culture and counterculture at large. When Tom Wolfe appropriates Clair Brush's 3,000-word description for the chapter "The Electric Kool-Aid Acid Test," she describes tripping on LSD in a way where a psychedelic lucidity is more evident than textual turbulence. Kesey's surrealistic passages also tend more toward the lucid, with his surreal lyricism. Interestingly, Kesey is also more spiritually inclined than Thompson. Thompson's psychedelic imagery is bizarrely surreal, but always in the context of a frenetic turbulence. In *The Road of Excess*, Boon states that:

> Psychedelics are powerful, direct activators and conduits of altered states. Psychedelics point out in a very direct and dramatic way that consciousness is mutable—not just in the slow, seemingly continuous fashion of everyday life—and that radical, rapid shifts in consciousness are possible [273].

Thompson's depictions of a hallucinatory state are imaginatively radical, with barrages of brilliantly original visions. Yet, the array of drugs used by Thompson was not limited to hallucinogens.

Over the course of his life, Thompson's mainstay drug was speed. In a February 2005 obituary on Thompson in *The Exile,* John Dolan pulls no punches on this fact. "A half-century on speed. It's an awesome achievement in itself, never mind the writing. Yes, speed. I'll say it again, since this crucial word seems to have been left out of every obituary I've read: speed. All the ex-druggies who run the California press, eager to airbrush the decades spent high on speed and coke from their official biographies, are squirming to find some way to avoid the word. [...] Nice try. But let's try to be a little bit honest, guys, just for a few minutes, in his honor. His drug of choice was speed. Crystal meth. Amphetamines" (*http://www.exile.ru/2005-February-25/ a_hero_of_our_time_ hunter_s_thompson_1937–2005.html*). The significance of this on the writing tone and style of Hunter S. Thompson's writing was more pronounced than his use of psychedelics. In *Fear and Loathing in Las Vegas* there is an unmistakably frenetic pace reminiscent of much of the Beat writing. There are also frequent bouts of paranoia in his sustained dithyrambic prose. Booth describes the impact of writing on stimulants, such as meth and cocaine, as follows:

> It is not just the volume of words that is fatiguing in stimulant literature, but the volume of ideas, each of which is in itself somewhat interesting and original, and which appears to be connected to the ideas that precede and follow it.
> [...] [E]ach thought is interrupted by the next one in such a way that the final text is more like a montage of phrases forced into coexistence than an organic whole [215].

It is not unreasonable to suggest that the two primary types of drug influencing the prose in *Fear and Loathing in Las Vegas* are speed and potent psychedelics. He stayed up for days at a time to write the manuscript, surely on speed. Also, while in the Las Vegas hotel tripping on acid and mescaline, Thompson wrote down imagistic phrases in a journal. One hallucinatory image is found on the opening page when he imagines that "the sky was full of what looked like huge bats, all swooping and screeching and diving around the car" (3). Yet, the pace of the narrative as a whole is a frenetic barrage of ideas and events. However, in this case, Thompson's montage only gives the illusion of being forced. In the parallel universes that Thompson creates—of his own fragmenting mind and the equally fragmented outside world—this novel succeeds in rendering an organic narrative whole.

On the surface, *Fear and Loathing in Las Vegas* promises the reader a traditional narrative based on reportorial coverage of two objective news events. Yet, this becomes a journalistic spoof on the conventional "news story." On page one of this fictionalized authobiography, the narrative promises a journalistic trip to Las Vegas filtered through a mind besotted with drugs. It doesn't matter that the "news stories" never come to fruition. What comes to fruition, instead, is a holistic story of fractured culture and fractured mind intimately juxtaposed. This fractured holism on Thompson's part, is a richly original paradox.

Like Gurney Norman, Hunter S. Thompson was born in Kentucky in the late '30s and found his way to the Bay Area in the early '60s. Both men structured their narratives as though there was a straight-ahead story to be told. Norman depicts hallucinations in a manner that furthers his plot and develops his main character in *Divine Right's Trip*. Thompson, on the other hand, is so ridiculously high in *Fear and Loathing in Las Vegas* that the hallucinations keep him constantly stumbling and careening around the plot where he is a reporter with a job to do. In this respect, Thompson as protagonist becomes an unreliable narrator in the classic literary sense. Ironically, the reader comes to trust him as a protagonist, not because of all the drugs, but because he is so blatantly honest about his malfeasance as a journalist. There is also a trust that the author, if he can risk being so bluntly straightforward about the drugs, then, logically, has no reason to distort the spirit of his observations. It is not the spirit, but the letter of his drug-addled, who-what-why-when-where reports that will never be deemed reliable by the reader. Also unreliable is any certainty on what is actually happening to this man in Vegas. This piecing together of Thompson's picaresque romp creates a literary tension that keeps the reader engaged. The author employs tight literary crafting: strategic backstory, hallucinatory effect, a paranoid reckoning with the consequences of his actions, and a spoof of his profession. Thompson wants to give an appearance of total chaos, but this is one more literary device in what is actually a tightly rendered narrative.

In contrast to *Trout Fishing in America* and *Slaughterhouse-Five,* Thompson's work does not toy with the traditional narrative form. *Fear and Loathing in Las Vegas* is an energeic narrative where the story unfolds with the actualization of potential in character and situation. At the end, the protagonist gets on a plane for the Rockies to lick his wounds and recoup his sanity, if such a thing were possible for Thompson. Unlike the protagonist in *Been Down So Long It Looks Like Up to Me,* Thompson's narrative has superior forward movement and a grander purpose in its more ironic design. Both books share a frenetic and fatiguing picaresque quality, but Fariña's work takes much too long in its development. *Fear and Loathing in Las Vegas* is more purposefully madcap, less constantly allusory, and thereby funnier.

Even though the protagonist's world was highly fragmented, the structure of the narrative wasn't refractory or juxtapositional. The main character, stoned in Vegas, tries to report on an off-road race that can't be seen because of the dust. The main character, still ripped, returns to Sin City to report on the District Attorneys National Conference on Narcotics and Dangerous Drugs where the presentations are outlandish. Every whacked-out adventure, twisted perception and ironic observation feeds off of this simple plotline.

If there is such a thing as Gonzo Journalism, it belongs as a subset of the New Journalism. The *New York Times Review of Books* article that came out in 1972, refers to the New Journalism as: "The form that reached apotheosis in *The Armies of the Night* reached the end of its rope in *Fear and Loathing [in Las Vegas]*, a chronicle of addiction and dismemberment so vicious that it requires a lot of resilience to sense that the author's purpose is more moralizing than sadistic" (Woods, July 23, 1972). Subjective journalism, of course, continues today, but what differentiates Thompson's work in *Fear and Loathing in Las Vegas* from Norman Mailer's *Armies of the Night* is in the autobiographical narrator's seriousness of intent. Mailer was not marching on the Pentagon to spoof anything.

Thompson is indeed the out-of-control chronicler, less in terms of the "news" he is hired to report, but on the story of himself as he lamely tries to do his job. Mailer established the humorous tone of his narrative by poking fun at his own foibles and opinionated personality. While this underscored the philosophical impossibility of any writer ever being fully objective, it also established the parameters through which the reader could trust the author's "journalism." Thompson, by comparison, lets the reader know in the opening not to trust the factual basis of his story. Mailer has every intention of wanting the reader believe in him as the reliable narrator of his anti-war protest story. The who-what-when-where-and-why serves as the spine of Mailer's narrative, a thread from which he can impart his political philosophy. Both authors in these radically different autobiographical renderings want the reader to trust in their more global observations about politics and American culture, though each goes about establishing such trust in markedly different ways. *Fear and Loathing in Las Vegas* is autobiography with a built in excuse for significant distortion.

Tom Wolfe, in *The Electric Kool-Aid Acid Test*, establishes himself, like Mailer, as a reliable narrator and journalist who will not only give the who-what-where-when-and-why of this story, but promises to take the reader inside the mind of his characters and to create the subjective feel of this world of acidheads. Wolfe is only marginally an autobiographical protagonist. Yet, all three of these authors created trendsetting works of literary nonfiction that were grounded in the premise of the journalistic feature story.

Hunter S. Thompson's immersive approach never changed over time, except that nothing he ever wrote before or after *Fear and Loathing in Las Vegas* was so thoroughly steeped in literary technique. Compared to his other narratives, the mind and state of the protagonist in *Fear and Loathing in Las Vegas* is much more the unfolding story than the external story being told. His later works remained autobiographically iconoclastic, but delved more extensively into social observation and the external story. Thompson continued writing and observing American culture from the wings of society until February 2005 when he died at his ranch in Aspen, Colorado from a self-inflicted gunshot wound. This bizarre and imagistic style allowed Thompson to speak for his times with a giftedness that was both perverse and probing. At his best he was ruthlessly funny and boldly insightful in how he spoke truth to power. As literature, *Fear and Loathing in Las Vegas* was masterful for its uniqueness of an interiority/exteriority that portrays the induced madness of mind within the induced madness of a city built on neon and indulgence. As countercultural literature, Thompson's work should be indulged as genuine artifact of this time.

13

The Fan Man (1974)
Missed Bliss of the Love Chorus

It's absurdly easy to lampoon the hippie, but in the case of *The Fan Man,* such exaggeration works to superb comic effect. With Horse Badorties, author William Kotzwinkle created the quintessential unreliable narrator, a protagonist with visions of grandeur and a chronic inability to see his own foibles. This comi-tragic hero is so filthy and trippy that if the reader isn't braced for a quirky ride, then all comic enjoyment will suffer. At the same time, he is never malicious, but wholly off in a dimension of his own continual remaking. The fan man, Horse Badorties, is part Bowery bum and stoner, part pervert and opportunist, and partly mad. Amplifying this unreliability, Horse tells the story in the immediate moments as it unfolds and happens to him. In these absurd actions, the reader can see what this first-person protagonist cannot. He's not your back-to-the-land, peace-and-love idealist, but a New Yorker of the Lower East Side who somehow evolved from the Greenwich Village beatnik scene into this denizen with surprising musical acumen and a disgusting survival shtick. Published in 1974, *The Fan Man* is the portrayal of one immensely colorful, down-and-out, inner city hippie in the waning years of the counterculture.

Kotzwinkle makes the novel work through the use of comic exaggeration. He employs the unusual narrative mode of first person, present tense. It's an uneasy, nonstop, up-close ride inside the mind of this wacky protagonist who moves the narrative forward, twitch-by-twitch and delusion-by-delusion. This keeps the action immediate, hot, and unrelenting. With only a couple of exceptions when Horse Badorties is not present in the current story, the story allows for no escape from his depraved mind. The comic twists are the result of this filtered point-of-view that reveals the preposterous eccentricity and antics of this odd man. The humor is constructed on a foundation of madcap delusion. It's the descriptive exaggeration, rather than the type of ironic juxtapositions seen in *Trout Fishing in America* or *Slaughterhouse-Five,* that are key to this novel's absurdist comedy.

First-person present tense, as a narrative strategy, hampers the author's ability to provide exposition. The reader is virtually always in the moment of the current story. In *Fan Man* it takes the reader quite a while to learn, for example, that Horse Badorties learned to play the violin at age two and was, by every indication, a legitimate musical talent. This comes out in bits and pieces, as does the fact that he grew up in the Bronx near Van Cortlandt Park. Horse mentions the park out of the blue, again and again, and Kotzwinkle uses the repetition to create a motif that becomes a viable obsession. At the end of the novel, the protagonist takes his sojourn to this place where he reconnects with his childhood.

The primary storyline concerns Horse Badorties' attempt to lead a Love Chorus of 15-year-old runaway girls. As the maestro, he is preparing them for a grand concert performance in Tompkins Square in the run-down Lower Eastside of Manhattan. If only the large shipment of $1.95 hand held fans arrives soon enough, then the collective battery-operated hum, along with the singing of the Love Chorus, will be sublime. These girls also serve as sexual prey for Horse Badorties who tries gamely to seduce the teens. However, he never quite consummates any of the sexual encounters shown in the novel. His spaced-out mind is always distracted, constantly sidetracked, continually diverted, and repeatedly turned in different directions. He also makes a practice of tenement squatting; he never pays the rent, and, while waiting to be evicted, Horse fills them so full of street rubbish that he can hardly make his way through his pad. His place is so disgusting that even his roaches have roaches.

The span of this novel is only a few days, and the reader inhabits the mind of this character who is so freaky that he makes the schizophrenically-impaired Billy Pilgrim in *Slaughterhouse-Five* seem bedrock sane. Every movement and gesture is an adventure with this character: "... it is not the sink but my Horse Badorties big stuffed easy chair piled with dirty dishes. I must sit down here and rest, man, I'm so tired from getting out of bed" (10–11). He frequently refers to himself in the third person like a prepossessed sports star, and, in almost every sentence, uses the ubiquitous hip term "man" as though it is a mantra to guide all stimuli entering his mind.

Horse Badorties also loves to smoke his special herbs. "Out of my moisture-proof herbalist's pouch I am removing a generous pinch of Mexican papaya leaf, man, to get my enzymes flowing" (32). As with everything he does, it's an adventure to get his hookah pipe lit, but finally smoking, "[t]he big bird is afloat, man" (32). At other points of the book, he smokes Peruvian mango skins, "a mild vegetable stimulant to help you see the iguanas in your eyeballs" (72). Later he finds his "little pouch of Panama Red turnip greens to ease the pain" (87). Then there is the "salty seaweed smoke harvested by Portuguese fisherwomen and dried on stones" (94), or "special culpepper's herbalist sprigs of wild asparagus leaves [...]" to get him "into outer spaced-out spaces" [100]. This will help him soak "up vital prana; the astral fluid of life, man" (101). Kotzwinkle excels with euphemisms to create a stream of palpable delusions for his unreliable narrator.

Marcus Boon in *The Road of Excess: The History of Writers on Drugs* describes the influence of cannabis on writing as follows:

> The subtle shifts in perception, the switching back and forth between the everyday and dream worlds that cannabis triggers, clearly lend themselves to utopian musings on the transformation of this world. Utopias are not merely impossible dreams or fantasies. They are visions of the transfiguration of our own world— visions that are often acted on [...] [166].

This is not to suggest that author Kotzwinkle was stoned while writing *The Fan Man,* but he certainly imbued the narrative with the type of stoner's energy described by Boon. Horse Badorties has a utopian notion of taking his Love Chorus on the road; he meanders toward the evening rehearsals; the big concert is in a few days; he approaches young female prospects with flyers to participate. Horse even manages to con NBC into televising the event. Somehow, blitzed, he plods through Chinatown, back to his pad, through the subway, by taxi to Central Park, to the Rockefeller Center, to Brooklyn Heights, into the Bowery and back again to his beloved Lower East Side with its familiar, comforting poverty. The reader is a part of every shifting Horse Badorties' perception. In the hippie era, if LSD was the potent moonshine, then marijuana was the nightly light beer. Horse was constantly stoned on the lighter stuff.

The Electric Kool-Aid Acid Test focuses on real life acidheads. *The Fan Man* is cannabis-driven with a highly interior rendering of a fully realized, urban hippie-bum. By comparison to Tom Wolfe's shallow characterizations, Kotzwinkle's portrait of Horse Badorties is masterful. However, this literary compliment must be taken within the context of this being a full-blown satire. This character is no more representative of the hippies than longhaired Tiny Tim playing "Tiptoe Through the Tulips" on his ukulele for Johnny Carson's *Tonight Show* circa 1970. Moreover, if the narrative were not so obviously a wild spoof of the hippie persona, then the story itself, with its depictions of statutory rape, drugged-out delusions, and racist attitudes toward Puerto Ricans, would be reprehensible. Through the spoof, though, the fictitious Horse Badorties is clearly established as his own worst enemy.

Beneath the preposterous exaggeration and outlandish humor, *The Fan Man* is full of clever allusions to the type of Eastern spirituality that was embraced by the Beat writers and many of the hippies who came on their heels. In his thoughtful article "The Ambivalence in Kotzwinkle's Beat and Bardo ties," Robert Kohn suggests that:

The Fan Man is a significant part of Tibetan Buddhist history in America and should be recognized as such. It is also a unique contribution to American culture, because its author anticipated the destructive influence of beatnik excesses upon the ancient religion. Because of Kotzwinkle's strong emotional ties both to the Beat Generation writers and to traditional Tibetan Buddhism, he experienced an anguished ambivalence of which American literature is the beneficiary. That ambivalence enabled Kotzwinkle to create a hero/anti-hero unique in literature and has made The Fan Man one of the most unusual novels of the mid-twentieth century [7].

It isn't easy to establish whether Kotzwinkle's motivation to write *The Fan Man* was rooted in anguish or if he simply wanted to create a comedy of someone fully steeped in the most excessive manifestations of Beat and hippie philosophy and lifestyle. Kohn, in his article, shows how many phrases in *The Fan Man* make plausible subtextual reference to specific Buddhist practices and beliefs as well as to some of the characters in the Beat writings of Jack Kerouac. More significant than the specific textual allusions, is Kohn's assertion that Kotzwinkle—through this satire—was highlighting a spirited controversy that occurred when "Buddhist meditation and ego nullification" was merged in the '50s and '60s with "the Beat Generation's glorification of psychedelic drugs and free love" (1). Kohn considered the Beat behavior "ominously excessive," but, caught up in the allusions, he loses sight of Kotzwinkle's robust humor that is very much contextualized within the dynamic of the story.

Clearly, Kotzwinkle has his pulse on the nature of excessiveness, and uses his manifestation of Horse Badorties to great comic effect as a way to illustrate the pratfalls of extreme hippie behavior. This is seen most clearly when Horse, blissfully ensconced at Van Cortlandt Park in the Bronx, thinks the Love Chorus concert is the next day. In actuality, the concert is being held at that same moment in lower Manhattan with NBC cameras rolling. In his stoned fashion, he misses out on his own great moment of accomplishment.

The author has set up this climactic irony through his superb characterization of the protagonist as he inhabits those "outer spaced-out spaces." This creates a surreal sense of time in the novel that makes his odd wanderings through the streets of New York (and the ending) so believable. Kotzwinkle, with what Tom Wolfe in *The New Journalism* calls "the detailing of status life" (48), creates the consummate example of hippie anti-status. Kotzwinkle's meticulous eye for the grotesque details of this life makes for impressive literature. Every original and wacky scene is anchored in evocative, concrete imagery. The imagery of Horse Badorties' pad, the strange people he meets, and all the odd places he finds himself serve the antics of this eccentric personality.

Wolfe was using Balzac as his example, but it could easily apply to the literary technique of Kotzwinkle in *The Fan Man* as he "piles up these details so relentlessly and at the same time so meticulously—there is scarcely a detail [...] that does not illuminate some point of status—that he triggers the reader's memories of his own status life, his own ambitions, insecurities, delights, disasters, plus the thousand and one small humiliations and the status coups of everyday life [...]" (33). In the case of Horse Badorties, the status life is hilariously one of anti-status, a wholesale rejection of the trappings of mainstream aspirations and accoutrements. Kotzwinkle plays this to the extreme and, from the detailed piles of evidence, the reader of this novel will be completely sold on the likelihood that this man would miss the most important event of his very here-and-now existence.

In one sense, the protagonist needed to find his bliss, to confront his past and the demons of his childhood, so missing the concert may have been better for Horse than attending. On the other hand, he is also an example of the myriad of human beings who have fallen through the cracks of society and have managed to eek along at the outermost fringes of society, passed by on the streets as though invisible, but unavoidably visible at the same time. In this, Horse Badorties is certainly an example of a hippie who is at the farthest edge of the declining counterculture. He is also a straight-out street bum, the kind with a shopping cart piled high, rather than a hopeful hippie seeking to find a sincere alternative lifestyle. Horse, in this respect, is more opportunistic bum than hippie, yet he is both. For example, beneath the surface of his Love Chorus created for homeless girls is the hoax of a degenerate man seeking to prey on innocent teens. If one is to find humor here—and humor, of course, is subjective—it is in how this situation is so over-the-top as to be ridiculously vile.

The most difficult scene to stomach is when Horse Badorties lures a runaway girl to his filthy pad, but has to leave for choir practice before they can have sex. He leaves a window open when he goes. The Hawkman, a Puerto Rican from the building next door, swoops in when Horse leaves. Rapping to the girl in broken stereotypical "Spanglish," the Puerto Rican rapes the girl:

"How you like eet, baby?" ask Hawkman, smileeng as he go out de weendow.
"You stink, man."
"Take it easy, *muchacha*," say Hawkman, flyin eento de air [156].

When Horse Badorties returns, he is more concerned that the Hawkman might have stolen some of his "precious" junk than he is with the girl who has been raped. The exaggeration is clearly for effect, but even as disgusting as Kotzwinkle wants to make his fictional protagonist, this scene is disturbing. Even without this extreme scene, Kotzwinkle succeeds in ridiculing much of the hippie lifestyle: the dangers of excess, being perpetually stoned, pursuing the limits of "free love," being in the "here-and-now," recycling the waste of others, being receptive to whatever signs the universe is sending, tending to one's karma, or working the situation to one's advantage. Through Horse Badorties' rolling monologue of mad hyperbole and nonsense, the author succeeds in his lampoon of the hippie. In doing so, he makes valid consideration of the propensity for male sexism during the hippie era. He also feeds the derision that has reduced all aspects of the counterculture movement to a phenomenon that was devoid of merit and any redeeming social impetus. Yet, such is the nature of satirical writing where exaggeration spotlights contradiction and flaw, and ironic detachment is the standard.

If Hunter S. Thompson viewed *Fear and Loathing in Las Vegas* as the epitaph of the counterculture, then Kotzwinkle seems intent on showing the world what became of the hippie after the counterculture was declared dead in so many circles. By 1973, "the hippie thing" may have been out of vogue in influential circles of the chic, but as a countercultural ethic and sensibility diffused into the mainstream culture, it was far from dead.

The drug culture, as noted in the chapter on *Fear and Loathing in Las Vegas,* still persists despite years of heavy effort by "the establishment" to curb the phenomenon through prosecution and incarceration, drug screenings for jobs, just-say-no-to-drugs education, or foreign and domestic curtailments at the source. Horse Badorties may love his assortment of herbs, but drug use and abuse and the human urge to self-medicate has always been much more of a pan-cultural phenomenon than simply countercultural. The difference, as seen with Horse's creative euphemisms for the pot he openly smokes, was that many of those in the counterculture brazenly embraced an open policy toward using illicit drugs. Except for limited efforts to legalize marijuana, few in today's drug culture risk public pronouncements opposing anti-drug legislation. Drug dealings and use, with its lucrative risks and personal dangers, are also kept much more covert.

It would be unfair to suggest that the creation of Horse Badorties was intended by the author to represent the epitome of the remnant hippie. Likewise, it is unlikely that Kotzwinkle was out to debase Eastern spiritual paths, promote sex with teen girls, or to lambaste the love and peace ethos. In fact, when Horse finds a semblance of inner peace at the end of the novel, Kotzwinkle seems to be saying that even the most despicable humans are redeemable. Or as Kohn states:

> It is true that Horse will eventually be enlightened. The end of the novel suggests that he will, and indeed it is a basic tenet of Buddhism that the worst among us, even murderers, will eventually, if not in the present lifetime then in some future lifetime, attain nirvana. In the meantime, Horse Badorties is visiting a lot of bad karma on the planet [7].

Also, it should be noted that Kotzwinkle is not relying on a Judeo-Christian sense of redemption or salvation to save Horse Badorties, but on an Eastern religious premise of individual spiritual attainment. This exemplified, not a repudiation of Western religion, which also features core themes of redemption, but the broader acceptance of spiritual awakening that, in America, rarely included an Eastern perspective prior to the counterculture of the '60s.

Even the fixation that Horse Badorties shows for all manner of rubbish and junk presaged a sensitivity that first surfaced in the early '70s toward recycling. This was one component of the burgeoning environmental movement that was a direct outgrowth of the counterculture of the '60s with its focus on ecological concerns. The first publicly funded pilot program for recycling occurred in Seattle in 1973 when the Honorary Mayor of Fremont, Armen Napoleon Stepanian, a longhaired hippie, established a neighborhood route to pick up recyclables. The newspapers were bundled for eventual use as insulation material, nonreturnable bottles were separated and crushed for remelting into new bottles, cans were collected and taken in for de-tinning, and the operation was staffed by juvenile delinquents sent to the makeshift recycling center by the municipal judges as community service sentencing. The counterculture and its new environmental movement was the unmistakable source of today's more mechanized, profitable, and comprehensive recycling industry. This was an example of the constructivism of the '70s that evolved from the reactionary iconoclasm of the counterculture of the late '60s.

Horse Badorties, as hippie junkman, is not so noble, but he is in his element when he buys an old school bus, a junkyard dog, air-raid siren, minesweeper, and subway-braking mechanism in Jersey with the idea of touring with the Love Chorus:

> NOW, I am off and away, onto the highway and heading back toward New York City, with a school bus at last, man, forty miles an hour in his own valuable vehicle. The things I can do with this bus, man, the incredible adventures and fifteen-year-old chicks I can get in here, man. But the first thing I must do is slow down, man, there is a sharp curve ahead ...
> ... slowing down, brakes working all right, but the wheels, man, [...] watch out, man, the bus is going off the road and over this bank, man, and down, man, my life is rushing past me, man, and I am bouncing down into New Jersey swamp grass, man, into a foot of water and mud and coming to a stop, man, in a swamp of tall weeds.
> [...] Coming over the hill is a police car. No time to get my dog out, man. The police will have to remove him. I've got to get the hell out of here, man, through these tall pussy willows, man, and continue off through the swampland.
> [...] Keeping my umbrella low, man, I proceed through the swamp grass and there are the state troopers, man, swarming over the school bus and scratching their heads, man, looking at my dog behind the steering wheel [77–78].

Note the first person, present tense where Kotzwinkle pokes fun at his protagonist's spaciness, while working hard to make Horse Badorties a close up, three-dimensional, one-of-a-kind character.

The author establishes Horse as not simply a loser, but a highly gifted loser. When it begins to surface in the novel that Horse is a refined musician, rather than just some stereotypical bum without an interesting history, the dimensions of the plot begin to take hold. The reader wants to find out what will happen to this gifted, yet filthy pervert. The period from 1966–72 is recognized as a musical highpoint in American and British history when amplified rock was notably vibrant and original. Horse Badorties, with his odd Chinese lute, shows that he can jam at a highly proficient level with a neighborhood saxophonist and trombonist. Impromptu street jazz was a Beatnik occurrence that carried through the hippie epoch. The saxophonist serves the novel as artifice in a couple of key junctures. He takes away the girl who was raped and gives her a safer place to stay. They are all in Horse's pad while Horse is lost in a mantra and repeating "dorky, dorky, dorky" for an entire day, so both the saxophonist and the girl are relieved to split. More importantly, and plausibly, the saxophonist is later available to conduct the Love Chorus on the day of the big concert when Horse is missing-in-action.

Throughout the novel, Horse's great obsession is music. He wears a "Commander Schmuck earflap cap"(16) in the summer heat so he won't have to endure the Puerto Rican music that accosts him. When he farts in the subway, he envisions it as a "Tibetan lama bass note," the kind made when Buddhist monks would blow on twenty-foot long horns in the Himalayans. Then, of course, there is the actual Love Chorus. Even though it is a near miracle when Horse is able to find his way to the rehearsals, there is a keen sense that the girls relish what they are doing and respect the musical leadership of their chorus leader. The author allows that the final concert is quite good. Perhaps this is Kotzwinkle's way of acknowledging the artistic renaissance of the hippie movement, one that centered more notably on the immediacy of music than on any other creative realm.

Of course, William Kotzwinkle was under no obligation to paint his character in any other way than how he did, and Horse Badorties is as original and fully-realized a comic literary caricature as can be found. He is a farting Siddhartha junkman in a cannabis cloud. However, it is indeed fair to note when Kotzwinkle's exaggerations become sexually and racially disturbing, irrespective of satirical context. It is also not necessary, because Horse is so masterfully rendered, to consider this character as one who is highly representative of the hippies. In one critique, Horse Badorties was called the consummate hippie. The comic exaggeration alone betrays the notion of consummate, a concept that implies a perfect representation of a member of that social group. David Ray "Divine Right" Davenport in *Divine Right's Trip,* comes much closer than Horse to being the consummate hippie. He was certainly far more representative than the highly exaggerated caricature of Horse Badorties. This does not take anything away from the comic brilliance of *The Fan Man,* but simply identifies that the author has accomplished what he set out to do—to create, not keen realism—but a very funny and thought-provoking novel featuring a wildly spoofed-up protagonist.

Like *Divine Right's Trip,* this novel is traditionally energeic and highly profluent from the first page to the last. Kotzwinkle never interrupts the continuous and vivid fictional dream. There is none of the self-reflective meta-fiction of *Trout Fiction in America* or *Slaughterhouse-Five.* The reader is immersed in the mind of Horse Badorties from beginning to end. Few stories would hold up to the unfolding immediacy of first person, present tense narrative throughout, but in this case the decision works exceedingly well. The author's decision to keep the narrative under two hundred pages was also wise. An epic 700-page saga unfolding through the iguanas in Horse's eyeballs would prove too reptilian for most readers. Ken Kesey's brilliant decision to tell *One Through Over the Cuckoo's Nest* through the eyes of Chief Broom was instrumental to the success of that novel. Likewise, William Kotzwinkle succeeded in creating one of the most memorable unreliable protagonists in literary history when he decided to force his readers to enter the perverse mind of Horse Badorties. And, even though Horse is a one-of-a-kind denizen, his mad ploddings reveal a fallen-through-the-cracks hippie in a manner that is both comic and probing. In spite of its satirical nature, *The Fan Man* portrays a genuine hippie casualty of the great countercultural bacchanalia of the 1960s. This novel is a largely forgotten classic of the hippie epoch.

14

Another Roadside Attraction (1971) and *Even Cowgirls Get the Blues* (1976)

A Shifting Zeitgeist

It was a dizzy period of transcendence and awareness: transcendence of compromised and obsolete value systems, awareness of the enormity and richness of a previously unsuspected inner reality. Its zeitgeist, despite what you may have heard, was only secondarily political. As much as it's been emphasized by uncomprehending journalists, the political movements of the time (be they pacifist, feminist, environmental, or racial) were largely the result of fallout from a spiritual explosion.

—Tom Robbins, from "The Sixties"

Tom Robbins started writing his first novel, *Another Roadside Attraction,* in 1968. It was published in 1971. Like Kurt Vonnegut's *Slaughterhouse-Five,* which uses a comic metafictional technique to contextualize a profound theme, *Another Roadside Attraction* also draws attention to its own narrative construction as a way to set the stage for exploring questions of Western and Eastern spirituality. Both novels share the distinction of setting the thematic stakes exceptionally high. Vonnegut's work focuses on the randomness of death, and our responsibility as humans towards the manner in which we engage our fellow humans with regards to war; Robbins' work tackles the pronounced shift taking place in the realm of religion and spirituality in America during the late 1960s. Never once does Robbins use the term "hippie" or "counterculture" in this novel, but his free spirited, gypsy-like characters—Amanda, John Paul

Ziller, Plucky Purcell, and, to an extent, Marx Marvelous—are very much at the cutting edge of the changing consciousness of the time. Vegetarian Amanda and her Tarzanesque husband, John Paul, operate a colorful hotdog stand and roadside zoo along Interstate 5 in the Northwest corner of the Pacific Northwest.

At one level, *Another Roadside Attraction* spoofs the emerging New Journalism of its time. The story's narrator, Marx Marvelous, who the reader eventually learns is the author, tells the story as though he's writing an objective report of the events that occurred. As part of the comic effect, the reader is never certain whether or not the author/narrator is an autobiographical caricature of the actual author or one more authorial artifice through which Robbins is constructing this multilayered story. However, unlike the New Journalism mainstays of the period—*The Electric Kool-Aid Acid Test, The Armies of the Night,* or even *Fear and Loathing in Las Vegas*—Robbins never promises that the narrative is in any way factual. In fact, the author revels in goofing with the reader in his use of Marx Marvelous as the fictitious narrator/author. Such is the impish, gleam-in-the-eye-humor of Robbins. At one point Marx states: "were I trying to compose the great American novel instead of factually documenting a particular event, I would draw my characters not from the Zillers, [...] nor from the young, long-haired itinerants who, by the scores, called at the Capt. Kendrick Memorial Hot Dog Wildlife Preserve as if it were a stopping-off place on a vast socio-religious pilgrimage; no my subjects would be selected from among the tourists and vacationers [...]" (241–242).

On many occasions during the narrative, Robbins, like Vonnegut, chooses to stop the action and draw attention to the manner in which the story is being constructed. This metafictional device, not only plays with the role of the author, but is an opportunity for the author to insert tidbits of information into the story so he can foreshadow the key narrative events which later surface, such as the coming arrival of "the corpse" that doesn't show up until two-thirds of the way into the novel. In another way, this technique characterizes the narrator as the chronicler and "objective" reporter of events through which the tenuousness of Marx's linear and rational "objectivity" become an overriding theme of the novel. Both Vonnegut and Robbins deviated from the continuous and vivid fictional dream. Neither author is so metafictional that they abandon the literary techniques of "social realism"—the techniques which Tom Wolfe points out were being abandoned by leading novelists of this period and successfully appropriated by the "New Journalists." Robbins took this trend full circle with Marx Marvelous as a fictional "New Journalist" of a clearly fabricated memoir.

Both Vonnegut and Robbins, unlike the New Journalists, fictionalized their accounts and benefited by not having to contend with the limitations of depicting real-life characters. Vonnegut, for example, spared himself a strict autobiographical rendering of his experience as one of the few survivors of the Dresden firebombing. Instead, he amplified the impact of the occasion through the creation of Billy Pilgrim, the Chaplain's assistant, who served as a purer embodiment of a fractured innocence in the face of manmade horror. The fictional Marx Marvelous engages in an ultra-rational discourse that serves as a clear counterpoint to the organic, free-spirited nature of Amanda. Robbins has full liberty to get inside their minds. When Tom Wolfe comments on novelists foregoing the techniques of social realism, he argues that this trend was washed up because these novelists also abandoned the "electricity" that such realism creates. Vonnegut and Robbins, however, offer two superb examples of novels that experiment—through metafiction and chronological disruptions—with the strict conventions of Modernism. Yet, even with the comic treatments, these two authors very much retain the "electricity" of mimetic realism. In other words, both of these novelists arrived at a happy medium between experimentation and convention. In fact, because Billy Pilgrim and Amanda are fictional constructs, these authors were able to infuse far more "electricity" into their characters than Wolfe did with the real-life characters in *The Electric Kool-Aid Acid Test* whose privacy he was impelled to respect.

Robbins never allows his core story to become "unstuck in time" to the extent that Vonnegut does, nor is *Another Roadside Attraction* as juxtapositional in structure, but he does play with the chronological rendering enough to tantalize the reader with events to come, or for richer characterizations. The schizophrenic representation in *Slaughterhouse-Five* is central to the theme that Vonnegut constructs, which warrants the pronounced fragmentation of time. Robbins, by comparison, creates a narrative structure based not on psychological dysfunction, but on a philosophical evolution of the protagonist. To accomplish this, the evolution of Marx Marvelous is predicated on a series of exchanges he has with Amanda on economics, politics, culture and foremost, religion. Though heavily didactic, these narrator essays "work" in the novel to the extent that, when strung together, they connect to the consciousness expansion of Marx Marvelous. Both Vonnegut and Robbins stray from the techniques of traditional narrative, but neither author, as they deviate from the "continuous and vivid fictional dream," lose sight of narrative profluence, the authorial propensity to hook the reader and carry him or her through the course of the story.

In the case of Marx Marvelous, it is Amanda who is forced to listen as he tries to make sense of a changing world. However, as the narrator/author falls in love with this woman—a mesmerizing character who is consummately Zen-like in her non-rational, here-and-now, sensual zest for life—he often finds himself relaxing his rigidly rational and logical positions. When he allows himself to be open to her wisdom, his consciousness expands.

Through this narrator/author, Robbins utilizes the façade of a reportorial technique to convey, through the guise of objectivity, the very essence of this consciousness revolution that epitomized the counterculture. As Amanda lightly undermines the "objective" posturing of Marx Marvelous, an undercurrent of narrative tension is created. Her koans of enlightenment not only change the narrator/author though the course of the story, but also elevate the narrative from that of an eccentric comic rant to one with profound spiritual implication. In other words, Robbins takes on the difficult task of exploring the most elusive, substantive, and difficult-to-grasp part of the change that occurred within the social tumult of the late '60s. He does this through Marx Marvelous, who comes to the Ziller's roadside zoo convinced that America is in the volatile throes of the old religion dying and a new one taking its place. Amanda and John Paul were at the psychic frontier of this change and Marx, by hiring on as the manager of their zoo and hotdog stand, wanted "to get close enough to the vortex, to the medulla of evolutionary outburst, so that [he] could experience it in a direct and tangible way" (164). Along the way Robbins mines popular American culture and counterculture to great comic effect, but he does so as a means to get at deeper philosophical concerns.

Amanda, in this regard, is an important character in American literature. Vivian Stamper, who strikes out independently at the end of Ken Kesey's *Sometimes a Great Notion,* can be said to exhibit an early feminist sensibility when she leaves her husband and his family, but wherever she's going, there's no sense that she will become unbound from the strong expectations of the "female" role of the early 1960s. This adherence to role expectation is absent from Amanda who, in *Another Roadside Attraction* just a few years later, is one of the first truly liberated female characters—sexually, materialistically and spiritually. She is one of the earliest and finest examples of a literary character that embodies the ascendance of feminism in America, a cultural progression—or shifting Zeitgeist—that surfaced forcibly in the early 1970s.

In *The Fan Man,* Horse Badorties is also immersed in a Zen outlook on the world, but the degree of comic exaggeration used by author Kotzwinkle renders Horse in a way that is much more stoned-out, spacey and dysfunctional than the characters in *Another Roadside Attraction.* This is a matter of degree, but Horse, as the hippified bum, is so cartoonish that the reader must abandon his or her attachment to verisimilitude in order to enjoy the comic ride. Some of the events in *Another Roadside*

Attraction are similarly beyond the realm of the plausible, but not the characters. Although Amanda is certainly eccentric and her husband John Paul even more so, the author maintains a tenuous believability that these are wildly expressive people one might actually meet. *The Fan Man* succeeds as a grand spoof and lampoon of the hippie and the Beat/Hippie sense of spirituality, but Horse is too cartoonish to be someone we might expect to meet. By comparison, Robbins draws his readers into the far out eccentricity of his characters as a way to engage a greater contemplation of the philosophical and spiritual questions being posed during this time. If anything, the spoofing in *Another Roadside Attraction* is not directed toward the counterculture, but at the mainstream society at large, with his targets including the Catholic Church, the FBI, and scientific rationalism.

In narrative terms, Amanda's character is traditionally rendered. *Another Roadside Attraction* is conventionally energeic in a manner that leads to a discernable climax—figurative and literal in this case. The plot, with absurdist comic twists, is largely linear and serves as a vehicle to develop the potential of the story's protagonist, Marx Marvelous. Amanda is the anchor point for the novel, the central spiritual figure, but does not change during the course of the novel. The three male characters pivot around her presence and energy. In respect to this spirituality, Robbins elevates her feminine Zen sensibility to a place that transcends the calcification of the Christian, male-dominated, establishment church. In one of the later conversations with Marx Marvelous, Amanda, in a manner that is indicative of the frequently didactic tone of the novel, says:

> "Jesus was a Jew. Judaism was a father religion. Christianity also grew into a father religion. But the *old* religion was a mother religion. We've had two thousand years of penis power."
>
> "Is that bad?"
>
> "It isn't a question of bad or good. It never is. But when the phallus is separated from the womb, when the father is separated from the mother, when culture is separated from the flesh ... then life is out of balance and the people become frustrated and violent.
>
> [...] "All I am saying is, tomorrow when you are sitting alone thinking about Jesus, open your window. [...] Open your window to the ducks and the fields and the river" [294–295].

Depictions of nature play an integral role as a metaphor for Robbins' primary focus on the shifting spiritual sensibility of this time. The author makes eloquent use of place as a motif to highlight his fresh blending of Eastern and Western spiritual thought. Specifically, the novel is set in the fertile Skagit River delta where the landscape between the craggy Cascade Mountain range and the sea is reminiscent of Holland with its colorful fields of tulips, black soil, dikes, and sloughs. However, it is through the oriental flavor of this place that Robbins anchors his East/West narrative:

> It is a landscape in a minor key. A sketchy panorama where objects, both organic and inorganic, lack well defined edges and tend to melt together in a silver-green blur. [...] It is a poetic setting, one, which suggests inner meaning and invisible connections. The effect is distinctly Chinese. A visitor experiences the feeling that he has been pulled into a Sung dynasty painting, perhaps before the intense wisps of mineral pigment have dried upon the paint [56].

The inner meanings and invisible connections confound the logical, linear-thinking of Marx Marvelous as Amanda and her husband, John Paul Ziller, promise public answers to the "meaning of meaning" at their eccentric roadside zoo with its tsetse fly, rare garter snakes, and circus of trained fleas.

The pastoral and thickly wooded richness of the Skagit Valley, a place with a mystical ambience, offers a distinctly rich setting that counterbalances the highly *un*conventional realism of the rebellious characters and whacky situations that Robbins develops. Robbins describes this eloquently, and in a manner that often contrasts starkly with his relentless comic barrages. However, many of his descriptions of setting are comic, too: "The day was rumpled and dreary. It looked like Edgar Allan Poe's pajamas" (306).

This is an example of how highly original similes are also used to playful effect throughout the novel. "[D]rool dripped from her mouth like pearls from the anus of an angel" (82), is one more example of the author's repeated attempts at outrageous twists of humor. Robbins is sometimes sophomoric, but frequently quite uproarious.

But even as caricaturized and eccentric as Robbins renders his heroes and heroine, the author never loses sight of their believable humanity, such as when Amanda and John Paul Ziller meet (and then quickly wed):

> Something almost angelic danced on the abrasive surfaces of his face. She carried her excitement lightly, the way a hunter carries a loaded shotgun over a fence. Warm chemical yokes burst in their throats. Ziller had the stink of Pan about him. Amanda heard the phone ring in her womb. In the magnetized space between them they flew their thoughts like kites. At last he reached out for her. She took his hand. As they disappeared far down the riverbank, the ringmaster and the Apache sat, stunned, in the kind of vacuum that forms in the immediate wake of an historic turn [24].

The tone is both powerfully real, yet comic. This an example of how Tom Robbins writes with an original and quirky charm crafted from the detritus of pop culture and psychedelia, yet grounded in the essence of the poignant moment.

In a 1982 interview with Michael Strelow in *Dialogues With Northwest*

Writers, Robbins, who was born in Virginia in 1936 and raised there, was asked why the rain, blackberries, mushrooms, caves, ranches and other distinctively Northwest things abound in his novels more than the imagery from his youth and college days. In answering, Robbins stated that "[e]vents, images, characters and places from my southeastern childhood do pop up in my novels occasionally. Generally, though, the stuff of the West is a wilder stuff. It speaks to my imagination more directly and with greater poetic authority" (100). Robbins has lived most of his adult life in the Skagit Valley of Washington State, and the vivid sense of this place infuses many of his novels. And, as has been pointed out several times in this study, the author's countercultural sensibility, "the wilder stuff," is of a strong West Coast persuasion.

Yet, as seen with Plucky Purcell in *Another Roadside Attraction* (or Sissy Hankshaw in *Even Cowgirls Get the Blues*), the Southern influence is also present. Plucky is a former Duke University football star who sells psychedelic drugs to a clientele made up exclusively of artists. He steals "the corpse," the mummified body of Jesus Christ, from the catacombs of The Vatican. A trademark of Robbins' style is to develop grotesque caricatures. Theses on Robbins's novels have referred to this as comic grotesque or American grotesque, but the tendency is decidedly more Southern than Northwestern. His wild heroes share the flavor of Flannery O'Connor's characters. O'Connor was the superb Georgia novelist and short story writer who died at the age of 39 in 1964. Her use of concrete details, strong sensory imagery, and an eye for the strange and ludicrous, such as the young bible salesman in "Good Country People" who steals the wooden leg from the spinster he is seducing, is not unlike the characters depicted by Robbins.

Plucky precipitates an absurd second coming of Christ when he steals the mummified body. What they choose to do with this startling news—information that would debunk any notion of the ascension of Christ into heaven and offer tangible proof of the greatest fraud in religious history—is the philosophical and pragmatic dilemma coursing through this novel.

While O'Connor was a devout Catholic, she, like Robbins, was not afraid to delve into the essence of faith through the depiction of unconventional characters in uproarious situations. A comparison of the characters of O'Connor and Robbins also serves to underscore the radical changes in American society from O'Connor's Southern world of the '40s and '50s, and Robbins' countercultural depictions of the Pacific Northwest in the late '60s and beyond. When he moved West in the early '60s, Robbins brought with him a Southerner's eye, but once ensconced in the Northwest he found himself at the edge of a "Manifest Destiny" that was not only *not* manifest, but destined for new frontiers of the mind and spirit.

The Beats and those that followed in the counterculture of the late 1960s explored the religious thought of the Far East and psychedelic realms where, as Plucky states in dealing these mind-expanding drugs: "I was selling people a new look at the inside of their heads, laying a lot of powerful energy on them that they could use to open up new dimensions to their existence" (288).

Similar to Ken Kesey in the Bay Area in 1959 and '60, Tom Robbins first ingested LSD in pharmacological laboratory tests at the University of Washington in 1963. Though Robbins portrays psychedelic drug use in a sympathetic light in his novels, he was never a public provocateur for the psychedelic experience in the manner of Kesey and the Merry Pranksters. Amanda, John Paul, and Plucky Purcell, however, lived very much in the vein of the Pranksters. On the wall of her bedroom, Amanda hangs "a cuckoos nest [...]. If one goose had flown over it, he had dropped no leaflets nor any other explanation of why he did not fly east or west like his peers" (332). The allusion to Kesey's first two novels shows where Tom Robbins stood in the great cultural divide of the '60s. At one point, Marx takes a short vacation from the roadside zoo by visiting San Francisco where "a lot of strange things were erupting [...] events with religious undertones that might bear looking into" (217). In *Another Roadside Attraction*, Robbins creates a set of characters that indulges in marijuana, hash, peyote, and acid, but draws the line against amphetamines and the addictive opiates. Plucky, though a dealer, has a history of pummeling the pushers of addictive drugs.

The novel, through these countercultural characters, is an exploration of life's Great Mystery. At the opening of the novel Amanda is asked by a priest what she believes in. She distills this down to birth, copulation, and death. To this, the narrator adds that Amanda also believes strongly in magic and freedom. *Another Roadside Attraction* features doses of all these things. As he creates this cast of characters who live at the expressive edge of American culture, Robbins establishes a discernable tone and intent. Foremost, there is the overt skepticism toward the Judeo-Christian tradition and toward all organized religion. As he says in his interview with Sterlow: "With the exception of Tantric Hinduism, every religious system in the modern world has denied and suppressed sensuality. Yet sensual energy is the most powerful energy we as individuals possess" (100). This type of sensuality is manifest in Amanda who exudes a palpable seductive quality that mesmerizes all the people in her inner circle. Amanda is armed with a spirit of playfulness.

In *Tom Robbins* by Mark Siegel, Robbins describes "playfulness as a form of wisdom and a means of survival essential to that most precious of all things, the human soul" (10). Siegel notes that the second coming of Christ is shown to be irrelevant (and too dicey to reveal to the world)

compared to the white magic of Amanda's love that enlightens Marx
Marvelous:

> Amanda's lessons are typically Zen. She knows from their first meeting that
> Marx must break through his resistance to the world in which he lives, a world
> to which he can only relate by manipulating its objects. He must become an
> equal part of things, rather than an obsessive person who sees himself as the
> center of the universe. Her first lesson, "You must learn to walk in the rain with-
> out flinching," is easily understandable to those familiar with Zen doctrine [16].

Robbins tone is decidedly less defeatist and pessimistic than that of
Hunter S. Thompson in *Fear and Loathing in Las Vegas*. Likewise, its playfulness is more hopeful than the writings of Beat era. Along with the Zen
sense of enlightenment, Siegel points out astutely that the characters of
Tom Robbins "win victories by carving out private pockets of freedom
from which to resist civilization. [...] They do not confront social authority, but outwit it, as do the heroes of traditional tall tales" (12).

In this novel, the roadside zoo and hotdog stand sit at a transition
point between a freeway and exquisite natural surroundings. Amanda
and John Paul Ziller are neither escaping the mainstream world
nor embracing it. They were, indeed, carving out a "private pocket of
freedom" by adapting to civilization as much on their own terms as possible. John Paul embodied the more primitive impulses of the counterculture with his pet baboon, loincloth, and bone through his nose.
He was a primal drummer and a Tarzan figure. He revered his "Jane"
and accepted Amanda's son as his own. He condoned his wife's sexual
openness to Marx and Plucky. "Sexuality ringed Amanda the way a
penumbra rings a shadow" (197). John Paul believed that all life ultimately is traced back to sunlight. This philosophy, like Marx's diatribes,
plays out at the end of the novel. After Plucky, with his heisted Jesus
mummy, is pursued to the Skagit Valley, he and John Paul escape with
the dead Christ. Plucky, unable to beat the system he always tries to outwit, is shot and killed in Florida by the authorities while liberating a large
helium balloon from a Naval Air Station. At the same time, in the same
way that Christ was raised up into heaven on the day of ascension, the
balloon, with John Paul, the baboon, and the bones of Jesus Christ, lev-
itates closer and closer toward the sun, "to energy, dissolving in the
essence that spawned all life" (326). The balloon and those in it are
never seen again.

Marx Marvelous is left behind at the roadside attraction with
Amanda and her young son. Thinking he might now have her white
magic love to himself, in one last koan, Marx learns that life is far too
transitory and Amanda, a transcendent soul "running away into the whirl-
wind of life, must move on. [...] In her face [he] notice[s] a terrible
beauty. Like the terrible beauty of nature itself." The reader is left to

wonder: "And if AMANDA is ALIVE ... And JESUS is DEAD..." (324). The FBI is downstairs and calling Marx Marvelous by his real name.

Metaphorically, Amanda, in her mystical enlightenment, is the spiritual ascendance of the awakened feminine. She was ascendant when Marx met her and when she left; it was he who changed because of her.

The rise of feminism in the early 1970s provides the framework for Tom Robbins's second novel, *Even Cowgirls Get the Blues,* published in 1976. The tone and structure of both his first two novels is similar, but from *Another Roadside Attraction* to *Cowgirls,* the author, as though segueing on Amanda's feminist spirit, identifies many noticeable shifts taking place on the vanguard of American culture by 1972–1975.

In his second novel, Robbins tones down the metafictional asides, though he can't restrain himself completely: "Hmm. The author can sense that Chapter 100 displeases you. Not only does it interrupt the story, it says too much and it says it too didactically. Well, a story about a woman with sugar-sack thumbs is bound to be a bit heavy-handed" (345). The punning, clever similes, and comic inventiveness in both books are offset by the author's philosophical mode. These pontifications do slow down the storytelling and, unless one hunts for the attributions, there is often little differentiation of voice between the pontificating characters. Occasionally, there is a bona fide polemic, such as between Marx Marvelous and Amanda, but more often those things being said are there to impart whatever ideas Robbins is intent on imparting. In other words, the proclamations of Amanda sound interchangeable with those of the Chink, except that a handful of years have past. In his philosophical mode, the words of the Chink blend into the words of Sissy Hankshaw (with the enormously oversized thumbs), or Dr. Robbins (the cleverly concealed viewpoint character of the author).

Such passages read like short essays rather than like carefully crafted dialogue designed to characterize or to move the story forward. Tom Robbins has a point-of-view to share with the world, and he makes certain to let the reader know that this will be part of the experience of reading his novels. As a result, the presence of the author always lurks and full immersion into the character and situation is denied the reader. But in his humorous manner, Tom Robbins comes clean about his intent: "If he has confused you, the author apologizes. He swears to keep events in proper historical sequence from now on. He does not, however, disavow the impulses that led to his presentation of the cowgirl scenes out of chronological order, nor does he, in repentance, embrace the notion that literature should mirror reality" (124).

The unwillingness of Robbins to mirror reality, and deviations from mimetic conventions, align him with many postmodern writers, however, as a whole, these first two of his novels very much adhere to a traditional narrative arc leading to a crescendo of dramatic tension. The deviation employed by Robbins lies in the intent of the author to create comic characters and situations that will accommodate his spectrum of philosophical asides. As Tom Wolfe suggests when discussing the "electricity" imparted through the literary techniques of social realism, Robbins certainly decreases the dramatic voltage of his narrative when he becomes didactic, but compensates for this in how the approach adds contextual depth and broader meaning to the surface events and situational tension.

At his most successfully audacious, Robbins integrates his comic inventiveness with this philosophical posturing. For example, when Sissy is swept up in the cowgirl's revolt against feminine hygiene products— the cowgirls are working on a ranch in the Badlands of South Dakota owned by a feminine products magnate—the author is able to infuse his absurdist instincts into what is also a substantive social commentary. When the cowgirls lead a coup d' état against the sexual reconditioning program, they end their educational session by encouraging that the women douche with natural herbs. Then they offer the female guests at the ranch "a little self-celebration. [...] [R]each down with your fingers and get them wet with your juices. Then you rub it behind your ears ... [...] It's a wonderful perfume" (157).

The comic twists and dramatic lags aside, Robbins is an astute social observer of his time. The story starts with Sissy coming of age in Richmond, Virginia during the Eisenhower years of the 50s, but during the 60s—other than posing as a model for the same said feminine hygiene products—she is in constant motion, using her prodigious thumbs to hitchhike around the nation and all over the world, never heading to a destination, but on the road for the ecstasy this freedom of movement gives her. In 1972, at the age of thirty, Sissy is a near innocent primed for a sexually awakening. The Chink, a sage-like character who lives on the butte above the cowgirl's ranch and is one of Sissy's lovers in the story, acknowledges how both he and Sissy had remained apart from the happenings of the past decade. They missed out on:

> riots and rebellions, needless wars and threats of wars, drugs that opened minds to the infinite and drugs that shoved minds into the mushpot forever, awesome advances in technology and confusing declines in established values, [...] corruption, demonstrations and counterdemonstrations, [...] oil spills and rock festivals. [...]
>
> But those young women down there on this ranch [...] have been dipped in the events of our times, immersed from head to toe. [...] Their parent's culture failed them and then their own culture failed them. [...]
>
> These ladies, however, they're making another attempt at something honorable, another try at directing their own lives [262–263].

Bonanza Jellybean, the lead cowgirl on the ranch, and another of Sissy's lovers, gives this perspective an overt feminist slant when she asserts that it is boys who are able to actually become the things they dream about being as kids, but "if you got a girl who persists in fantasizing about a more exciting future for herself than housewifery, desk-jobbing or motherhood, then you'd better hustle her off to the child psychologist. Force her to face up to reality. We girls have about as much chance of growing up to be cowgirls as Eskimos have got being vegetarians" (149). Robbins loves the clever simile.

In addition to using these bisexual, "New Age" cowgirls as a construct to explore the feminist assertions of the early '70s, Robbins also corners a discussion on the rise of the environmental movement when he has the last fifty whooping cranes in North America land at a small lake on the ranch. Eventually, the rare cranes are at the center of conflict between the cowgirls and the Feds during the showdown at the climax of the novel.

With his comic flare, Robbins makes a case for these spiritually poor Westerners to rebuild the fires of paganism, to be their own master, their own Jesus, their own flying saucer, all by rescuing themselves. The dilemma is great. His protagonist Sissy, who is married to a very mainstream Native American, is "simultaneously in love with an elderly hermit and a teen-aged cowgirl" (278). The whooping cranes are on the brink of extinction and, as Dr. Robbins asserts "[l]esbianism is definitely on the rise [...], it's a cultural phenomenon, a healthy rejection of the paternalistic power structure that has dominated the civilized world for more than two thousand years" (279).

Dr. Robbins in *Cowgirls* and Amanda in *Another Roadside Attraction* share the same perspective about the two Christian millennia of what Amanda calls "penis power." And, even though Sissy floated through the '60s, the author doesn't ignore the hippies of the early to mid–'70s. Like Kesey, Brautigan, Hunter S. Thompson, and Gurney Norman who all shared an insider's perspective on the counterculture, Tom Robbins was also born in the mid–1930's. He turned thirty-one in 1967 when the term "hippie" was first widely applied to the teens and early twenty-somethings who were part of psychedelia and the countercultural upheaval. Even though Robbins didn't embrace the term hippie as a label for himself or his writing, as a novelist he promulgated a countercultural sensibility, especially with his application of "play as power." His novels serve as powerful edicts for suggesting a philosophy on how the individual should adapt to society. The author's hope implies that adult expressions of playfulness, in a myriad of manifestations, might impact the nature of our society. In this, the author sends a message of hopefulness about changing the world, an ethos he shares with his fellow counterculturalists. Siegel points out that:

The goal of Robbins's art is to alert us to the sacred, to get us to see things in a new, intense way—to get us to let go of our own limited perspectives by exciting us into a new awareness of the world.

The mysterious, hip, comic, and apparently discontinuous narrative voice that Robbins employs seems to mislead many readers who don't perceive the ultimate seriousness of his playfulness or the sense in magic [34].

From 1972 to 1975, young American men were no longer being drafted for Vietnam, "The Movement" had splintered. When *Cowgirls* was being written by Robbins, many hardcore hippies had ventured back-to-the-land in a communal mode not unlike what the cowgirls were attempting on this South Dakota ranch. While the so-called Woodstock Nation was shifting out of the spotlight at the center stage of American social change, the two most significant successor movements to emerge were feminism and environmentalism. However, as becomes evident at the end of the novel, the spirit of collectivism exhibited by the cowgirls dissipates into the larger, individualistic society in the manner of what happened with the counterculture. Likewise, at the end of *Even Cowgirls Get the Blues*, Dr. Robbins and Sissy hook up on their own road to domestication.

The writerly palate of Tom Robbins is by no means narrow or simplistic. Into his *Cowgirl* weave appear the hippies, FBI Agents, capitalists, media members, Indians, rednecks, cosmetic surgeons, and cosmetic deodorizers. As for the hippies, when Sissy is first heading down the back road to the ranch, she sees a "VW Microbus. It was painted with mandalas, lamaistic dorjes and symbols representing 'the clear light of the void'—quite an adornment for the vehicular flower of German industry." The bus pulls up with a man and a woman inside who are about twenty-four years old. "The female in the middle spoke. 'Are you a pilgrim?' she asked." They had thought Sissy was there to visit the Chink, whom they had heard was a sage. The young man warns her: "The crazy bastard tried to stone us to death" (131).

One hundred twenty-five pages later, after Sissy and the Chink are lovers, and as a hint of the Chink's earlier motivation as "the crazy bastard," he says:

[T]o worship the natural at the exclusion of the unnatural is to practice Organic Fascism—which is what many of my pilgrims practice. And in the best tradition of Fascism, they are totally intolerant of those who don't share their beliefs; thus, they foster the very kinds of antagonism and tension that lead to strife, which they, pacifists one and all, claim to abhor [257].

Tom Robbins, through his spokesperson/characters, is most intolerant of intolerance. Not only does he lampoon the excesses of these hippies, in a widely publicized article in 1979 he coined the term "feminismo" to point out the danger of feminist extremism. In *Cowgirls* this extreme is embodied in Dolores del Ruby, the man hating, cowgirl-in-black. Yet, even she softens after a Third Vision comes to her while high on peyote during the standoff with the FBI. The author's depictions of institutional intolerance toward threats of a communal nature, played out in eerie fashion in the early 1990s when Federal agents unleashed a barrage of firepower toward sect members holed up in a Waco, Texas church and toward a family of survivalists sequestered in a private homestead on Northern Idaho's Ruby Ridge. Even Robbins' use of the name del Ruby was prescient.

In the spirit of things "natural," the Cowgirls have their brown rice and bean sprouts, the reconditioning of the sexual reconditioning program, and a communal configuration where they must reckon with issues of territory, power, and interrelationship, as well as how they must posture themselves toward the larger world outside their gates. And if the challenge of surviving in a communal enclave is not hippie enough, the cowgirls alter the engrained migratory habits of the exceedingly rare whooping crane when Dolores del Ruby's peyote is mixed into the birdfeed. Some of the cowgirls are even indirectly linked to what Robbins calls the "League of the Acid Atom Avatar" of California of the '60s. In *Cowgirls*, Robbins presents many remnant elements of psychedelia and its counterculture that were still filtering through American society throughout the decade of the 1970's. In his essay, "The Sixties," Robbins notes that this transformative decade was "a fleeting moment of glory, a time when a significant little chunk of earthlings briefly realized their moral potential and flirted with their neurological destiny; a collective spiritual awakening that flared brilliantly until the brutal and mediocre impulses of the species drew tight once again the thick curtains of meathead somnambulism" (94). The standoff between the cowgirls and the authorities embodies such "somnambulism."

The author, as effectively as any other observer of the vibrant fringes of America's modern frontier, juggles a "hodgepodge of confounding ideas" (279). This hodgepodge is part of the fabric of the postmodern frontier like Brautigan's junkyard sale of a pastoral trout stream. Or as Seigel points out in a manner similar to Kesey's use of the wilderness as motif:

> To Tom Robbins, the wilderness seems to be all around us in the confusion of our culture, in the chaos of the events of our days—and in the virgin land of each individual's capacity for new experiences.
> [...] Robbins seems to say: Let's all move out there, to the borders of our conscious minds, to the frontiers where our selves meet creation [48, 51].

Out of the cauldron of the '60s came pronounced changes in attitudes and behavior. The linkages and fresh disconnections of these changes during this period of only a few years can be traced in a consecutive reading of *Another Roadside Attraction* and *Even Cowgirls Get the Blues*. Robbins has both a comic story to tell and many things he insists on telling the world. With his ardor for the freedom and magic of the human spirit, he succeeds far more than most novelists in his balancing of the dramatic and the didactic.

15

An Essay on Slouching, Hippies, and Hitchhiking

On the last day of 2005 while riding a ferry back from San Juan Island, I sat reading Joan Didion's breakout essay from 1967 called "Slouching Toward Bethlehem." A young woman, about twenty, came up and asked to use my cell phone. Her scarf partly covered a semi-mat of blonde dreadlocks, and the fabric almost matched a gauzy, East Indian skirt that drooped to her ankles just above a practical pair of boots. I wondered whether she was traveling with the young man who also had a scruffy backpack and similar, but shorter, hair. He had walked through the ferry by himself a few minutes earlier asking for a ride to Bellingham. I had told him, sorry, but we weren't going there.

The young woman took my phone, dialed, and sat on the bench across from me. She began telling a friend how not enough was happening on the Island so she was "flowing with it" and might be dancing that night somewhere in Bellingham for New Year's Eve. The enthusiasm never left her voice, though her forehead furrowed momentarily when she determined that the person on the other end wasn't taking her suggestion to drive to the ferry depot to pick her up. Ending the call, she stood and stretched toward me to hand back the phone. Dirt clogged her fingernails, and when she extended her arms, a natural-colored wool sweater rode up and exposed a wrinkled t-shirt and a bit of bare waist. Her bright eyes looked me over, but she didn't suspect the least bit of hippie in me.

Didion's article, first published in the *Saturday Evening Post* in September 1967, launched her career as a major American essayist. To write her story, she went to the Haight-Ashbury District in the spring of 1967 and fell in with several uprooted kids in their late teens that had found their way to San Francisco. It can't be said that she interviewed them because there seems to have been no formalized Q and A between Didion and her subjects. Didion, to use Kesey's term, was not "on the bus"

217

even though she copped an inauspicious manner in order to play the participant/observer. From the manner in which she described herself in the essay, Didion actually wasn't much of a participant. She was more like Oedipa Maas from *The Crying of Lot 49* in the way she reacted to her changing surroundings. These were two intelligent, young California women who, with fairly conservative inclinations, were being assaulted by seemingly darker forces they couldn't fully grasp. Didion was actually part of what Martin Lee and Bruce Shlain referred to in their book *Acid Dreams* as "the beginning of a concentrated media assault on the Haight-Ashbury. Soon it became the most overexposed neighborhood in the country as reporters from all over the world zeroed in on the psychedelic playground" (163).

By comparison, two years earlier in 1965, "Haight-Ashbury was a vibrant neobohemian enclave, a community on the cusp of a major transition. [...] The new hipsters had cast aside the syndrome of alienation and despair that saddled many of their beatnik forebears. The accent shifted from solitude to communion, from the individual to the interpersonal" (141–2).

When I was twenty, I hitchhiked on spring break from Seattle to San Francisco. I had little money and a slip of paper with an address on it where my hippie cousin supposedly lived. When I knocked on the door of the address, the woman who answered told me that my cousin didn't live there anymore, but since my cousin was their friend, they were cool with me crashing on the couch. The apartment wasn't in the Haight, but I visited the neighborhood during my stay. I wasn't expecting a hippie Mecca actually, but went there curious to see what all the commotion had been about. Nine years after the notorious Summer of Love, I thought there might be some remnants of what had made the neighborhood so infamous. In the spring of 1976, Haight-Ashbury was all but rid of any traces of hippiedom.

At the apartment I recall how one night some guy stopped by to sell cocaine. My hosts were ticked off because they got burned and the stuff wasn't coke at all. One morning I managed to find my cousin who seemed dazed to see me. We ate breakfast at a coffee shop, but I continued crashing at her friends' pad. After four days in San Francisco, I hitchhiked north. I stood for an especially long time under clear March skies on the freeway onramp waiting for a ride when another hitchhiker, an Englishman, showed up. I had mixed feelings about this since it's much tougher to get a ride with two males holding out mortal-sized thumbs. Other than that, the Brit seemed nice. When we talked, I used the expression "shooting the breeze." He'd never heard it before. When you think about it, it's a pretty strange phrase.

At long last, a muscle car with glass-pacs that barely muffled the sound of the engine pulled over for us. After they said they were headed to Redding, a good ride north, we climbed in back behind the two greasers. They asked us if we could help with gas money. We only had a couple of bucks each to offer. We handed this over to them when they stopped at the nearest truck stop. They suggested we go inside to buy some snacks. While cruising down one of the aisles, they bolted toward the door. As quickly as we figured out they were ditching us, we chased after only to see their car squealing off. We ran toward them in t-shirts, fearing the worst for a long trip to the still cold Northwest. The closer we got to the parking space, the faster we ran. Our breath came back when we spotted our backpacks dumped by them on the asphalt.

Other than the one time I rode with some way-too-drunk guys into Pullman, that was the worst experience I've ever had in those several years of hitchhiking. Unlike Sissy Hankshaw, I was thumbing rides, not just to be hitchhiking, but to get to some specific destination. When we got to Portland, I left the Englishman to go visit my grandparents. They told me they were really happy that I'd visited my cousin, but they didn't like the idea of my hitchhiking. They bought me a ticket on Greyhound and I spent the last 180 of my 1600-mile trip tightly wedged into a seat on the bus to Seattle.

The free spirited young woman on the ferry didn't surprise me when, following the use of the cell phone, she worked us for a ride, especially once she found out we could get her part way to her destination. "Is there anything I can offer you in trade?" she asked, and looked down at her soiled Guatemalan cloth purse as though it held an assortment of artifacts to barter. I wish that I'd asked her what she had in mind so I might know her sense of cosmic fairness, but when I thought back on all the hitchhiking I'd done I let her know that we expected nothing. Whatever grand scheme of giving and taking she had going in her life, she knew how to engage beneficent souls with a disarmingly charming style. Still, she didn't win our blissful trust. She tried to act like she was alone, but we sensed she wasn't. This was all a social game between strangers, a sizing up that cut both ways. With two kids in our family, we filtered our decision. She was petite and benign and only mildly trippy, so our home-ride security wasn't a concern.

Earlier that day at the used bookstore in Friday Harbor, I asked the proprietor what she thought of Didion's latest work, *The Year of Magical Thinking*, the one about her husband's death, the one for which she had just won the National Book Award.

"I lost my husband five years ago," the bookstore owner said. "I couldn't have read this book a few years ago, but enough time has passed now." She took a deep breath and rang up my purchases. "She got it right," said the woman.

I mumbled something resembling a condolence and looked forward to reading the "Slouching" essay. This whole mercurial hippie thing isn't easy to get right. I asked the bookstore owner if she knew of any buses going across the island to Roche Harbor. (We had left our car at the ferry landing on the mainland.)

"Not this time of year," she said. "How many of you are there?"

"Four," I said.

"I was going to say that you might hitchhike. That's very common on the Island, but that's probably not practical with so many of you."

With my copy of *Slouching Toward Bethlehem* in a plastic sack—along with *Steppenwolf, The Greening of America,* and Didion's *The White Album*—I was impressed that I was in a place where the mortification of giving rides to strangers didn't exist in the way it does on the mainland. In an American culture steeped with a fear of all that might go wrong, hitch-hiking has diminished many-fold since the 1970s. Of course, without a ferryboat or plane ticket, or boat or plane of ones own, there was no way off the island.

"Slouching Towards Bethlehem" opens by pointing out how "[a]dolescents drifted from city to torn city, sloughing off both the past and the future as snakes shed their skins, children who were never taught and would never now learn the games that held society together." I'm confident that this hitchhiker, for all her neo-hippie manner, absolutely knew the games that held society together, but was at a space and time in her life where she simply refused to be part of the glue. Didion's phrase, "would never now learn" struck me as a cold indictment of the youngsters in her essay. I couldn't see condemning any of the hippies I'd ever met—including this second generation, Woodstock Nation/eco-Village kind of kid—to a life of never now learning, or becoming, or transcending the lessons or obstacles that they would come to face in life. In Didion's essay, all the transient kids were high or coming down or waiting to get high again. On the ferry this young woman acted quite sober. That's not to say that I could not have imagined her getting high, with and without drugs, but she did understand one of the most fundamental elements of societal functioning: She knew how to reciprocate.

On San Juan Island, a highly affluent place of waterfront homes and rural seclusion near both Seattle and Vancouver, a hippie sense of free-spirited mobility was in play to an unusual extent. After buying the used books we heard one neo-hippie, who was grabbing an espresso through the outside window of a kiosk, being asked by another neo-hippie, who had stopped in the middle of the road in a beat up pick-up, if he knew about anything going on. To me it sounded like the guy in the truck was sending veiled signals to the one sipping coffee that he was receptive to hanging out on New Year's Eve. Pretending not to be listening, we walked on and never heard the outcome.

Going to Friday Harbor, I had no intention of writing a personal essay to include in this book. Then I was reading Didion's essay and encountered the neo-hippie character on the ferry. These things connected in my mind to Denis Johnson's essay called "Hippies" which he wrote about a Rainbow Gathering in 1996. In "Hippies" he commented on how it was "astonishing to see so many youngsters on the cusp of twenty, as if perhaps some segment of the sixties population stopped growing up" (27). So, on the cusp of 2006, thinking about this twenty-or-so-year-old hitchhiker and about when I was a twenty-year-old hitchhiker three decades earlier, I concluded that a period of free-spiritedness is a rite of passage for many coming-of-age youth.

So here I am writing this essay to link these two other essays into this book. Of all the forms of essays, the personal essay is the least rhetorical in the Aristotelian practice of rhetoric. The personal essay approximates narrative in the way Aristotle defined dramatic actualization in *Poetics*. This type of essay is a form of story as well as an argument or method of persuasion through dramatic actualization. This is playing out here in the incredibly high stakes tension I've created while deciding whether to offer a ride to a strange nouveau hippie after she interrupted my reading and my thinking about other essays on hippies. I mention this in this late chapter within *The Hippie Narrative* because I want to feel justified, rhetorically, in using the personal essay to impart a bit of narrative denouement to my dramatic arc of literary studies that show how the hippie phenomenon unfolded and, in cultural impact, never fully died. Like that one metafictional aside of Tom Robbins, I don't repent this method. It's a way of noting how this postmodernist technique of meta-essay is stopping the vivid continuous dream of my riveting primary essay by acknowledging its structure as a narrative form with rhetorical intent. It's a deconstructionist approach to storytelling and a trippy way to write.

Most of Denis Johnson's essay is about how he was tripping on psilocybin mushrooms at the Rainbow Gathering in the Ochoco National Forest of eastern Oregon in 1996. At the Gathering there were:

[t]en thousand or more hippies touring along paths here in the American wilderness just as we did up and down Telegraph Ave. in Berzerkly almost thirty years ago. Yes! They're still at it! Still moving and searching. Still moving along the thoroughfares ... [22–23].

When I read "Slouching Toward Bethlehem," I was struck by Didion's bleak 1967 perspective about how we in American society had "aborted ourselves and butchered the job, and because nothing else seemed so relevant I [Didion] decided to go to San Francisco. San

Francisco was where the social hemorrhaging was showing up. San Francisco was where the missing children were gathering and calling themselves 'hippies'"(85). So off she went to find her tightly defined target group. In fairness to Didion, she defines "hippie" as the equivalent of what today we call homeless street kids. For the purposes of my book, published four decades later, I used a broader definition by categorizing hippie as those voluntary and pacifist adherents of that period's counterculture.

In her essay, Didion demonstrates superb talent for a New Journalistic approach, though her conclusion was simplistic:

> Of course the activists—not those whose thinking had become rigid, but those whose approach to revolution was imaginatively anarchic—had long ago grasped the reality which still eluded the press: we were seeing something important. We were seeing the desperate attempt of a handful of pathetically ill-equipped children to create a community in a social vacuum. Once we had seen these children, no longer could we overlook the vacuum, no longer pretend that society's atomization could be reversed [122-3].

Even today, I could imagine traveling to inner city Vancouver, Seattle, Portland or San Francisco to find a startling overabundance of rootless street kids strung out on meth or heroine. I could talk to them, give them rides and write about their disorientation, drug taking and lack of goals in life. However, unlike Didion, I wouldn't conclude from such depraved excess that society was being atomized. Many of her observations strike me as boldly honest and astute, and obviously she identified a systemic problem in North American society, but to call it "atomization" implies that the mainstream society was being blown into tiny particulate matter, an analogy that's misleading.

Didion's use of "atomization" was a rough way of saying we have an increasingly privatized society. Yet, society wasn't atomized, but simply connected, more and more, by a mass culture. What was once handled within networks of extended familial ties had unraveled (as Didion acknowledges in her essay). The option of individuals to uproot and move Westward Ho to the frontier was no longer viable. The institutions of the mass culture have a limited ability to replace the extended family, but that's not to say that an evolving re-configuration of society into a dynamic of mass culture was "atomizing," or, to carry out the logic of her analogy, exploding into minute, particulate matter. Even though individuals within the mass culture are more depersonalized, not unlike atomic specks, the institutionalized mechanisms of social control, despite the chaos, were well in place. In the essay she talks about one narcotics cop making 43 busts in one week. The crackdown was part of an orchestrated effort by the authorities. A year or two earlier, the same authorities had taken a hands-off approach to the bohemian goings-on in the

Haight. In the larger context, it was the fabric of a viable social safety net that was in tatters. In fact it was the great misuse of American institutional military might that was directly agitating so many of draft age youth in 1967. And this from the single institution in the world best positioned to literally atomize society. Didion's term "atomization" helped sell magazines, but it was poorly conceptualized.

What happened in the latter part of the '60s was in part about creating new forms of community, but as Diggers Emmett Grogan and Peter Coyote portray in their respective memoirs about the Haight Ashbury scene, it was more than a handful of pathetically ill-equipped children attempting this feat. The hippie fringe of society was also the product of the federal government's direct role in opening a Pandora's Box with the hallucinogenic drug LSD. Without the secretive MK-Ultra program funding those CIA sponsored experiments on American civilians in the late '50s and early '60s, one should doubt whether psychedelia would have occurred. Once LSD—this kingpin of all the drugs of the '60s—was discovered, chemically produced, and widely distributed on the street, the Box was open and this mind-expanding substance altered the way its users dressed, created art, engaged one another, and perceived the world around them. Or as Tom Robbins asserts in his essay, "The Sixties": "I think it need be established, firmly, flatly, and finally, that what we call the 60's would never have happened had it not been for the introduction of psychedelic drugs into the prevailing American paradigm (94)."

The government then reacted to stem the tide, to deter the public from using and experimenting with this substance. LSD was far from the mind-controlling drug for interrogation that the CIA was trying to find when conducting its experiments. The anti–LSD campaign of the late '60s and '70s was fiercely waged. In *Acid Dreams,* the authors state that:

> LSD was singled out as Public Enemy Number One by the mass media, which whipped America into a virtual frenzy over psychedelic drugs. It wasn't enough to convey the false impression that LSD probably caused permanent insanity; all of a sudden the press conjured up the frightening prospect of couples giving birth to some kind of octopus because acid had scrambled their chromosomes. However, when the Army Chemical Corps ran in-house studies to assess the potential hazards of LSD "from a tissue or genetic standpoint," it could not duplicate these findings. "Although human chromosome breaks have been reported by others, we found them much more frequently from caffeine and many other substances," stated Dr. Van Sim, chief of clinical research at Edgewood Arsenal during the 1960s and 1970s [154–5].

There was, of course, the bad trip, and in a few people, lysergic acid caused a horrible reaction—even the psychotic reaction of suicide—but there was undeniable official hypocrisy when so many people in the intellectual and artistic elite, including tenured Harvard Professors such as

Richard Alpert and Timothy Leary, comedian Steve Allen, writers Ken Kesey and Tom Robbins and many others, could take the drug in a manner tacitly approved by the government, and then, suddenly, when psychedelia erupted, the drug, according to the official word, was the worst imaginable thing that a human could possibly ingest short of croaking by drinking poison. LSD is, irrefutably, a highly potent hallucinogen with a profound neurological effect that the government, since the mid–'60s, has chosen to censure rather than to continue studying.

The Haight, as the center of psychedelia, became depicted as an alternative frontier, even though this artistic, bohemian neighborhood didn't have the institutional resources to handle a huge influx of runaways. Didion described a self-selecting assemblage of young, homeless street kids descending en masse to a place they had read and heard about that offered wild fun and refuge. Attracted to San Francisco by word-of-mouth and increasing mass media attention, these kids hitchhiked into town with their youthful excess. In line with a raw, laissez faire capitalism, most needed to hustle on the streets to survive. Drugs were both escapist and part of a currency of survival. In "Slouching," Didion stopped short of seeing any hope in the effort of these "children to create a community in a social vacuum."

Far more than involving just street kids, the counterculture generated a critical mass of momentum that was creating alternative community out of what Didion called a "vacuum." The anti-war protest movement, communal lifestyles, drug use, explosion of hard rock, spiritual exploration, civil rights efforts, and reaction to what was widely perceived as a cabalistic governing body, all coalesced with such a momentum and purpose that the then-called "establishment" was forced to reckon with this upsurge on many fronts.

"The Movement" had so many movements contained within its defiant momentum that it was difficult for the government to define this new "enemy" that was so freedom loving, freewheeling, and largely leaderless. Yet, the momentum of "The Movement" was full of participants who were designing solutions of their own through communalism, new spiritual paths, political activism, and earth-friendly environmentalism, including healthier approaches to eating and health care. For a brief time, the "alternatives" seemed primed to overwhelm everything that was "tried and true." In his essay, "The Sixties," Robbins goes on to say that "(for a time, the "counterculture" functioned as the dominant culture), music was less superficial then, authority less respected, violence less tolerated, love less fettered, wealth less worshiped, power less coveted, guilt less shouldered, depression less indulged, and fear less shivered with (93)."

The dialectical nature of this countercultural antithesis to the status quo resulted, over the next decade, in a profound resynthesis of society that became neither like the mainstream culture that went before or the counterculture that withered over time. The nature of this revolution was not an overt overthrow of a political or economic system, but of radical shifts in the shared cultural values and consciousness once a critical mass of individuals within American society exacted this shift. In the first decade of the new millennium, we still have our street kids, our rampant consumerism, drug problems, and, in many ways, we still have a divided society in how America approaches war and the social role of government. Yet, rock music blares ubiquitously, organic foods share space at the grocers, high tech innovations ushered in the information age, industry pollutes less, equal opportunity and cultural diversity are the norm, heterosexual men hug heterosexual men, and even the most conservative Joe can have a "bummer" day.

Again, in fairness to Didion, she wrote her essay in 1967 as the counterculture was just flourishing. She did recognize that these children were attempting to create community in a social vacuum. Over the next few years, the hippie lifestyle with its communal manifestations offered the hope of refuge, and, for many, filled a deep-seated yearning for meaningful human connections. Sincere efforts to establish alternative communities were by no means limited to Didion's street kids. According to *Acid Dreams:*

> By early 1967 a number of thriving alternative institutions already existed in the psychedelic city-state [of the Haight]: the *Oracle*, the Community Switchboard, the Hip Job Coop, Happening House (a cooperative teaching venture), Radio Free Hashbury; in coming months the Free Medical Clinic would open its doors. Even the neighborhood merchants formed a business council, HIP (Haight Independent Proprietors). The idea of building a parallel society smack-dab in the belly of the beast held great appeal to many a shell-shocked pacifist who'd grown weary of sit-ins, demonstrations, and police violence. For these people the futility of trying to reform the system was amply confirmed by the landslide election of Ronald Reagan as governor of California. They were ready for a different approach; rather than try to overhaul the social and economic structures of mass commercial society, they would simply try to outflank them [168].

Over the next couple of years, this momentum shifted from a primarily urban focus to a rural one. The back-to-the-land movement was sincerely believed by large numbers of participants and observers to offer new modes of living together that would be more nurturing and enlightened than the dominant privatized model. Today, gated communities sell the appurtenances of the commune with shared clubhouses, pools, and common spaces, but the sequestering is elitist and the collectivist overtures superficial. The mostly failed attempts at communal living in the '60s have been judged as romantic idealism, but it made realistic sense in the social vacuum that Didion partially depicted in "Slouching Toward Bethlehem."

She failed to recognize how constructivist this new collectivist spirit would be in its many manifestations.

A hippie communal spirit was evident at the 1996 Rainbow Gathering that Denis Johnson described when a communal circle formed in the middle of a large meadow:

> As the sunset reddens the west, black thunderheads form in the south: a lull, a dead spot, a return of the morning's silence as the Rainbow Family watches a squall gathering, bunching itself together in the southern half of an otherwise clear ceiling [33].

When I hitchhiked to an earlier Rainbow Gathering in 1981, nature didn't intervene on the unified voices that grew in volume under blue sky at noon on that Fourth of July. The early afternoon crowd formed a circle in Meditation Meadow. I joined the throng. From the hum of those gathered, an "om" started softly and grew like a swarm of honeybees circling the hive. The tone was collective and human. The "om" of several thousand voices seemed to whirl more and more loudly above my head until it was overhead. I tilted my head upward. Above us, a helicopter approached and descended. In order to photograph our bliss, it loomed above our moment of peace. For a photograph of our collective hope, we weren't bombed. Instead of storm clouds, our harmony was obliterated by the chopper.

Didion, like Tom Wolfe, was an outsider looking in on the counterculture. Such a perspective affected the tone and selectivity of her writing. She presented her covert findings in shocking detail. Her considerable eye for detail and compositional talents brought her readers an unsweetened look at the "Flower Child" phenomenon. She watched the Diggers using trippy, street-mime techniques to unsettle public consciousness. She found troops of other reporters there as well as cops cracking down on the scene, and she uncovered ample evidence of youthful excess, some of it atrocious. She recognized that these kids were adapting to dislocation.

Didion failed to see, seek, or find the esprit of any hopefulness. By her account, her young subjects were doomed. Many of those shooting heroin or crystal meth probably were. I would never expect to find the likes of the young woman on the ferry sleeping in a heap on Skid Row. With her articulate, creative manner, it wouldn't surprise me to find her in a few years in most any capacity, still living alternatively, or as a part of the mainstream flow of glue. Even Didion's use of Yeats' metaphor "slouching" implies only bad posture. This makes sense considering how the author limited the scope of her essay to a portrait of the most down-and-out street kids. The approach, however, ignored the collectivist spirit of hopefulness, or the individual quest for spiritual peace. Like Tom Wolfe, Didion gave a mainstream readership reason to fear this whole hippie phenomenon, but she, by no means, gave a rounded picture. Instead, the great fear of our time—atomic annihilation—was now Didion's convenient metaphor for the great social change in play in 1967. These hippie kids were victims—particulate matter of The Bomb.

She ends the essay by depicting a young child whose hippie mother continually allowed the little girl to be high on acid or peyote. Didion used this extremist illustration to sum up her case of society breaking apart:

> "Five years old," Otto says. "On acid."
> The five year old's name is Susan, and she tells me she goes to High Kindergarten. [...] For a year now her mother has given her both acid and peyote. Susan describes it as getting stoned,
> I start to ask her if any of the other kids at High Kindergarten get stoned, but I falter at the key words [127–8].

In her life beyond writing this essay, one wonders if Didion actually protected her journalist's source, or if she reported the mother of this child to the authorities on grounds of severe abuse. Was this not a situation where the social "game" of journalism, of which Didion clearly knew the rules, should have been violated for the sake of this young child? Or would Didion "never learn" that the welfare of this child was part of her social and moral engagement as a member of this society in a way that transcended her role as a writer/reporter/journalist/essayist?

I visited San Francisco again on New Year's of 1978–79. The Grateful Dead—former denizens of The Haight—played the last concert at Winterland. Ken Kesey and some Prankster friends were at the edge of the stage. While Haight-Ashbury was still sterile of its hippie heritage, this Dead concert that kicked off at midnight and played until dawn, had an auditorium filled with countercultural zeal:

> Bill Graham, to his credit, had not overstuffed the place. Winterland was full, but not a crammed mob scene. There was ample room for everyone there. The New Rider's of the Purple Sage, old friends of the Dead, opened the evening. The potpourri crowd of Deadheads ranged from fading hippies to their teenage children, cowboys to freaks, bikers to the bourgeois chic. I wondered what percentage of the audience had been active participants in the acid tests and the Summer of Love. Meandering earlier that day, [...] I visited the Haight Ashbury district. A dozen years after the Summer of Love, there was scarcely a trace of hippiedom in the Haight, but looking around the concert, the old movement seemed well represented. [...]
> The Dead had helped the San Francisco counterculture erupt. Now everyone waited for the rocket ship to land. With pulleys and a revving engine, Bill Graham, in his joint-shaped space vessel, descended from the back of the Winterland Arena. A cannon exploded. 1979. The crowd roared. Let the bacchanalia begin. The spirit of Dionysus floated in amid the letting go of balloons. As they cascaded onto our heads, the music drifted in—a sunshine daydream at midnight [Seattle *Sun*].

Ten years later in 1989, I visited the Haight again. This time, shops trading in hippie regalia, memorabilia and paraphernalia had popped up. This was tourism—the hippie epoch was a commodity sterilized of its earlier political and sociological threat.

By the end of the '80s, the hippie culture had long since dissipated, only grouping now and then in the cracks of mainstream society. The Rainbow Gathering that Johnson described in 1996 was a vestige, but very much the real thing. In his essay, those assembled are watching the gathering squalls:

> Then a rainbow drops down through the pale sky.
> The sight of it, a perfect multicolored quarter-circle, calls up a round of howling from everywhere at once that grows and doesn't stop, and the drumming starts from every direction [32].

The young woman on the ferry, after we offered her a ride, began showing us her two wick balls on a chain. Though these fist-sized clumps of wicks probably had a hip name that she mentioned, I didn't catch it. She swung them in circles and said that, at night, when they were dipped in lamp oil and lit, the effect was very trippy. She didn't strike me as atomized, but quite adaptive at living a free-spirited rejection of mainstream norms as she worked to ingratiate herself to us.

She told us she would be swinging her lit up wick balls at Burning Man in the summer. I didn't ask her, but maybe she had been to a Rainbow Gathering herself. Denis Johnson describes the freedom and magic of that same storm in 1996:

> Then it's a double rainbow, and then a triple, and the drums and howls can't be compared to anything I've ever heard, it's a Rainbow Sign from Above—*Loving you!*—then a monster light show with the thunderheads gone crimson in the opposing sunset, the three rainbows, and now forked lightning and profound, invincible thunder, every crooked white veiny bolt and giant peal answered by a wild ten-thousand-voiced ululation—a conversation with the Spirit of All at the Divine Fourth of July show! Far fucking out! The Great Mother-Father Spirit Goddess-dude is a hippie! [33–34].

Even though we never left the United States, our Evergreen State Ferry had originated on Canada's Vancouver Island. After we passed through the Homeland Security checkpoint for customs, she was standing alone at the edge of the parking lot above us, smiling freely, looking more transcendent than the clean-cut passengers filing along behind her. Politely, she let us know that she had found a different ride to Bellingham—probably with her friend. Our young hippie could have slouched away without a word to us, but she stood tall. She knew her social graces and we wished her luck.

Denouement

16

Postmodernism
Reconstructed

"Hippie" and "postmodernism" are both terms of uneasy distinction. The hippie phenomenon has been said to encapsulate the postmodern state of being. Not until late 1966 was "hippie" used as a label by the mainstream media to typecast the multitudes of teens and young adults who were growing long hair, questioning authority, and participating in the throes of psychedelia, a phenomenon that took root most strongly on the West Coast of the United States, but which spread contemporaneously through major cities across the United States and Europe. This nascent counterculture created a whole lifestyle rooted in a disaffection that challenged core precepts of the mainstream culture on questions of war, health, consumer habits, spirituality, sexuality, ecology, and institutional constraint on personal liberty and expression.

"Poststructuralism," as a theoretical approach of literary "postmodernism," emerged as an outgrowth of related youthful discontent and protests in France in 1968. Just as many longhaired, pacifist, and antiestablishment adherents of the counterculture eschewed the term "hippie" for its mainstream pejorative connotations, the term "postmodernism" was similarly elusive, as explored in the chapter on *The Electric Kool-Aid Acid Test*. The American sobriquet "hippie" was promulgated by "outside" media wanting an easy label for the youth who were partaking in this unrest. Similarly, the leading poststructuralists believed that any definition for postmodernism must come from the "outside," even though, according to postmodernist reasoning, there is no "outside" from which to "objectively" label the present. Perhaps the Postmodernists recognized that, once labeled, this school of critique, like the freshly labeled hippie, could be more easily scorned, ridiculed, and dissected.

The philosophical question of whether there *is* or *is not* such a thing as "objectivity" lies beyond the scope of this book. Yet, within the postmodern argument, one finds the corollary that there can be no such thing as "realism." To make this argument, the fundamental unit of *meaning* for the poststructural deconstructivist is linguistic and derived from the signifier or sign that cannot be "objectively" delineated.

The "electricity" which Tom Wolfe refers to in the "New Journalism" is an emotive response of the reader to narrative created through the literary techniques of social realism. With such conventional narrative writing, *meaning* is derived, not primarily from signs and signifiers, but from the dramatic whole. Terry Eagleton in *Literary Theory: An Introduction* states that, for the poststructuralist, "meaning, if you like, is scattered or dispersed along the whole chain of signifiers: it cannot be easily nailed down, it is never fully present in any one sign alone, but is rather a kind of constant flickering of presence and absence together. Reading is like tracing this process of constant flickering than it is like counting beads on a necklace" (128). In other words, a constructivist literary critique looks at story in terms of how effectively it has built towards the dramatic whole, while the poststructuralist starts with the text and deconstructs toward the smallest linguistic unit, the signifier. To do this, poststructuralist literary theory looks at the interrelationship of the reader and the text.

Within *Poetics* Aristotle diagrams a conceptualization of speaker/audience/subject as an integrated model for understanding how drama functions. This evolved into the triangulated model of author/ reader/ text as the conceptual basis of several pre-structuralist literary theories-: phenomenology, hermeneutics, Reception Theory and New Criticism. Yet, unlike these prominent 20th century literary theories that privilege the reader, author, or text, Aristotle did not elevate one element over the other two. Deconstructivism concerns itself with analysis based on reader/text. Missing in such analysis is the role of author in the creation of the text. Also, recent literary theories based on linguistics (structuralism, post-structuralism), economics (Marxism), psychology (psychoanalysis) or gender studies (feminism) are essentially interpretations, or deconstructions of literary text, that do *not* focus on the crafting of literature. The authorial role is inherently "constructivist" rather than "deconstructivist."

Tom Wolfe was speaking about literary novelists of the 1960s and '70s when he commented on the abandonment of the techniques of social realism and the "electricity" this approach renders. Such "electricity" implies an integrated author/text/reader perspective whereby the author, through strong depictions of social realism, has created a text that will "jolt" the reader. Dramatic actualization, rather than a string of signifiers as the conduit of meaning, is best analyzed through the integrated analysis of authorial design, textual construct, *and* reader response.

Within the hippie phenomenon, the parallel to this was in its Dionysian dialectic. There was a prevailing construct of culture, its countercultural deconstruction, and the yielding of a new cultural construct. In the literature of the 1960s and '70s, one prominent experimental approach featured the metafictional technique of authors writing self-referentially to discuss within their texts the construction of those narratives. Kurt Vonnegut and Tom Robbins were notable as metafictionalists. The hippies of the late '60s were railing against mainstream society in a highly deconstructivist manner, but as seen in Gurney Norman's *Divine Right's Trip*, the phenomenon evolved into one where those hippies found constructivist adaptations on the edges of American society. After the initial bacchanalian upsurge, many fully immersed hippies withdrew into creating an alternative lifestyle with shared expectations for attaining a harmonious coexistence with one another and with the environment. This included healthier eating habits, greater thought regarding the impact of what they were consuming, a pacifist and collectivist credo, and striving to find a higher level of spirituality, as well as coming to grips with overly escapist drug use or how to engage in core relationships. The hippies redirected their reactionary and iconoclastic spirit of 1966–1968 toward alternative approaches that, by roughly 1969–70, began looking in earnest to "change the world," mostly through the contagious energy of lifestyle example. As utopian and idealistic as the hippies were, the most conscientious of them attempted to take their frustration and alienation beyond a state of ennui, the postmodern condition that the current postmodernist tenet holds to be ontologically inevitable. In other words, there was a hopefulness being exhibited through the creation of alternative lifestyles. This was constructivist, not deconstructivist.

Even Hunter S. Thompson, whose ennui falls on the most jaded end of the countercultural spectrum, took part in the back-to-the land exodus. James Stull in *Literary Selves: Autobiography and Contemporary American Nonfiction* points out that:

> Hunter S. Thompson's journalism pieces often conclude with the author's self-imposed exile (from society). This real and metaphorical escape to his Woody Creek home [in Aspen, Colorado] coincided with the counterculture's rural retreat at the decade's end and prefigured the therapeutic quest for selfhood that followed in the 1970s. These cultural trends corresponded with two distinct and at times overlapping ways in which literary journalists conceptualized and presented the self through the 1970s and into the 1980s. Instead of focusing on the urban milieu as the setting and subject of their works, which characterized much of the New Journalism of the 1960s, many literary journalists and nonfiction writers [...] revealed an increased interest in rural, regional, ecological, environmental, and historical subject matter [119].

As Stulls suggests, the energy of the counterculture became less urban and more diffuse as it "retreated" into rural enclaves. The diffusion of countercultural values through the mainstream, of course, resulted from much more than the hardcore hippies going back-to-the-land. At the same time as this exodus occurred, a spectrum of hippie values were being absorbed or rejected by those within the mainstream culture— rural, suburban and urban.

In dialectic terms, the *thesis* of the Eisenhower era was turned on its head with the *antithesis* of social tumult in the late Sixties. At the beginning of the decade the diffuse stirring of cultural unrest was depicted aptly by Ken Kesey in both *Cuckoo's Nest* and *Great Notion*. Into the middle years of the decade, the proto-hippie, communal antics of Kesey and the Merry Pranksters became the subject of Tom Wolfe's biographical *Electric Koolaid Acid Test* in a way that captured the cultural manifestations of a burgeoning psychedelia. On the political front, Norman Mailer's *Armies of the Night* portrayed the antiwar element of this *antithesis* of rebellion. Then, as an outgrowth of this Dionysian reaction, a *synthesizing* cultural absorption of new values, behaviors and production began to occur when many of the constructivist alternatives were commoditized or otherwise integrated into mainstream society. Tom Robbins, especially, was tuned into this shifting zeitgeist with *Another Roadside Attraction* and *Even Cowgirls Get the Blues*.

The 1970s and '80s witnessed an acceptance and cooption of many countercultural alternatives—organic foods, tempered militarism, mainstreaming of hard rock music, longer hair, relaxing of social protocol, more acceptance of diversity, and the legislation of more environmental and ecological protective measures. At the same time there was a wholesale rejection of other hippie tendencies through anti-drug crackdowns, eradication of many communes through zoning and health code restrictions, or cultural dismissal of non-monogamous sexual relationships. The mainstream American society of the 1970s became somewhat more hip and somewhat more authoritarian as a consequence. American culture was changing as a result of the tension with its counterculture.

When John Gardner talks about three kinds of novel—energeic, juxtapositional and lyrical—and presents the concept of profluence to depict the manner of keeping a story moving forward, he is being constructivist; he is speaking about the way authors write dramatically effective narrative. In *The Art of Fiction,* he states:

> Seize the trunk of any science securely, and you have control of its branches. [...] Since metafiction is by nature a fiction-like critique of conventional fiction, and since so-called deconstructive fiction [...] uses conventional methods, it seems more important that young writers understand conventional fiction in all its complexity than that they be too much distracted from the fundamental [xi].

The Art of Fiction was published in 1982 before the term postmodernism was widely used in literature. *Trout Fishing in America* is an example of a compellingly wrought work of juxtapositional fiction; *Slaughterhouse-Five* is highly metafictional with an energeic core to its "unstuck in time" juxtapositioning. Both works gained favor with a burgeoning counterculture that was open to ironic depictions of alienation where humans were trying to adapt to the modern condition.

Rather than engage in a postmodern discursiveness, *The Hippie Narrative* has employed the "trunk of the science" as the analytical benchmark and tool from which to study these key countercultural narratives of the era. Specifically, in taking Gardner's precept a step further than he did in *The Art of Fiction*, the theoretical basis of creating conventional fiction is viewed as one which is built on a profluence of prose that is embedded with an energeic dynamic—the crafting of narrative so that it is dramatic and forward-moving and driven by an actualization of potential in character and situation. Of the works examined here, *Trout Fishing in America* departs the most from the "trunk of the science." *Divine Right's Trip* adheres most closely to the conventional energeic form and best captures the verisimilitude of the hippie scene of 1969 and '70 through its representative profile of a callow, trippy, and idealistic hippie couple. With verisimilitude comes the "electricity" of which Wolfe is speaking. The other countercultural works studied here deviate to a varying extent from the "trunk of the science" with its profluence and energeia.

When examining these countercultural works, there is no simple segue from Late Modernism to Postmodernism. What is notable, instead, is a broadening of authorial techniques. Reflected in this diversity of writing was a decided shift from the conventional realism of the Late Modernist to the more unconventional realism depicting the initial stages of the postmodern era in the 1960's. Techniques of realism were never completely abandoned, but comic surrealism, a fragmented juxtapositioning, and self-referential metafiction were part of the experimentation used by authors to gain specific narrative effects. For example, *Slaughterhouse-Five*, as it depicted the psychological impact of the horror of war, benefited greatly from its highly fragmented, juxtapositional irony that, nevertheless, culminated in an energeic climax. The depiction of the firebombing scene near the end of the novel, not only unified the many narrative fragments, but served as the story's climax in a way that actualized the potential of its protagonist as a schizophrenic victim of both modern war, the alienating society in which he found himself in 1968, and his abduction to the planet Tralfamadore, a place that served as a grand metaphor for the utopian confines of a repressed man's escapist yearnings.

The most ironic literary development of the 1960s came with the propensity of non-fiction writers to adopt the literary techniques of social

realism at the same time that serious novelists began abandoning such
realism in favor of increasingly metafictional and juxtapositional methods. As the conventions of the establishment order were being challenged on many social fronts, it was not surprising that the writers of the
era also challenged the conventions of literary depiction. However, the
writers of nonfiction appreciated more than the writers of fiction those
narrative advantages gained by employing the literary techniques of
social realism.

The postmodernists, through deconstructivist theoretical techniques, became adept in the 1970s and '80s at what Eagleton states, "is
a power-game, a mirror-image of orthodox academic competition. It is
just that now, in a religious twist to the old ideology, victory is achieved
by *kenosis* or self-emptying: the winner is the one who has managed to
get rid of all his cards and sit with empty hands" (147). For the creator
of literature such an approach is irrelevant, because the author is constructing text, not deconstructing it. In fact, the author, when constructing a narrative, is interested in issues of whether or not what he or she
is writing holds together as a finished text. The poststructuralists deconstruct text; the societal "bacchanalia" of the nascent counterculture was
also reactionary and, in the sense of Euripides' play, sought to tear down
the proverbial walls of the "City-State." The genuine cultural production
of a literary work is inherently constructivist, just as out of the bacchanalian chaos of the late '60s, the attempts of the hippies to create genuine alternative lifestyles became constructivist. By not looking at the
constructivist process of the author, the poststructuralists have created
a seemingly inviolable postmodern discourse featuring a "being-within"
way of thinking that is held captive to a sometimes indecipherable, discursive language.

Discussing this postmodern discursiveness in the realm of literary
criticism by no means suggests that the tumult of the '60s did not contribute to significant change in how novelists engaged the world and created innovative depictions of the condition of modern man. The term
postmodernism implies the loss of faith in the capacity of modern society and its attendant expressions of modernism to improve the lot
of mankind. In this, it is an apt term for describing the "advanced" societies of the mid–1960s and beyond. The counterculture opposed
the mainstream's blind allegiance to the "progress" of science and technology. The hippie disaffection toward institutional authority, and a
yearning for the grander possibilities in life, manifested itself in a "consciousness revolution" as a way to adapt spiritually to the postmodern
circumstance. *The Armies of the Night* articulated with eloquence the postmodern condition of these young people in 1967. For them he held out
a guarded hope that America, in the face of its "technology land" and

"corporation land," might rediscover a renewed humanity in its midst. Yet this hope was ultimately constructivist. Mailer, in making this statement, was looking beyond the deconstructivist moment of his narrative where protesters were marching on the Pentagon and decrying the war policies of the American government. He was talking about the role of these youth in reshaping the political landscape of the United States.

So, if Late Modernism—when the "grand narrative" still dominated literature—could be seen to change into a different kind of Modernism, then Mailer's observation was at the core of this shift. The shift altered the kinds of narrative construction that audiences/readers were willing to watch or read. In this, Postmodernists accurately identify the attributes of postmodern literature. These include disconnected images, fragmentary sensations, simulacra, flippant indifference, self-referential fabulation, pastiche (farce), or bricolage. Such prose, by constructivist terms, seeks not the emotive connections derived from the continuous fictional dream of traditional narrative, but intellectual stimulation and humor through ironic juxtaposition. However, very few postmodern narratives, *Trout Fishing in America* notable among these few, totally eschew the energeia and profluence of traditional narrative and solely employ a juxtapositional structure.

So, if one is to accept that this is a postmodern era, then the broadened array of structures seen in these hippie narratives implies simply that the trunk has been allowed to branch out robustly, and that, in many instances, the branches of juxtapositional or metafictional techniques grant the authors of fiction more creative possibilities for sharing their conceits. Interestingly, collections of postmodern writing, without clearly defining the editorial criteria for inclusion, yield samples from the highly "realistic" writing of the New Journalism to the most fragmented juxtapositional prose. When David Simpson in *The Academic Postmodern and the Rule of Literature* notes that "[g]rand narrative is out of style, with its rhetoric of truth and progress and its covert corollaries of masculinization and Eurocentrism," he seems to imply that biases based on late capitalism, gender, post-colonialism, or race—which are unrelated to formulations of narrative structure—have contributed to a postmodern predilection favoring the experimental over the conventional. In such shunning, however, Simpson asserts that it "would be foolish to pretend that little narratives are true alternatives to grand ones, rather than chips off a larger block whose shape we can no longer see because we are no longer looking" (29). What was no longer being looked at is the "trunk of the Science" in creative writing, and the "electricity" of its social realism.

The array of hippie narratives discussed in this study demonstrates how, in the spirit of openness in the '60s, a literary vitality benefited from the broader spectrum of constructivist possibility, conventional and experimental. In other words, the conventional narrative form should not be viewed as a contributing factor to culturally driven biases; it is simply the "larger block" of a value-neutral narrative mode of construction that postmodernists have ignored in favor of more experimental novelistic forms. In a similar vein, what Robbins (through his narrator/ author Marx Marvelous) noted as the socio-religious pilgrimage toward the limits of the psychic frontier in *Another Roadside Attraction*, certainly heralded a changing (postmodern) spirituality in America. However, while Marx Marvelous was noting the decline in conventional Church-going, this section of prose and Amanda's openness to spiritual possibility no more negated the essence of Christ's message than deviations from the traditional narrative form negated the validity and vitality of an energeic novel expressing its conceit through a continuous and vivid fictional dream. If readers of literature were no longer interested in the traditionally rendered story, then the shift from Late Modernism to Post-modernism would be a matter of the narrative form and methods of execution changing toward these "true alternatives." Rather, with the experimentation of form came a critical postmodern preference for these offshoot styles and an odd disregard for the "larger block." This is akin to Ken Kesey's comment that both Buddhism and Christianity hold perspectives from which the other would benefit, not a scenario where one religion negates the other. Juxtapositional irony, for example, can be the basis of experimental narrative, but is also a common fixture in today's traditionally rendered narratives. "Postmodernism Reconstructed," consequently, is simply an assertion that the energeic "trunk of the science" is the "larger block." A deconstructivism which ignores both this and the constructivist precepts of the author, relegates itself to the realm of self-emptying or *kenosis*. In intellectual terms, this creates a discursive isolationism.

This constructivist distinction offers a fundamental departure from the deconstructivist approaches of most contemporary literary analyses. Constructivism is the craft of storytelling and constructivist critique is directed toward how aspects of craft in a text adhere to the dramatic whole. In light of how poststructuralism and feminism, especially, are outgrowths of the profound social tumult of the '60s, such a constructivist approach offers insight into the emergence of these phenomena in the postmodern realm.

Again, this is not to say that constructivism obviates analysis by deconstruction. By employing a constructivist analysis, this study privileges a look at the creation of these "primary" texts of the counterculture, how they are crafted as stories. Taken chronologically, these works parallel the discernable changes in Western society that occurred during this time. Simpson references the time-held potency of this approach:

> [...] for all our [academic postmodernist] professions of subject positionality, politicality, and theoretical integrity, we are really in search of some basic forms of happiness that have not changed much through time. [...] Editors, critics, and theorists of all genders, sexual preferences, and generations are captured by the spell of authentic passion and by the power of writing to bring it back to life [174].

Philosophically, the emotive response to the literary techniques of social realism may or may not be objectively "real" in poststructural analysis of the sign and signifer, but the "electricity" of compelling dramatic actualization is at the core of literary appeal, of these "basic forms of happiness." Explaining how and why such traditional narrative approaches work so well in eliciting strong emotive response should be an area of more rigorous academic and scientific inquiry.

When Tom Robbins uses metafiction to pontificate, he is engaging in his own grand narrative on truth and progress. His techniques of social realism—in his case humorous exaggerations of concretely described, offbeat characters and odd situations creating the core narrative—cause an "electricity" of comic response. Robbins has been widely considered a postmodern author; the difference between his approach and that of Late Modernism is that his engagement with finding "truth" is presented intermittently through his narrative; it breaks up the continuous and vivid fictional dream and, at the end of the two novels examined here, the drama is not neatly tied up in one profound climactic epiphany. His denouement leaves open future mystery and is not carefully summed up and tidy.

The point here is to embrace the dramatic form of the energeic narrative, and recognize this "trunk of the science" as a core, but not exclusive, method for portraying the dramatic conflicts within Western society. Such conflicts can include sexism, militarism, racism, overdevelopment, distribution of wealth, social deprivation, psychic dysfunction, or interpersonal unenlightenment.

The narratives chosen for this study remain, to this day, strong literary works with very different points of emphasis. All are genuine reflections of either the rise, crest, or ebb of the hippie phenomenon. Although varying in narrative structure and dramatic intent, there is enough similarity in voice, tone, roguishness, iconoclastic whimsy and anti-establishment sentiment to consider grouping these narratives as a distinct body of countercultural literature. The Beat movement was defined and led by its authors, and, as this book has documented, the bohemian philosophy of the Beats served as the foundation from which the counterculture exploded in the late '60s. The counterculture itself was much more diffuse and diverse than the Beat movement and the authors attempting to portray the time were not part of any coordinated effort that could be considered a literary movement. Taken chronologically, these works offer a robust excursion through this period of American history that was most unique for its "great and terrible vitality." This vitality included bold rebelliousness and shaky experiments in lifestyle that moved beyond a collective ennui to seek rebirth in the ideals of hope, in trying to live out the ethos of peace and love. And "so it goes," if we "care to listen" that the writers—Vonnegut, Robbins and the others—"Snatch that essence from its wild background and isolate it from commotion and myth." The hippie phenomenon and these hippie narratives left a lasting imprint on American culture and literature. The diverse works examined here and written over a period of a decade-and-a-half from *Cuckoo's Nest* (1962) to *Even Cowgirls Get the Blues* (1976) are of lasting significance as literature and warrant stature as the embodiment of a countercultural canon.

Bibliography

Abbott, Keith. *Downstream from "Trout Fishing in America."* Santa Barbara: Capra Press, 1989.

———. "Garfish, Chili Dogs, and The Human Torch: Memories of Richard Brautigan and San Francisco, 1966." *The Review of Contemporary Fiction*, 3,3 (Fall 1983): 214–9.

Adams, Tim. "Bonfire knight." *The Sunday Observer.* http://observer.guardian.co.uk/comment/story/0,6903,1340080,00.html, 10/31/2004.

Allen, Brian. Personal conversation. Portland, Oregon, 6 August 2003.

Allen, Steve. *Beloved Son: A Story of the Jesus Cults.* Indianapolis: Bobbs-Merrill, 1982.

Aristotle. "Poetics." *The Pocket Aristotle.* Ed. Justin Kaplan, Trans. Ingram Bywater. New York: Washington Square Books, 1958.

Baldick, Chris. *The Concise Oxford Dictionary of Literary Terms.* Oxford: Oxford University Press, 1990.

Barthelme, Donald. *Snow White.* (First published 1967.)

Begiebing, Robert. *Acts of Regeneration: Allegory and Archetype in the Works of Norman Mailer.* Columbus, Mo.: University of Missouri Press, 1980.

Bhagavad-Gita. Trans. Franklin Edgerton. New York: Harper & Row, 1964.

"Books by Gurney Norman." Review in http://www.appalachianbooks.com.

Boon, Marcus. *The Road of Excess: A History of Writers on Drugs.* Cambridge, Mass.: Harvard University Press, 2002.

Boulby, Mark. *Hermann Hess, His Mind and Art.* Ithaca, N.Y.: Cornell University Press, 1967.

Brautigan, Ianthe. *You Can't Catch Death.* New York: St. Martin's Press, 2000.

Brautigan, Richard. "A Long Time Ago People Decided to Live in America." *Revenge of the Lawn: Stories 1962–1970.* New York: Simon and Schuster, 1971.

———. *Trout Fishing in America* [etc.] [selections]. (Originally published Grove Press, 1967.) Boston: Houghton Mifflin, 1989.

Buda, Janusz K. "Richard Brautigan 1935–1984." *Otsuma Review* (July 1985): 20–6.

Bufithis, Philip. *Norman Mailer.* New York: Frederick Ungar Publishing Co. 1978.

Burroughs, William S. *Naked Lunch.* New York: Grove/Weidenfeld, 1959.

Capote, Truman. *In Cold Blood.* New York: Signet Books, 1966.

Carson, Rachel. *Silent Spring.* Boston: Houghton Mifflin, 1962.

Caudill, Anne. "Gurney Norman." Http://www.english.eku.edu/services/kylit/norman.htm.

Chabot, C. Barry. "The Problem of the Postmodern." *Zeitgeist in Babel: The Postmodern Controversy.* Ed., Ingeborg Hoestery. Bloomington: University of Indiana Press. 1991.

Clayton, John. "Richard Brautigan: The Politics of Woodstock." *New American Review*, November 1971.

Cook, Bruce. (Back cover quote.) *The Hawkline Monster: A Gothic Western*. By Richard Brautigan. New York: A Touchstone Book, 1974.

Cooke, Douglas. "Pursuit of the Real and Escape from Reality." http://www.rich ardandmimi.com/beendown.html, 2001.

Cowley, Malcolm. "Ken Kesey at Stanford." *Kesey* (Volume XVI, Numbers One and Two of the *Northwest Review*). Eugene, Oregon: Northwest Review Books, 1977.

Deloria, Frank. "Foreword." *Black Elk Speaks*. Nicholas Black Elk and John G. Neihardt. (Originally published 1932, Foreword copyright 1979.) Lincoln: University of Nebraska Press, 2000.

Didion, Joan. "Slouching Towards Bethlehem." *Slouching Towards Bethlehem*. (Originally published September 1967 in *The Saturday Evening Post*.) New York: Noonday, 1990.

_____. *The White Album*. New York: First Pocket Books, 1979.

_____. *The Year of Magical Thinking*. New York: Random House, 2005.

Dolan, John. "A Hero of Our Time Hunter S. Thompson 1937–2005." *The Exile*. http://www.exile.ru/2005-February-25/a_hero_of_our_time_hunter_s_ thompson_1937-2005.html.

Durbin, Karen. "Together: When Love Thought It Could Defeat War." Movie Review. *New York Times*, 19 August 2001, final ed.: Sec 2, page 9, column 1.

Eagleton, Terry. *Literary Theory: An Introduction*. Minneapolis: University of Minnesota Press, 1983.

Euripides. *Medea, Hippolytus, The Bacchae*. Trans. By Philip Vellacott. New York: The Heritage Press, 1963.

Everson, William. "Dionysus and the Beat Generation." *The Beats in Criticism*. Ed. Lee Bartlett. North Carolina: McFarland, 1981.

Faggen, Robert. "One Crying in the Wilderness: Excerpt from an Interview with Ken Kesey." *The Paris Review*, Spring 1994.

Fahey, Todd Brendan. "Comes Spake the Cuckoo, Ken Kesey: The Far Gone Interview." www.fargonebooks.com, 13 Sept 1992.

Fariña, Richard. *Been Down So Long, It Looks Like Up to Me*. New York: Viking Penguin, 1966.

Festa, Conrad. "Vonnegut's Satire." *Vonnegut in America*. Kinkowitz, Jerome and Donald Lawler, eds. New York: Delacorte Press. 1977.

Fitzgerald, F. Scott. *The Great Gatsby*. (First published 1925.) New York: The Penguin Modern Classics, 2000.

Frank, Joseph. "Spatial Form in Modern Literature." *Sewanee Review* (Spring, Summer, Fall), 1945.

Friedan, Betty. *The Feminine Mystique*. New York: W.W. Norton, 1963.

Gardner, John. *Art of Fiction: Notes on Craft for Young Writers*. New York: Vintage Books, 1985.

Ginsberg, Allen. "Howl." *Howl*. (First published 1955.) San Francisco: City Lights Books, 2003.

Goodman, Fred. *The Mansion on the Hill: Dylan, Young, Geffen, Springsteen, and the Head-On Collision of Rock and Commerce*. New York: Vintage Books, 1998.

Grogan, Emmett. *Ringolevio: A Life Played for Keeps*. (First published 1972.) New York: Citadel Underground, 1990.

Heinlein, Robert A. *Stranger in a Strange Land*. (First published 1961.) New York: Berkley Science Fiction, 1983.

Heller, Joseph. *Catch-22*. (Originally published 1961.) New York: Scribner, 1996.

Hesse, Herman. *My Belief: Essays on Life and Art.* Ed. Theodore Ziolkowski. Trans. Denver Lindley. New York: Farrar, Straus, Giroux, 1974.

_____. *Siddhartha.* (First published in German, 1922.) New York: Bantam, 1971.

_____. *Steppenwolf.* New York: Henry Holt, 1990.

Howe, Irving. "Mass Society and Postmodern Fiction." (First published in *Partisan Review* in 1959.) *The Decline of the New.* New York: Harcourt, Brace and World, 1970.

Hubbard, L. Ron. *Dianetics: The Modern Science of Mental Health.* New York: Hermitage House, 1950.

Huxley, Aldus. *Doors of Perception.* New York: Harper. 1954.

I-Ching. Trans. James Legge. New York: New American Library, 1971.

Iacchus, Priest. "What Is the Church of All Worlds?" www.caw.org/articles/WhatIs Caw.html, 1995.

Jezer, Marty. *Abbie Hoffman: American Rebel.* New Brunswick, N.J.: Rutgers University Press. 1992.

Johnson, Denis. "Hippies." *Seek: Reports from the Edges of America and Beyond.* New York: Perennial, 2001.

Kerouac, Jack. *On the Road.* (First published 1957.) New York: Penguin, 1999.

Kesey, Ken. "Earthshoes." *Spit in the Ocean 7.* ed. Ed McClanahan. New York: Penguin Books, 2003.

_____. Interview. (www.sputnik.ac/interview%20page/trip.html)

_____. *Kesey* (Volume XVI, Numbers One and Two of the *Northwest Review*). Eugene, Oregon: Northwest Review Books, 1977.

_____. *One Flew Over the Cuckoo's Nest.* New York: Signet, 1962.

_____. *Sometimes a Great Notion.* New York: Viking Press, 1964.

Kitchell, Kaaren. Personal interview. Vista del Mar, California. 20 December 2005.

Klinkowitz, Jerome. *Vonnegut in Fact: The Public Spokesmanship of Personal Fiction.* Columbia: University of South Carolina Press, 1998.

Klinkowitz, Jerome, and Donald Lawler, eds. *Vonnegut in America.* New York: Delacorte Press. 1977.

Koch, Stephen. "Prophet of Youth: Herman Hesse's *Narcissus & Goldmund.*" *The New Republic.* 13 July 1968.

Kohn, Robert E. "The Ambivalence in Kotzwinkle's beat and Bardo ties." *College Literature,* http://www.findarticles.com/p/articles/mi_qa3709/is_200004/ ai_ n8896696. Spring 2000.

Kotzwinkle, William. *The Fan Man.* (Originally published, 1974.) New York: Avon Books, 1979.

Krassner, Paul. *Confessions of a Raving, Unconfined Nut: Misadventures in the Counter-Culture.* New York: Simon and Schuster. 1993.

_____. "An Impolite Interview with Ken Kesey." Reprinted in *Garage Sale.* Ed. Ken Kesey. New York: The Viking Press, 1973.

Lee, Martin A., and Bruce Shlain. *Acid Dreams: The Complete Social History of LSD, The CIA, The Sixties, and Beyond.* New York: Grove Press, 1985 and 1992.

MacFarlane, Scott. "Dead Heads, Winterland and the Wrecking Ball: New Year's in San Francisco." *Seattle Sun,* 6, 4 (January 24, 1979).

Mailer, Norman. *The Armies of the Night: History as a Novel, the Novel as History.* New York: Signet Books. 1968.

Marshall, Brenda. *Teaching the Postmodern: Fiction and Theory.* New York: Routledge, 1992.

McCleary, John Bassett. *The Hippie Dictionary: A Cultural Encyclopedia (and Phraseicon) of the 1960's and 1970's.* Berkeley: Ten Speed Press, 2002.

McNally, Dennis. *A Long Strange Trip: The Inside History of the Grateful Dead.* New York: Broadway Books, 2002.

Merrill, Robert. *Norman Mailer Revisited.* New York: Twayne Publishers. 1992.

Mojo: Special Limited Edition. "Psychedelic." London: EMAP Metro, 2002.

Morse, Donald E. *The Novels of Kurt Vonnegut: Imagining Being an American.* Westport, Conn.: Praeger Publishers. 2003.

Mungo, Raymond. *Famous Long Ago: My Life and Hard Times with Liberation News Service.* Boston: Beacon Press, 1970.

Newhouse, Thomas. *The Beat Generation and the Popular Novel in the United States, 1945–1970.* Jefferson, N.C.: McFarland, 2000.

Norman, Gurney. *Divine Right's Trip: A Folk Tale.* (First published in somewhat different form in *The Last Whole Earth Catalog,* 1971.) New York: Bantam Books, 1972.

_____. KET Television "Living by Words" Interview. Guy Mendes, producer/director. http://www.ket.org/livingbywords, November 28, 2001.

O'Connor, Flannery. "Good Country People." *The Complete Stories of Flannery O'Connor.* New York: Farrar, Straus, Giroux, 1971.

Patterson, William. Editor of *The Heinlein Journal.* Comments made on Heinlein Panel. National Conference of the American Culture Association and Popular Culture Association. San Diego, California, 25 March 2005.

Perry, Paul. *Fear and Loathing: The Strange and Terrible Saga of Hunter S. Thompson.* New York: Thunder's Mouth Press, 1992.

_____. Personal conversation. Culver City, California, June 23, 2004.

Perry, Paul, and Ken Babbs. *On the Bus: The Complete Guide to the Legendary Trip of Ken Kesey and the Merry Pranksters and the Birth of the Counterculture.* New York: Thunder's Mouth Press, 1990.

Pynchon, Thomas. *The Crying of Lot 49.* New York: Bantam Books, 1966.

_____. *Gravity's Rainbow.* New York: The Viking Press, 1973.

_____. *V.* New York: Lippincott, 1963.

_____. *Vineland.* New York: Little, Brown & Co., 1990.

Pütz, Manfred. "Transcendentalism Revived: The Fiction of Richard Brautigan." *Occident,* 8 (Spring 1974): 39–47.

Radford, Jean. *Norman Mailer: A Critical Study.* New York: Barnes and Noble Books. 1975

Reich, Charles A. *The Greening of America.* (Originally published Random House, 1970.) New York: Bantam, 1971.

"Review of Richard Brautigan." *London Review of Books.* 14 December 2000.

Ritter, Jess. "Teaching Kurt Vonnegut on the Firing Line." *The Vonnegut Statement.* Jerome Klinkowitz and John Somer, eds. New York: Delacorte Press, 1973.

Robbins, Tom. *Another Roadside Attraction.* New York: Ballantine Books, 1971.

_____. *Even Cowgirls Get the Blues.* New York: Bantam Books, 1976.

_____. "The Sixties" (Originally part of Remarks made at the Northwest Book Fest, 1996). *Wild Ducks Flying Backwards.* New York: Bantam, 2005.

Rooks, Kristen W. "Lessons Plan Library: One Flew Over the Cuckoo's Nest." http://school.discovery.com/lessonplans/programs/cuckoo/, 2005.

Schneck, Stephen. "Review of Trout Fishing in America." Ramparts, 6 (December 1967): 80–7.

Schnit, Stanley. *Kurt Vonnegut, Jr.* Boston: Twayne Publishers. 1976.

Schott, Webster. (Back cover quote.) *Snow White.* By Donald Barthelme. New York: Atheneum, 1967.

Sherrill, Rowland A. *Road-Book America: Contemporary Culture and the New Picaresque.* Urbana: University of Illinois Press, 2000.

Siegel, Mark. *Tom Robbins.* Boise, Idaho: Boise State University Western Writers Series, 1980.

Simpson, David. *The Academic Postmodern and the Rule of Literature.* Chicago: University of Chicago Press, 1995.

Somer, John L. "Geodesic Vonnegut; or If Buckminster Fuller Wrote Novels." *The Vonnegut Statement.* Ed. Jerome Klinkowitz and Jerome L. Somer. New York: Delacorte, 1973.

Stevens, Catez. "Post-Modernism and the Jim Jones Potential." http://allthings 2all.blogspot.com/2004/11/post-modernism-and-jim-jones-potential.html. 17 Nov 2004.

Stover, Leon. *Robert A. Heinlein.* Boston: Twayne Publishers, 1987.

Strelow, Michael. "Dialogue with Tom Robbins." *Northwest Review of Books* (Eugene, Oregon), 20, 2 & 3 (1982).

Stull, James N. *Literary Selves: Autobiography and Contemporary American Nonfiction.* Westport, Conn.: Greenwood Press, 1993.

Tanner, Stephen L. *Ken Kesey.* Boston: Twayne Publishers. 1983.

Thompson, Hunter S. "The Battle of Aspen," *Rolling Stone Magazine,* 1 October 1970.

_____. *Fear and Loathing in Las Vegas: A Savage Journey to the Heart of The American Dream.* (First published 1970 in *Rolling Stone Magazine.*) New York: Random House Modern Library, 1996.

_____. "The 'Hashbury' Is the Capital of the Hippies," *New York Times Magazine,* 14 May 1967.

_____. *Hells Angels: A Strange and Terrible Saga.* New York: Ballantine Books, 1966 and 1967.

Tibetan Book of the Dead. New York: Quality Paperback, 1998.

Timpe, Eugene. "Hermann Hesse in the United States." *Hermann Hesse: A Collection of Criticism.* Ed. Judith Liebmann. New York: McGraw-Hill, 1977.

Triance, Tavis Eachan. "Richard Brautigan: A Poetics of Alienation." *Half Empty.* http://www.articles.halfempty.com/art/00-03-19.htm

The Upanishads. Trans. Juan Mascaro. Baltimore: Penguin Books, 1965.

Updike, John. (From review of *Divine Right's Trip* in *The New Yorker.*) (www.edmc clanahan.com)

Vanderwerken, David L. "*Trout Fishing in America* and the American Tradition." *Critique: Studies in Modern Fiction,* 16,1 (1974): 32–40.

Vonnegut, Kurt. *Slaughterhouse-Five, or The Children's Crusade: A Duty-Dance with Death.* New York: Delacorte Press, 1969.

Waters, Frank. *Book of the Hopi.* New York: Viking Press. 1963.

Welch, Bob. "Kesey, Oregon Are Inseparable." (Newspaper Column) Eugene, Oregon: *The Register-Guard,* 15 November 2001.

Wilson, Cintra. "The Awful Truth." *Salon.* www.salon.com/weekly/meany960930. html, 22 June 2005.

Wolfe, Tom. *The Electric Kool-Aid Acid Test.* New York: Farrar, Straus & Giroux, 1968.

_____. *The New Journalism.* New York: Harper & Row, 1973.

Woods, Crawford. "The Best Book on the Dope Decade." *New York Times Book Review,* 23 July 1972.

Index